About the co-author

Richard Torné is a journalist and the editor of the English language Costa Almería News newspaper in Spain. He has written extensively on film making in Almería, as well as the illegal property crisis in the region and the Palomares nuclear incident of 1966.

He has also been a feature writer and columnist for the UK-based monthly magazine, *Everything Spain,* in addition to writing political articles for *Open Democracy.*

He is currently working on a novel about expats in Spain.

DAVID LEAN'S DEDICATED MANIAC - MEMOIRS OF A FILM SPECIALIST

DEDICATION

"To Kathleen, who has been everywhere with me for forty years (lucky me) and whose opinion David always asked for."

Eddie Fowlie

Eddie Fowlie & Richard Torné

DAVID LEAN'S DEDICATED MANIAC – MEMOIRS OF A FILM SPECIALIST

AUSTIN & MACAULEY

A CIP catalogue record for this title is
available from the British Library.

ISBN 978 1 84963 041 2

www.austinmacauley.com

First Published (2010)
Austin & Macauley Publishers Ltd.
25 Canada Square
Canary Wharf
London
E14 5LB

Printed & Bound in Great Britain

ACKNOWLEDGEMENTS

"I looked long and hard for a writer who would listen to, and understand a dedicated maniac when he saw one. My thanks to Richard Torné for all his hard work and understanding."

Eddie Fowlie

"I learned that a zebra could kick sideways – although I must confess I wasn't quite sure how useful that knowledge would be in the future."

Eddie Fowlie

"Eddie was the only one who told it to me straight. Everyone else on the crew thought it might be OK, so that I was the one who fell in it if it wasn't."

David Lean

"If the director wanted a thousand butterflies on the set the next day, Eddie would say 'no problem'."

Geraldine Chaplin

FOREWORD

The first film Eddie made with me was in 1966. *How I Won The War* was filmed first in Germany, then Almería, and finally in England. After a week of night shooting near Hamburg and three plane journeys, I arrived in Tabernas, near Almería, where Eddie was waiting to show me a possible location area for the next day's shoot. Hot and thirsty, we climbed over the hills looking for areas to represent the film's North African locations. We reached a point which seemed suitable and I said, "This spot will be fine, Eddie."

He looked round and replied, "You've just come 800 fucking miles to find this set-up; why not go the last fifty feet to the top in case it's better there?"

I didn't realise it at the time but that had encapsulated Eddie Fowlie's principle of life and film-making. He was always prepared to give everything to the cause of a film and had little time for people who were not prepared to push themselves to the limit to serve the attempt to make a great film.

Undoubtedly, Eddie's enthusiasm resulted in behaviour which in normal circumstances might be considered certifiable, but like a whirlwind force of nature, was aimed purely at serving the director he worked for. If you wanted a frozen lake for shooting near Madrid in July, Eddie was your man. A giant chessboard with dogs and monkeys as the pieces, "no problem".

Sometimes, things did not go quite as planned. On *The Three Musketeers*, we had a scene, shot in Toledo, where D'Artagnan, having just acquired an elegant suit of clothes, bumps into a rat collector, who was advertising his profession by carrying a pole supporting a line of dead rats.

As the shot was being prepared, I checked with Eddie that he had the rat catcher's dog and the rat pole. I saw the merest flicker cross Eddie's face. "Sure, they're in my truck." Slightly suspicious, I asked to check them as we would be shooting the scene within the hour. Eddie climbed into the truck and soon returned with a face like thunder. "Some fucker's stolen them off my truck!" Before I had a chance to discuss the likelihood of Toledo's criminal element lying in wait to make off with Mr Fowlie's four dead rats, Eddie said, "Give me ten minutes." Thinking this would be too good to miss, I quietly observed Eddie round up a group of children from our crowd of extras, and hand them all money. They soon returned with a few cages of pet hamsters. Eddie shouted for the crew's painter for a pot of grey paint and disappeared into the bowels of his truck. Four tiny squeaks were heard. Eddie reappeared, tying bits of string, representing tails, onto his painted hamsters, the scene was shot on time. Just another problem solved, on a film with Eddie Fowlie.

Richard Lester

Contents

Somebody at the British Film Institute phoned me about a year ago, asking me if I'd be willing to provide details of my life, so that they could add them to their archives. I have to admit I thought it was a slightly cheeky request, seeing as I was not going to get paid for it, so I told him to buy my autobiography when it came out, instead. I guess it was not exactly the answer he was expecting and after a short silence he changed tack and asked me where I had learned my trade, perhaps hoping I'd tell him about some fabulous film school I may have attended during my formative years. I'm sure I heard his jaw drop when I told him I learned everything playing in Hampton Court Palace and Richmond Park as a boy. Perhaps he thought I was being awkward for the sake of it, but the truth is no one had ever heard of a bloody film school when I started. The only requirement was to be a dreamer.

Dealing with highly eccentric film directors was just another quirk that came with the job, and I've met many in my career, from one-eyed cigarette-rolling gamblers and crazies willing to throw live horses over a precipice, to panic-stricken individuals who seemed to be on a permanent knife-edge. There were, however, just a handful of geniuses. One of them in particular was often irascible and awkward, but they didn't come much bigger or better than David Lean. I never figured out if he was hard on the outside and soft on the inside or the other way round, but during the thirty-five or so years I knew him I learned more from David than any other director. He once said: "People remember pictures, not dialogue." I couldn't agree more. Film critics (never the best judges of his work) would probably scoff, but as David once said he wouldn't trust one of them to shoot a close-up of a teapot. He insisted on nothing less than absolute perfection, that's why he expected others to have the same exacting standards all the time. If you failed – and actors in particular came in for a rough time, especially if they could not, or would not, do things his way – he could become a bit of a tyrant, but he never was towards me. The film industry has changed a lot since I stopped working some fifteen years ago, so you can imagine how far it's changed compared to that day, some sixty-five years ago, when I first walked up to the Warner Brothers' gate in Teddington Studios to enquire about a job – any job. Nowadays, they have all sorts of fancy names to describe what I did: you can be a Production Designer, an Art Director, an Assistant Art Director, a Buyer or whatever else the film unions and the accountants can come up with; they even have a man in charge of trees and greenery! In my time a Prop Man did everything, down to the tiniest detail, such as calculating how long a cigarette should burn for, or helping to design and build a Spanish Galleon. Although I no longer work, I could still do it now; I could still find the answers to the problems, except that I can't get about very much these days. My routine is mostly limited to feeding sixteen hungry mouths; the stray moggies who turn up at the door of my beach house in Carboneras every morning at six o'clock sharp. But I can still dream – that's why I got into the film business in the first place.

CHAPTER 1

INTRODUCTION

I recently saw *Lawrence of Arabia* for the first time from start to finish. It may surprise some, but I only viewed a few rushes when it was being made and never bothered to see the end product – I never did with the films I worked on, based on the view that once I finished my job the rest mattered little. And yet, with the perspective of time, I must admit I was quite pleased with the end result. What's more, I felt my own contribution wasn't bad at all, especially the Wadi Rum set. When I saw the size of the camp, everything seemed grander and more lavish on screen, and I realise what a huge undertaking it had been to prepare. For a long time I was convinced that I had about three hundred tents in place (all done without a computer in sight), but it's clear to me now that I had erected far more than that, spread out over three to four miles wide. It may seem like we went to a lot of trouble just to have the camp appear for a brief instant on screen, but it was worth it: we were helping a genius to conceive his vision.

In fact, the thing that struck me most about watching the film some forty-seven years after it had been made was how David Lean kept the audience in suspense. Timing was the other thing, not just between each cut but between the actors. It was all done by David because he gave them strict and very precise instructions about that. I could find fault with the film, but nothing with my work or David's.

Watching the film decades later gave me a deeper understanding of why David asked me to prepare props a certain way. Right at the very end when Lawrence is about to go back to England, I remember David asking me to polish the top of the desk so that it would reflect like a mirror. If you look at the scene carefully as Lawrence leaves, he goes through a see-through curtain, but in the bottom of the frame you see the top of the desk…and Lawrence's ghostly reflection; the impression of a man who's finished.

Tortured souls, tragic heroes (always men) facing dilemmas and forced to question their actions were the central themes of most of David's leading characters. Perhaps they spoke for him through their actions, projecting his own inner doubts. David would never talk about his fears to anyone, but in the same way the beautiful images he created on film often made words redundant, we developed an almost telepathic understanding that helped to transform his visions into reality. That bond between us would remain until the day he died.

The film school
I think it finally dawned on me that I was leading quite a unique and exciting life when we were about to blow up the bridge on *The Bridge on the River Kwai*. I was in the water helping to place the dynamite, and as I surfaced I saw David Lean looking down at me. "Bloody millionaire's stuff!" I remarked. It neatly summed up what we were all doing, playing with trains and blowing up bridges, like the games we used to play as children, save for the all-important difference that only millionaires could do it this way. The last time I had been this interested in trains was when I was two years old, waiting at the gate of our little house in the hope of catching a glimpse of a scary red dragon screaming past me and spewing sparks from the long, thin horns on its head. The dragon was actually the local tram which ran backwards and forwards along the main road, and I was waiting for my father to come flying off it on his way back home from work. It was August 1924, I was about to turn three and for some reason I wanted that dragon, or a toy one just like it. I didn't get either, but I made up for it with my imagination. I found a paradise in which to live out my fantasies a stone's throw away from where I lived in the huge, green open spaces of Hampton Court Palace, Kew Gardens and Bushey Park.

My Scottish parents – like many before them – fled the Highlands before I was born and happily settled in the south-east of England at N°.5, Fairfax Road, Teddington, on the outskirts of London. My father, Jock – or Ned, as my mother Mary called him– was a skilled motor engineer who worked making hand-built AC Cars. He later became the chief of a fleet of huge Daimlers for a funeral company. It was a sign of the times, as they had just decided to change over from black, Belgian horses to motorcars. Jock was a good dad, but occasionally the relationship soured (usually the result of my being informed upon by my mother of a misdemeanour of mine). He would then make use of his considerable strength to whack my bare backside with his hand. If it was more serious, he would use a strap. It acted as a sure-fire deterrent, and I kept mostly to the rules or, better still, tried to not get found out.

Keeping out of sight was a wise move, so I quickly learned how to climb a big horse-chestnut at the bottom of the yard where I'd hide for hours. I say 'yard', but to me it seemed more like a huge forest – my father may have been a good engineer, but he was no gardener. Fortunately for me, his lack in landscaping skills was my gain. The shrubbery grew wild and out of control and the resulting 'jungle' became my stage; an ideal private playground that was free from the influence of stern-faced grownups and their inflexible rules.

I did not get any pocket-money, but as I got older I found out one could earn money in a variety of ingenious ways. I earned a penny for turning the handle of the mangle, or half a penny by polishing the brass knobs on door handles. Most of my earnings were spent on sweets because fun didn't cost anything, especially if you were creative. In those relatively traffic-free days, the most you could expect to see was the milkman on his horse and cart; the baker with a hand-pulled barrow; or the muffin man with the tray on his head and the bell in his hand. If it got really busy, the rag-and-bone man; the coal man; or the Spanish onion man riding on his bike would also make an appearance.

But being a kid, all I was really interested in was having a good time. As I grew up I realised I didn't feel comfortable being part of the pack, and one particular event taught me the importance of standing out from the crowd. The boys and girls in my street were all equal in the group until one day, when kids from another street invaded our patch and I was suddenly propelled towards the front of the pack to square up to them. Words were spoken but we came to the quick conclusion that there was nothing that couldn't be sorted out with a good punch up. Being rather civilised about it, it was left to the leader of the street gang and me to solve our differences. I agreed to take up the challenge as a matter of honour, and although older than me I gave him a handsome black eye. It felt good, but that evening his enraged mother came knocking on our front door, demanding summary justice from my bemused father. "Don't worry about it – I'll punish him," my dad assured her. The woman left satisfied, no doubt convinced that I was about to get a good smacking. I have to say I shared her feelings about the likely outcome. My dad closed the door and turned to me. Bracing myself, I tightened my buttocks and got ready for another taste of the strap. But to my surprise, I saw a smile on his face. "If you'd lost I would have given you a bloody good hiding!" he said with a wink. It was a lesson I never forgot: I learned that it pays to win. It was also typical of my parents, who taught me to stand on my own two feet from an early age.

One activity that helped me on my path to independence was learning to read. Mum and dad had the habit of going out to the pub with their friends every Saturday evening and I would be sent to bed early with comics like *Comic Cuts* or *Chips*, which contained strips with a comment below each individual picture. That way, in the gas light, I learned to identify and interpret individual words. It didn't say much for the educational system at the time, but it worked for me. My bed piled high with comics, I invariably ended up falling asleep to dream of the stories and the characters. As I grew older, I progressed from annuals to books and *Comic Cuts* and *Chips* gave way to *Arabian Nights*, *Aesop's Fables*, *Treasure Island* and *Robinson Crusoe*. These became treasured possessions that helped to shape my imagination and boost my self-confidence. With loving care I made brown paper dustcovers for each to put on bookshelves, which I fashioned out of orange boxes, complete with a little curtain in front.

School was a totally different matter, however, as I spent more time honing skills which had little to do with the development of academic knowledge. We had no luxuries such as pen and paper, and had to make do instead with a slate and slate pencil, eventually progressing to steel pen-nibs and ink-wells. But progress, if you could call it that, was a double-edged sword. Now, the dreaded ink blot betrayed our mistakes and became a customary feature in schoolchildren's exercise books. It was rather easy to blot paper and as a result I got whacked a lot, but I didn't care, which was just as well as you got an extra ration for flinching. The teachers, it has to be said, had a penchant for inflicting physical punishment, the legacy no doubt of their public school upbringing. For worse misdemeanours, such as talking in class, I was regularly called up to the front of the class to get a whack across the palm of my hand. In fact, out of about sixty boys in our class I gained a reputation for breaking the record in canings and for never flinching. I made sure I never wiped my hand down my trouser leg (which was a dead giveaway). It was something I could at least feel proud of. In fact, I got caned so often I got to know in detail the different types of canes used and learned that the swishy ones made the most damage. But there were certain records my pride and the sorer parts of my anatomy were prepared to renounce. Determined to put an end to one of the teachers' favourite pastimes, I sneaked into the empty classroom, took the canes from the top of the cupboard and threw them into a fire. I never got found out, but my satisfaction was short lived. Days later, the teachers were soon furnished with new, even swishier canes.

Public transport was limited to those who could afford it. In my case, walking was the only option. We did the half-mile walk to school all year round, come rain or shine, four times a day on most days. Those in the group who were a bit bolder occasionally jumped on the back of a horse and cart to hitch a free ride. This was called a 'whippey' on account of the driver turning round and flicking the long whip at the opportunistic free-loader whenever one of us shouted 'Whip behind guv'!'

We had no school dinners, either. Packed lunch for most consisted of bread and drip: two thick slices of bread, known as doorsteps, with beef dripping between them and wrapped in newspaper, were usually eaten in the playground below street level. This was a grim, dark cellar, enclosed within arches that supported the school building. Despite the diet – literally dripping with animal fat – none of us were overweight. There was also almost no truancy, either. If someone failed to answer his or her name during register, the truant officer rode on his bike to the offender's home to find out why and drag him back into the classroom by his ear to be caned. It wasn't all sore bottoms, though.

About half-way along the half-mile journey from school there was an old, disused clay pit just off the main road, which our gang used as a playground. Without doubt, the best ride we devised was a steeply sloping track which was slippery, and we discovered that if you urinated on it the slide down was even better. Boys and girls would pee on it from top to bottom, demonstrating a practical approach to equal rights long before it became fashionable to do so. Along the main road there was also a turreted, stone building with narrow windows, set far back in the shadows of the huge chestnut trees and hidden behind a row of high walls, spiked railings and big iron gates. When we later found out it was the lunatic asylum, we almost shat our pants in terror. Our imagination ran amok and we started conjuring up tales of creatures – half-men, half-animal – that were kept in cages. We were pretty sure we could hear them howling at night and decided that we would never walk on that side of the road again. I think this was my first attempt at script writing.

Down our road we were the only ones who went anywhere with the family. As a special treat, every now and again we'd go on a paddle boat trip from London to Margate. The boat, the *Golden Eagle*, was full of Londoners playing accordions and singing bawdy songs like 'Knees Up Mother Brown', with the women waving their skirts, dancing and laughing cheekily as the men cheered them on. I decided I liked Londoners and their unique zest for life. Even in those days London was a hub of social activity. The Lord Mayor's Show; Bertram Mills' Circus at the Olympia; pantomimes at the Lyceum; the Palladium; and the Zoo at Regents' Park were all seats of learning for me.

On one occasion, on a steam boat trip to Scotland, my father got permission to take me to the engine room and down through the narrow iron gangways. We walked in amongst the huge, shiny steel shafts and pistons that surged madly up and down like the boots of giants – it was the scariest thing I had ever seen, worse even than the lunatic asylum. Observing my fear, dad gently guided me up to the ship's bow. As we looked down over the edge we spotted a bloom of jellyfish swirling in the water. We stood silently in awe, watching the jellyfish glinting under the moonlight. It was a special moment. No words were spoken, but the experience brought us even closer. Later that day he opened up to me for the first time and told me how he had managed to survive four hellish years fighting in France during the Great War. He had either been very lucky or very smart, but I suspected the latter. He confessed he never went 'over the top' first: "Somebody's got to be last," he wisely remarked. He reasoned that one's chances of survival increased dramatically just by being a little bit sharper than the rest.

He lived to see the war through, but cancer eventually caught up with him and he died at the age of sixty-two from smoking woodbines – his only real weakness. He lay in bed in agony for two weeks, but he put up a brave front for the sake of the family. "I've got a cancer but we've got to keep it secret from mother," he pleaded with me. Despite the pain he kept his dignity right until the end. At the funeral they took the hearse past all the pubs he used to drink at, right down into Sussex. With his death I lost my inspiration and the person I had most looked up to, but rather than withdraw into myself I turned to films for solace.

My initiation into movies was the same as most other people's. In the junior years a few of us could afford to go to the pictures on Saturday mornings at the Super Cinema in Kingston. Despite being very old, dilapidated and infested with rats, we were drawn to it like a magnet, and for the modest fee of threepence we got to sit high up in the gods. As there were no seats, we sat on the steps almost knee-deep in discarded peanut shells. Watching expectantly, we waited for the main feature to appear, and if the screening didn't get us excited a small blaze, which happened more than once when the film caught fire in the projector, was sure to get us cheering. The stuttering black and white films were silent, so a piano player added impromptu melodies to accompany the action which, with our excited screams of 'behind you!', gave a whole new meaning to the concept of interactive entertainment. The piano joined in during moments of high-tension, or when there was a need to get the old waterworks going during the more romantic scenes. The crowds also did their bit and shouted out just as they do today during a pantomime. It was pure theatre.

We left the pictures on a high to re-enact most of what we had just seen in Bushy Park. We were suddenly transported from Surrey to the Wild West to become Will Rogers, Tom Mix, and Bill Cody. I decided, however, that playing alone was not satisfying enough and began to put into practice my budding entrepreneurial skills. By the Hampton Court side of the park I started hanging around the maze by the palace to show lost people the way out in return for a small, financial reward. It turned out to be quite a profitable venture and it set me up for the summer. With money came a bit of power, followed by a stirring in my loins and a budding interest in the opposite sex. One of the best hunting grounds for a horny young man like myself was to be found at Goose Green, where one of London's great funfairs was held twice a year. There were merry-go-rounds and jellied eels, with big steam-traction engines generating the electrical power. Boys chased the girls and they, in turn, chased the boys, giggling and squealing with equal enthusiasm while wearing funny hats with 'kiss me' messages stuck on them. But school was always a sobering reminder that life was more than just about having fun.

When I reached the age of eleven I had to pass an exam if I wanted to move up to senior level. I failed, of course, and I was shunted to another school, which in itself didn't bother me. My next stop was a fairly new school with playgrounds and gardens closer to home. There were an equal number of boys and girls in the classes – about twenty of each – sitting on either side of the room along long desks, with a narrow space down the middle which we exploited to pass surreptitious messages of love whenever the teacher's back was turned. As it turned out, being 'demoted' to that school worked out fine. It was much better than the gloomy old place I'd left behind, where there were probably as many as fifty or sixty of us to a class. For a start, we enjoyed the luxury of having a different teacher for each subject. Some things never changed, though, and just like at my old school I got caned a lot. I began to measure my success at a subject by the frequency of canings. I got caned quite a lot at History for forgetting dates, but I must have been reasonably good at Geography because it was the one class where the palm of my hand didn't look as red as a tomato.

I definitely couldn't complain about life: we could play sport, the girls were close at hand, the canings were within bearable limits…and the films at the cinema simply got better. Out went the cowboy flicks of Tom Mix, Hopalong Cassidy, donning Stetsons and Colt 45s, and in came Fu Manchu, torture chambers and Chinamen with long beards and evil grins. Getting the hell scared out of us was a new thrill and we couldn't get enough of it. We soon upgraded to watching flicks of dead people draped in black cloaks and lurching out of coffins (invariably to get a stake through the heart by the film's end). At times, it was a close call. The vampire bat we had just seen hovering over the victim's bed, or following behind the coach, would later flap his wings outside my bedroom window, perhaps to get his own back. Terrified, I'd pull my bed sheets over my head (it was best not to be seen as they could suck all your blood out). Needless to say, I lived to see another day.

But it wasn't just our tastes that were changing. The arrival of 'talkies' sent shockwaves through the industry and revolutionised the way films were being made. As in any field undergoing a large transformation there were those who lost out and got left by the wayside. Many silent stars whose voices did not match their good looks were unable to make the transition and saw their careers fade into oblivion. The fans, who until now had idolised their erstwhile heroes, proved to be a fickle bunch and quickly forgot them. We now paid sixpence, nine pence or a shilling to see a feature, but the rising cost didn't put anyone off and the queues outside the cinemas simply got bigger. Audiences became more demanding and craved to see bigger productions. In response, cinemas screened an ever increasing number of films and it became the norm to watch two features and a short. The cinemas also got larger and plusher in order to feed the public's insatiable appetite for celluloid. In Kingston, we soon had five cinemas as well as one in Teddington, called The Savoy. During the half-hour interlude we had a mighty Wurlitzer organ rising from below the theatre and changing colour like a giant pinball machine to accompany the ice-cream girls.

Cinema's golden age had well and truly arrived, and with it the first tentative steps at exploiting the vast commercial possibilities on offer. The faces of film stars began to appear on cigarette cards, which we swapped or bartered to complete sets, sometimes two or even three for one. There seemed to be millions of these cards about and we all became avid collectors. But I yearned for bigger thrills, and one of my favourite pastimes was dodging fares on trams. My best friend Mick and I would often race up to the open-top deck, where we stayed put until the conductor showed up to charge the fare. We then bolted downstairs just before a stop and jumped off to get on another tram. We'd do this all day, all across London. Not only was it a cheap way to travel, but it was an ideal method of finding your way around the capital.

One of our favourite spots was the Kingsway tunnel, where the tram travelled underground at Aldwych. Another was the embankment where we watched the pleasure boats loaded with the well-to-do steaming from Richmond to Windsor. For some reason we never learned to dodge the fare on these and riding on a pleasure boat remained an elusive dream. In any case, as I got older I needed more cash to fund my more expensive tastes which, like most teenagers, I had become accustomed to, so I got a job as a baker's rounds man, helping to deliver bread and cakes from a horse and van from Teddington, Hampton Wick and Hampton Court. I worked on Saturday because it was the busiest day, selling more cakes for the weekend and collecting people's weekly bills. At half a crown a day – two shillings and sixpence – I started at eight in the morning and finished at eight at night. Setting out from Hampton Wick, I travelled to Teddington as far as the Physical Laboratory and then circle round and end up at the Tide End Cottage pub, beside the film studio. It was while taking a break, sitting at the back of the van with the door open and eating breadcrumbs, that I first noticed the imposing brass gate entrance at the Warner Brothers' Film Studios. I stopped munching and craned my neck to peer inside, but the building refused to give away any of its secrets; these I was to discover much later on. Right now I was more excited at the prospect of delivering cakes to the houses of stars such as comedian Max Miller and actress Jessie Matthews.

However, most of our customers were old ladies who lived in grace and favour apartments in Hampton Court Palace. These were given by the King to famous people and their close relatives such as Lady Shackleton, widow of the Antarctic explorer, Sir Ernest Henry Shackleton. While the baker went to the bar of the Mitre Hotel to enjoy a few drinks and, it has to be said, end up pissed out of his mind, I delivered the cakes and bread to all four corners of what had once been Henry VIII's palace. On damp and misty winter nights, walking along the dimly gas lit passageways and cobbled courtyards was quite an unnerving experience. A basket was lowered on a string from the stairwell by women I never even saw. I simply placed the usual bread loaf in and up it went as if pulled by one of the ghosts we'd been told regularly haunted the place. I hurried through the shadows, my footsteps echoing down the halls. I was pretty nervous and half expected Anne Boleyn's ghost to appear at the next corner carrying her head under her arm. Alas, she never made an appearance, and after I finished my round, I waited for the baker to stagger out of the Mitre Hotel looking the worse for drink. It didn't matter much, though, because the horse always knew the way home. Unfortunately, we encountered a new problem when the horse was retired and we got a motorised van. The idea of driving didn't bother me unduly and I eventually learned to handle it well enough to be able to drive along the straight road from Hampton Court to Hampton Wick, albeit at a horse and carriage's pace. Just as well there weren't many motorised cops around at the time.

As I started earning more money I eventually saved enough to go on my very own first trip overseas…well, to the Isle of Wight (it only required taking a three-mile ferry ride across the Solent). Having successfully failed my exams to continue schooling – considered a badge of honour in the mind of most of my peers – my self-esteem was high. I had confidence by the bucket load and my zest for learning gave me all the motivation I needed. But I knew that dreams were pretty useless unless I made a conscious effort to make them come true. I was also aware I'd need a lot of luck, which I was destined to have, but not yet. Shortly after turning fourteen, I started working.

CHAPTER 2

The voyage begins

Almost immediately after leaving school I got a job at the Hawker Aircraft Company in Kingston, where I got stuck in helping to build Osprey and Super Fury bi-planes. The company manufactured motorbikes before turning to the production of combat aircraft during the First World War, the most successful of which was the legendary Camel. My contribution to the building process was to fix soft iron wire onto small parts, which were then hung up like fillets of smoked salmon and spray painted with a sticky substance called P.O.V. in specially-constructed booths. Girls applied a strong-smelling glue called dope onto the canvas cover of the aeroplanes, which was toxic and could make you quite woozy, hence the expression 'dopey'.

Soon I was moved to the electrical plating shop where I learned rather more, and the jobs got harder and more dangerous. We handled corrosive substances such as trichoethylene degreasers, which when inhaled had an effect similar to being drunk. It's an irony of life that what was once considered a work hazard has now become a pastime for many young people. All in all, between feeling woozy and getting drunk, it was quite a hazardous existence at the factory, and for my pains I got eleven shillings a week for forty-eight hours work – with deductions if I was late clocking on.

It wasn't long before I was moved again, this time to the machine shop. It was a place that almost defied description, but Charley Chaplin's film *Metro* faithfully re-enacted the hellish conditions in which we had to work. About three hundred yards long, the shop floor was strewn with lathes, grinders, milling machines and heavy presses, all crammed together and driven by leather belts actuated by a great central shaft high above in the apex of the roof. Above that was a dirty skylight where the light struggled to get through. The noise of hundreds of leather belts thrashing about wildly, mixed with the oil and the dirt, made life unbearable at the factory, yet many of the men would end up doing it for their entire working lives. Some machines which did the more repetitive tasks were operated by boys, and I was one of them. I still got the same wage, but could earn more if I stepped up production. I guess it wasn't much of an incentive because I never earned any extra cash.

To while away the time, the setter in my section often took me on the back of his Triumph Speed Twin motorbike to the river at Kingston for a swim during the summer months, and on the way home we raced up and down the new Kingston bypass road to dry off. I was learning to mix with adults and although I still went out drinking with my dad, thanks to my job I could now go to different pubs thriving with their own atmosphere. In one of these, the pianist at a pub in Hampton Wick – a man called Randall – had been a victim of the 'talkies'. He had played the piano at the Super during the age of silent movies but was now relegated to playing at the Rose and Crown. I often sang Tin Pan Alley songs there, and when I realised I was going down rather well I decided to try my luck in other pubs. I must have done something right because I usually got a pint of beer for my troubles.

Despite it all I still treasured my solitude. I had moved on and given up on most of the friendships I had forged at school and in my street, but I still kept in touch with Mick, who lived next door to me. He loathed drinking and billiards but he liked girls, and that was good enough for me. At weekends we went down Kingston's 'monkey parade' in the main street to pick the most gorgeous looking girls, who in turn walked down in twos and threes to flaunt their stuff and tease the lads. If we thought they were worth it we'd chat them up. But it was a delicate balancing act. It was important to find out where they lived in case they expected to be seen home (that was an added financial burden as it meant buying them the bus fare back) then, within ten or fifteen minutes we had them down the river bank in Canbury Gardens. It was evidently a popular place for lovers because we had a hard time walking there without tripping over used condoms, not that that bothered the couples on the ground. It was all too much for poor old Mick who, as a devout Catholic and altar boy, always confessed his 'sins' before we went on the pull, or so he claimed.

On Sundays, while he went to Church, I would go for a long ramble on my own that lasted for most of the day. The walk gave me an opportunity to clear my head, especially after a few pints at the Rose and Crown. During one such walk I made up my mind to leave the hell-hole that my job at the factory had become. Back to work that Monday, everything seemed clearer to me. The sunlight, which always desperately tried to shine through the grime and dirt on the skylight, seemed brighter than usual. I watched for about a minute and then shut the machine down, marched across the factory floor, and walked out of the front gate without stopping once. The gatekeeper told me to clock out, but I was so euphoric I ignored him – I could have clocked him instead. It took a few days to get rid of the soluble oil which had impregnated my skin, a nasty reminder of what my job at the factory had been like. My departure also coincided with a new chapter at the factory where they started to build the prototype of a new kind of mono-winged fighter plane: the legendary Hurricane. Now they would have to do it without my help.

It was clear I wasn't cut out for factory work and within a few days I had a far better paid job working outdoors as a trainee sports groundsman at St Mary's Hospital.

The hospital had a very big sports ground with a good Rugby pitch grandstand, a cricket field, a hockey pitch, and six hard clay courts for tennis. Unsurprisingly, Saturday was always a very busy bar day. I helped to look after all the installations and never counted the hours as I happily learned all the tricks of the trade, knowing that one day I would probably be the head groundsman at Lord's or Wembley. Being able to drive was a bonus as I could harrow the acreage and tow the harrow behind an old bull-nosed Morris. I took the most care with the cricket wicket's bowling pitch. It had to be perfect; not too hard and not too soft and perfectly swept clean of the smallest specs. It was an obsession for perfection I would later carry into films.

After a rugby match on Saturday and after the players had bathed in the pool-sized communal tubs and fixed their cuts, bruises and occasional broken collar bones, they would all crowd into the bar. The men, mostly young student doctors in their early twenties, asked me to put their name in chalk on one of the wooden beer barrels that were stacked up in tiers against the wall at the back of the bar counter. Everybody sang rugby songs whilst topping up their beer jugs, and they only had enough when the barrels became empty. That was the cue for them to get into their open-topped sports cars and drive away. They never had an accident, but many of them were to die tragically in the war soon afterwards, fighting to preserve their way of life. In fact, rumblings of war had already started. There was a lot of talk on the wireless and in the pubs that there might be a war with Germany.

Most people took little notice, and those who could still remember the Great War were sceptical. But the rumours soon took on a greater urgency. The newspapers began reporting on Hitler, his Nazi party and the great force of bombers the Germans were building. We were told that the new way to fight a war was to bomb the cities flat and to wipe out the civilian population. It made for grim reading, but it was to be far closer to the truth than we suspected. Then, at 11a.m. on a Sunday morning, with the whole country listening, Neville Chamberlain gave a speech on the wireless that would change history. The Prime Minister's shaky voice and sombre tone ominously foretold the tragic news: the invasion of Poland had lit the touch paper and we were at war with Germany.

It was September 3, 1939, and I had just turned eighteen, almost a month earlier. I was dumbstruck like the rest of the country and decided to go out for a walk in Kingston to clear my head and hear what was being said in the pubs. On Sundays they didn't open until 12 o'clock but I thought on this unusual occasion they might. Suddenly, the air sirens wailed out and everyone around me looked up, desperately scanning the sky above to catch a glimpse of the feared bombers and the accompanying blitzkrieg. Many rushed for cover, but soon the sirens sounded the all-clear. It was the start of the phoney war; a period during which very little fighting actually took place, but it was a sobering foretaste of what was to come. I made my way to a pub and sat down for a drink, listening intently to the people around me, the majority of whom had plans to build bomb shelters. Everyone was apprehensive, dreading the unknown but certain their lives were about to change forever. The world was about to become embroiled in six years of horrific death and destruction and I would not be immune to any of it – my own blissful, happy-go-lucky existence and the job I treasured included.

In spite of it all, I accepted life with a sense of fatalism in much the same way the rest of Londoners did – whatever would be, would be. That same afternoon I went into a passive air defence post and joined the war effort, not quite sure what I would be asked to do. I was given a steel helmet, a gas mask, and an arm band and told to be on standby with the others – shovel in hand – and to be ready to rescue people. For a moment I thought I was going to be asked to go into battle without a rifle. Instead, I learned the basics of tunnelling into rubble, took part in a first aid course, and was eventually in charge of a full squad of men. It was all rather pointless, mostly because there wasn't anybody waiting to be rescued. But of one thing I was certain; I would never return to the lovely sports ground again.

The bombs began falling on London but the Germans found the nut wouldn't crack and it all went quiet again. I had been 'deferred' from joining the army as an essential worker and been reviewed several times, but now that things had calmed down a bit I tried to join once more. Prior to this I'd been to the Marines, who were very exacting in their requirements, then I went to the RAF who told me I had good eyesight and thought I could make a good gunner. I froze. The idea did not appeal to me one jot because everyone knew gunners were more exposed and far more likely to get killed. Fortunately for me, the army called me up on the same day, and that decided it for me. I joined the army and learned all sorts of ways to kill the enemy – all of which were invariably brutish and I never got round to doing – and discipline, which I wasn't very good at.

Things were looking up, however. Eighteen months later I was discharged after damaging my leg in an accident while on manoeuvres in Salisbury Plain. Pondering my next move while recovering in hospital in Bath, a soldier in the bed next to me told me he had worked in a film studio before the war. I don't remember quite what he did but whatever it was sounded easy enough and I was sure I'd be able to handle it. On being discharged from hospital I was told I would have to appear before a board of army officers and doctors to decide my future in the armed forces. I was hoping the news would be good. It was.

I was discharged from the army forthwith and my rather short service for King and Country came to a sudden end. I went back to my parents' home to recuperate before getting out and about once more, and found things had changed radically since the last time I'd paid them a visit. The pubs were overrun with thousands of American and Canadian troops. The Canadian battalions were based in Richmond Park, while the American Army and Air force had built a huge base in Bushy Park, littering the surrounding area with anti-aircraft guns. All my stomping grounds were overflowing with rich soldiers and highly-impressionable girls. It was almost a war zone but today no one would ever know there had been tens of thousands of troops based in huge camps there. Watching all the activity around me and being on the sidelines made me edgy, but fortunately I soon felt physically able to work again. I remembered what the soldier had told me at the hospital, and that the Warner Brothers' studio was next to the Angler's pub in Teddington. I made a conscious decision to have a stab at working in the film business in whatever capacity presented itself. It was morning and the studio was open for business. I took a last swig of my pint for Dutch courage and limped towards the imposing gates, emblazoned with the big brass 'WB' in the centre. To one side was the gateman's office. Wearing my old battledress, as I had no money to buy new clothes, I walked up to the gatehouse and tapped on the sliding glass window. A big bloke peered out, eyeing me suspiciously. "Do they need anyone here? I'm looking for work." I asked. Before I gave him time to respond I explained that I had been discharged from the army and showed him the relevant paperwork. It did the trick. He opened the door and invited me into his comfortable looking office.

"What can you do?"

"Anything and everything." I cheekily replied.

"They need a boom operator. You could learn to do that quickly enough."

"Of course I could." I was riding my luck, but the security guard and I seemed to hit it off, so I saw no harm in being bold. "What does a boom operator do?"

He explained that the job consisted of holding out a long pole or boom with a microphone at the end of it over the top of the actors, making sure one didn't interfere with the lights or intrude the camera's view.

"I can do that. How much does a boom operator get paid?"

"Four pounds and ten shillings for a forty-eight-hour week."

The low wages instantly put me off. "What else do they need?"

He shuffled a few papers in front of him and mumbled to himself, "They need a set dresser."

"Who does he dress?" I naively asked. With a smile he explained about dressing sets with props. It could be a house, garden or anything that would appear within shot. The job appealed to my sense of freedom.

"How much does a set dresser get paid?"

"Seven pounds for a basic forty-eight-hour week, with a lot of overtime paid at time and a half."

41

"Look no further," I interrupted, "I'm your man."

With a smile he picked up the phone. A young boy, known as a runner, strolled to the gates and escorted me to the front office of this strange, make-believe place. I was about to start my life in a 'let's pretend' world for real.

Set up the easel and start the fun

Captain Horatio Hornblower R.N. – UK /US (1951) 116 minutes. Warner Bros.
Director: Raoul Walsh. Producer: Gerry Mitchell. Writers: Ivan Goff, Ben Roberts, Aeneas MacKenzie (based on the novel by C. S. Forester).
Cast: Gregory Peck, Virginia Mayo, Robert Beatty, James Robertson Justice, Denis O'Dea, Terence Morgan.

The site beside the Thames and the weir in Teddington was excellent. It had once been the big garden of a house, unimaginatively called Weir House. In the earliest days of moving pictures a small studio with a glass roof had been erected in the corner of the garden and, little by little, became a fair-sized stage. When Warner Brothers took over they got rid of everything except the old stage, and with the introduction of new buildings helped to transform the site into a proper film studio. A film distribution building, where cans of films were stored in fireproof vaults, stood nearby. Next to the vaults was a lab where rows of girls, running to and from cutting room machines, checked returned film before sending it out again. It all formed part of a huge, movie-making machine. American companies that wanted to show their movies in the United Kingdom were required by law to invest in the British film industry, and they did that by churning out low budget films, popularly known as 'quota-quickies'. They proved to be quite successful at the time and were the studio's main operation. In between the 'quickies' I managed to make a number of good films with top name British actors and actresses, as well as the Australian Errol Flynn, who was eventually shipped out to the USA to become a screen legend. The biggest building on the lot, four storeys high and extending all along the river bank, was the property building. It contained a huge collection of props and antiques used for dressing the sets of most of their films.

There was everything from Chippendale to Sheridan, and even the odd kitchen sink. We bought furniture at auctions from great old houses that had been closed because of the war, including silverware, bronzes, pianos, harpsichords, full-dinner services, and quality carpets of every shape and description. It was a veritable treasure trove, and the wizard in charge of it all was a cockney property master called Harry Hannay. We became good friends and spent most days out in a van, 'totting' or looking for the props we might need. Some things were bought and others rented. Whether the set was a suburban room, a hospital ward, a pretty garden or a hovel for tramps, my job was to dress it with suitable props, down to the last detail – and no detail was too small or insignificant. It could be a piece of paper in a typewriter, or a slipper tossed carelessly by a rumpled bed. It was all a question of using one's own imagination. Much to my surprise I learned that black and white films were anything but. We applied a blue dye to cloth bed sheets and tea for the smaller surfaces, because anything truly 'white' did not show up on film. We introduced blotting paper between sheets to prevent them making a rustling sound and tipped a bit of lighter fluid on candles to help them light up instantly. Those little details went unnoticed but they were just as important as the rest of the set. Whenever I was stumped for ideas I referred to old books or pictures on the subject. The main aim was to get a set to look right and to enjoy the work while it lasted. I did; it was like being transported back to Bushy Park, except this time the toys were real and far more expensive.

I was just getting the hang of my job when one day a runner came to tell me that I was to report to the studio manager's office. A chill went down my spine. You only ever went to the front office when you were in trouble, and this felt like being summoned to appear before God. In this case God was Doc Salomon, an American from Burbank who had been a long-time friend of the great man himself, Jack Warner. Despite feeling nervous and apprehensive I plucked up all the courage I could muster. I knocked on the door and Salomon's gravelly voice boomed back at me, summoning me to enter. Salomon looked and sounded just like Jimmy 'Schnozzle' Durante, which gave him a somewhat comical appearance. I must have had a similar effect on him, too. He looked up at the dishevelled figure standing before him in an old battledress on his shag carpet. "Are you a deserter?" he growled.

"You know I'm not." I stiffly replied. "The personnel at the accounts department have seen my discharge papers."

"Then why do you come to the job wearing your army uniform?"

"I'm saving to buy civvy clothes," I answered, defensively.

He leaned forward on the desk and almost whispered to me, "I'm going to pay you more, but don't tell those bastards out there, they've got a trade union." And that was that. My first meeting with a studio big nob and I'd got a pay rise without even asking for one. I was on my way. About two weeks later the shop stewards told me to join the union. I agreed, but only because I was in a Catch-22 situation: if you didn't join the union, you couldn't get a job, and you couldn't get a job if you weren't a member of the union. There's a general consensus of opinion that Britain's industrial malaise was brought about partly by workers' apathy and disinterest. It's no secret that the unions were responsible for much of this – I was a witness to it. By joining the union I was now one of them, but it quickly became apparent that it didn't matter if one was good at his job or not. The fact that I enjoyed my work irritated many of the other union members who felt put out by my enthusiasm. Some of them went as far as to suggest I show restraint and take a more lackadaisical approach to my work. The shop stewards – and there were quite a few of them – had their hour-long works' committee meeting at four o'clock every afternoon after the tea break in the canteen, which started at 3.15p.m. and lasted about half an hour. There was a special committee room set aside for these 'brothers' where, amongst other things, they decided if a member would be allowed to work overtime. If the department head had not put the request in before four o'clock that same evening it was rejected. There were strict union rules for everything and no one was allowed to even touch things from the other departments. I once saw a stage hand who worked for the construction department carefully sweeping around a fallen ivy leaf because it was termed a prop. It was a crazy set up and I instantly rebelled against the system.

One of the better quality films I worked on was *Mr Emmanuel*, starring Felix Aylmer, an old star of the period. One of the scenes called for a number of teenage girls, and as I watched them on the set I picked out one who seemed to be the most confident, and certainly the prettiest. She was a fifteen-year-old and appeared to have more talent and charm than the rest. Her name was Jean Simmons. The next time I met her was in Cambodia many years later while working on *Lord Jim*, a film her then husband Richard Brooks was directing. Without being conscious of it, I was beginning to do a bit of talent spotting of my own.

The war in the meantime continued its unrelenting course. The Germans tried to dive bomb the River Weir beside the studios with what I guessed were a couple of Stukas, but they missed us. The bombs exploded in the river instead and the water became full of dead or stunned fish. The big old studio cat had a field day, standing at the bottom of the steps and hooking them out with his claw. There were winners even after a bombing raid, I mused. The Germans then tried another tactic and started deploying unmanned flying bombs, or V-1 rockets. They made a lot of noise coming in; a sound not unlike that of a thousand scooters, but it was when they stopped buzzing that one had to worry. They often glided downwards for quite a long time, comparatively speaking, but they could just as easily fall out of the sky without any warning. You could watch, or even run and take cover, but there was not a lot you could do, except hope it wasn't your turn to kick the bucket. These 'doodlebugs', as Londoners called them, didn't penetrate the ground but they caused a lot of widespread damage. They also managed to kill more than five thousand people and injure some sixteen thousand throughout the south-east. They came in at twenty-minute intervals, and you learned to judge your moment for doing things – you didn't want to be caught literally with your pants down.

Inevitably, all this made it difficult to shoot a film on the sound stage, so we looked for a solution and developed our own version of an early warning system. A man was posted on the roof with a pair of binoculars to judge if the next doodlebug had our name on it. If he thought the rocket was flying towards the studio he would press a button which rang a bell on stage, thereby alerting the stage crew to take cover behind a sand bag shelter. But our luck eventually did run out. Fortunately, when it did most of us had all left the building. It was 7.30 in the evening and only Doc, the studio manager, the head of security, and three other men – all passionate poker players – were in Doc's office playing a round when the V-1 fell on them. The bomb exploded on the diesel fuel tanks of the studio's generator station, and everything except the prop building and the film vaults

– both of which were down by the river and protected by the big stage – was reduced to great piles of blackened rubble and twisted girders. Whilst searching among the ruins I made a gruesome discovery. I stumbled upon Doc's hand which I instantly recognised as his thanks to the great big wedding ring he always wore. We had been creating a world of make-believe, oblivious to the sickening reality of war, until now.

Next day, everyone was fired except for the chief accountant, the chief purchase controller, the chief engineer, Harry Hannay and me. We put the glass back in the prop room and everything back in place in an effort to return to normality as quickly as possible. I suppose I could have gone to another studio, but I had such an affinity with Warners' at Teddington that I literally spent my life in the prop room. At night, I slept inside a pair of Chesterfields; a long settee with the rolled back and arms of the same height. Turned on top of one another like a cave in case a bomb sent shards of glass flying everywhere, it became quite a safe shelter. The prop room was very different at night and the chandeliers tinkled every time a bomb went off in the distance. I made sure I spent nights comfortably by retiring into 'the cave' with a bottle of 'Scottish medicine' and a book which I chose from the fine old collection available in the prop room. To make life a little more bearable we grew tomatoes and kept a few chickens and rabbits on the big flat roof. I even cooked pork chops obtained from friendly shopkeepers.

One day, after a quiet spell from the bombing raids, there was an enormous bang which had apparently been caused by a huge gas explosion at Chiswick. It later transpired that the Germans had a terrifying new weapon in their arsenal: the V-2 flying bomb. This clever little device carried a one-ton explosive charge and, in contrast to its predecessor, the V-1, the V-2 rocket was supersonic and gave no previous warning to the unsuspecting civilians below. The Government was at a loss as to how to respond to this potentially catastrophic weapon, so they decided to keep quiet about its existence at first and attributed the explosions to accidents. But they could only keep it a secret for so long. The following day we heard two more blasts, which we later discovered had been a V-2 striking the Firestone tyre factory, killing a large number of factory workers, many of whom were young women. Thankfully these proved to be the last attacks, and when war ended in Europe we started rebuilding the studios.

It didn't take long to build or equip, and it was better than before – we even had lawns and gardens. Gerry Blattner became our new studio manager and he put in place all new department heads. His main anchor was the new construction manager Peter Dukelow; a tough, hard living, hard drinking, no-nonsense Irishman from County Wexford. We were destined to become great friends and work together on several classic films during the next fifty years. To coincide with the opening of the new studio, Jack Warner came along to see us shoot scenes of his new movie, *Yankie Doodle Dandy*, in colour. We then got involved making black-and-white feature films, which were a far cry from the quickies of old that we stopped making. The unions were just as strong but they got short thrift from Peter, who scared the hell out of most people.

The studio now made films mostly for independent producers, and when Blattner came he brought a young man whom we assumed to be a friend of a friend from Elstree. His name was Ken Adam; the future set designer for the James Bond films. He was quite a flamboyant character and drove around in a monster open-top American car with a giant German shepherd that sat on the back seat. A top art director called Paul Sheriff also came and asked if Ken could learn with me. Starting from scratch, Adam didn't know the difference between a sofa and a Chesterfield but I don't suppose it mattered if you ended up making James Bond films. It was not all serious work, though. For a specific scene we had to build a set that was supposed to represent the sea using a flat sheet of cloth, which we stretched out and covered with glitter. A couple of prop men were under it to gently rock the scenery and during one of the takes one of them violently broke wind. "Cut!" yelled the director, who was momentarily lost for words. "We'll try again without the belly rumbles from under the ocean."

It was round about this time that I started dabbling with special effects and, more specifically, explosives. I was doing a scene for another film at Teddington in which Hollywood star and all-time baddie Peter Lorrie had to pull the big breaker switch in the opera house. The Director asked me to add a big spark effect, which I did with a bit of photo-flash powder. Feeling a bit mischievous I made sure I put in a tiny pinch more. All of a sudden Lorrie, who was supposed to be playing a fearless villain, became a scared little lamb. It looked good, but he was so shaken that he fled into his dressing room and was not seen again for the rest of the day.

On another occasion I was involved in a muddy battlefield scene by the riverbank. The actor playing the hero, a British officer, had to have a shell explode beside him, and before we started shooting I showed him where the charge was hidden. The actor in question was a very young Richard Attenborough who was totally unfazed and ran so close to the bomb when the charge went off that he was spattered with mud and, after stumbling a few paces, continued his charge.

Yet all this was a mere taste of what was to come – my first major break. Warner Brothers' decided to make a film adaptation of C S Forrester's story of *Captain Horatio Hornblower R.N.* with Gregory Peck in the lead role and Virginia Mayo as his romantic co-star. Director Raoul Walsh, who was an old friend of Jack Warners', was a tough, down-to-earth character who just got on with things with the minimum of fuss. His one distinguishing feature was a black eye-patch he wore to cover an empty socket; it didn't bother us and it certainly didn't seem to bother him, either. He never missed a trick, but he had one strange habit. He used to hand-roll thin cigarettes one-handed, while pouring a very loose dark tobacco called 'Bull Durham', which he kept in small soft leather pouch around his neck, with the other. The odd thing was that after going to the trouble of making the cigarettes he would throw them away without even looking at the finished product. He then started the process all over again. During the big action scenes he'd roll the cigarettes at a frantic speed and, just occasionally, light one up by taking a red match from his pocket and striking it against whatever was close. He was the first person to arrive at the studio at the start of the day, often to take up position at the main door. He had a little note book and a pencil he would use, not to make notes on his staff but to ask those in the know their tip for the day's horse racing, which he then put to good use to compile his bets. Not one to do things by half, he relied on inside information from someone in the studio, which was of course totally illegal but very common at the time.

Before we began shooting, Gregory Peck arrived in London to an apartment Warner Brothers had rented for him near the American embassy. I was told to arrange things and went to pick him up. As I was walking up the sweeping staircase to the apartment I noticed a couple of young boys leaning over the balustrade, carelessly hurling objects down on me. "Hey fellah! Watch out for the bombs!" they yelled. I felt like belting them but I suspected they might have been part of Peck's entourage, so I bit my lip and said nothing. They could not have been more different to Peck, who was one of the quietest people I ever met.

The rest of the cast threw up few surprises. A young and relatively unknown Christopher Lee was to play the baddie, a role he would make his own over the next sixty years. I found him to be a very pleasant man, but James Robertson Justice was a different character altogether. Arrogant and aloof, like most of the characters he played in films, his most irritating habit was continually taking snuff, most of which dangled on his upper lip and gave his prominent beard an odd ginger hue. *Hornblower* would be a very big picture; too big for our small studio, so Warner Brothers' decided to shoot the film at the biggest studios in Europe at the time; Denham in west London, which also had the biggest sound stages in the world.

During the war Denham had been handed to the American forces as a giant storehouse. Filming re-started after the war, but aside from making a few films such as *Treasure Island*, not much else went on. Shortly afterwards, it was shut down and all the personnel were fired. But when the job was given to us we reopened it and I moved in as the Property Master to hire new staff. At Denham we had no problem with the unions as we started from scratch with men carefully chosen by Peter Dukelow. Peter, like the stunt men, could be hard to keep up with, but he promised higher wages if they did overtime – it was an arrangement which suited everyone. There were no pointless works' committee meetings because there was nothing to discuss, we just got on with the job to earn as much as we could. At the height of the battle scenes Peter and I virtually lived in the studio, preparing the action during the night in readiness for the following day's filming. On Stage Four, Peter built a life-scale British Man-o-War. It was in fact not a sea-worthy vessel, but an ingenious device hollowed out below the water line, its bottom replaced by hydraulic rockers. There were no tops to the masts either, as there was no room to accommodate that and the roof girders to the stage. The makers of *Elizabeth: The Golden Age* recently made a big deal about building something similar, but we got there first almost sixty years earlier, and without the aid of computer animation.

49

The art department was in charge of making most of the working drawings for the ship. The designer was a top man called Tom Morahan who, like Peter, was Irish but did not get on well with him. Morahan was a bit of a know-all who got under people's skin. He also had a reputation for having fired every draughtsman who'd worked under him. Peter, on the other hand, was very much his own man and simply ignored Morahan, which also helped me as he kept him off my back. New materials were being introduced at this time by companies such as ICI, and I was the first person in films to use a liquid plastic called Velvic to make many new props, including swords and grappling hooks. These were safe to use but did not look very convincing in close-up shots. Nonetheless, it gave film makers another useful tool and I took full advantage of it, even doing a crash course on how to bake the stuff.

Swords for fighting had until then been made of laminated leather, stitched together for strength, but I eventually found a better material than this – Tufnell. It was the insulator board material used for big switch panels and made of layers of linen compressed together with resin. It was strong but safe and could be machined.

As we were going to film a 19th century naval battle we had no option but to master the workings of a cannon. We had a whale of a time firing cannons of all types, including single shot, chain shot and broadsides, for months on end. Although quite dangerous to use, the end result was worth it as a full broadside could be felt as far as Denham railway station, a quarter of a mile away. We built model boats that carried two men, one to steer and the other to fire the small cannons. During the height of battle the noise inside the stage was deafening. We installed great big fans that blew gusts of wind and hoses to spray water on the decks. In the meantime the rigging would come crashing down and disappear into the make-believe sea below. We had tremendous fun playing at war with huge galleons day after day, but the picture wasn't just about battles – there was also a romantic story involving Virginia Mayo, whom Gregory Peck had been persuaded to rescue from somewhere in the Caribbean and whisk back to England.

During one of the romantic scenes, Walsh wanted them on deck in the moonlight while a very gentle breeze fanned their lovelorn faces, and that's where I came in.

I arranged the tiniest breeze to disturb their hair at the right moment. It had to be inaudible otherwise the microphones would pick up the noise – and heavy breathing, after all, was Peck and Mayo's job. They were both great to work with and I felt I was doing more than just a job; I also wanted to help and be part of what they were trying to transmit. When there is intensity and sincerity on the part of the actors it all becomes real, until one hears the word 'cut!'

Peck did a splendid job playing the role of the imperturbable Royal Navy Captain as only he could, standing motionless on the ship's deck while the scenery crashed all around him. It was all rigged so that the falling masts missed him by a few feet, of course, but it took nerve and it required the utmost trust in what we were doing. The stunt men in the film were all a close-knit bunch who also doubled as the ship's crew. I became good friends with them all. It was just as well because we had to work together and they were a pretty hardened lot, on and off the job, and totally off their rockers. In between shots they played murderous games of poker for very high stakes, with often dire results. On one occasion they started a terrific fight in the dressing rooms. Taking their roles as brawling sailors a bit too literally, they smashed furniture along with the wash basins and even some of the toilet bowls. And that was during their lighter moments. One guy found out that another stuntman friend of his had been having it off with his wife. His solution to the problem was totally in keeping with his profession. He decided to rig the chap's car with dynamite and blow him to Kingdom Come. Fortunately, he got found out in time and went down for two years. But they were all good blokes...no, really.

While the crew went to Elstree to shoot interiors, Peter modified what had been a Royal Navy ship into a larger and more decorated Spanish galleon. We worked day and night to get it ready so that we could later smash the whole thing up. No question about it, we were earning double and having a lot of fun in the process. The ships had to sail on the open seas, so Peter set about building a water tank filled with millions of gallons of water. It was only about five feet deep but it was spread over a huge area on the back lot near the river, from where the water was drawn. One end of the tank spilled into a false horizon, beyond which Peter built a backdrop the full width of the tank, some ninety feet high and made of steel and cement. It leant backwards so that the light fell on it correctly. In front of it, on a rail track, were two steel towers that travelled along the face of the backdrop. One had painters on to paint the sky and the second one to paint the clouds on. At the shooting end of the tank were the wave machines, and at the sides six old fighter planes were tied down to create the wind effect. A touch of copper sulphate was added to colour the water for the fifteen-foot long model ships to play on. While this was being prepared – and as I had little to do – Warners' decided to send me to work on another film, this time in San Remo in northern Italy. But as I was getting ready to leave on my first trip abroad, I was told to return urgently to Denham to meet Peter. When I arrived, the tank had been emptied and along one side there was some undulating scaffolding with a mock cliff built over it. On top of the cliff stood a fort which guarded the entry to the harbour. As we stood in the tank Peter cast his hand across the cliff top.

"Can you make that into the coast of France?"

"No problem," I replied. I was then told to have it ready in three days.

"I want to start putting water into the tank when you're finished," Peter added, almost as an afterthought. If I flinched, I didn't show it. I went straight back into my old office and heated up the phone lines. I took on some crew and phoned up all the studios to borrow prop men for the weekend's overtime. I got in touch with estates and gardens to get all I needed, including scale-size pine trees, clippings by the thousands, Cumberland sea-washed turf and as much moss as I could gather. The crew were joined by colleagues from other studios to dress the set and by Sunday evening the mock French coast was looking pretty good. Peter started up the big pumps and we went for a celebratory pint of beer. Next morning we stood on the side of the tank, its floor well covered with water rushing in from the big slush pumps. Tom Morahan, the designer who had not had a great deal to do with the cliff set, came in and stood beside us. He gazed at the green cliff, complete with matching trees, but instead of thanking us for our hard work, he had a fit.

"What is this? Who did this?" he fumed. We seemed to have ruffled his feathers.

"I did," I replied, a bit smugly.

"Don't you know there are drawings for those trees?"

"You're kidding me Tom."

He drew himself up close and barked an order to his sidekick, a skinny man known to everyone in the studio as Johnny 'Hosepipes' Hoseley on account of his tight trousers.

"John! Go and get the drawings!"

Johnny hurried as quickly as his tight pants would allow. In the meantime, an increasingly flustered Morahan was getting nowhere with Peter, who pretty much ignored him. When Morahan's shadow arrived with the drawings, they were thrust into my hands.

"You were supposed to make these trees!" he said, jabbing at the plans. I looked at them and laughed. There were thousands of gnarled trees, far too many than were needed, or could realistically be built.

Upon seeing my reaction Peter lost his rag. "Just bugger off Tom, the water's going in and we're about to start shooting. That's the way Gerry wants it and that's the way it's going to be done." Tom went off in a sulk and there the matter ended.

Many years later, on a nostalgic visit to the area, I went down a little wooden staircase by Kingston Bridge where they used to tie up the big river barges. Close by, there was a small pub called The Row Barge. It appeared abandoned, but the door pushed open and I entered. In a dark corner a lonely old man sat staring at an empty beer glass, looking somewhat dishevelled. Feeling curious, I ordered a pint for myself and one for him. His eyes lit up in gratitude and he invited me to sit by his side. As we chatted, it slowly dawned on me that I was talking to Tom Morahan. He confessed he'd been out of work for a long time following a heart attack but despite being broke, he dreamt that one day he would make his own films. I didn't want to shatter his illusions and bought him another drink. He passed away not long afterwards and I was genuinely saddened. I felt no sense of triumph because, by then, I knew full well that the film industry regularly chewed decent people up and spat them out without a second thought. But I was determined that would not happen to me.

A Different Kind of Break

I'll Get You for This (1951) US – Director: Joseph M Newman. Writers: George Callahan, James Hadley Chase, William Rose. Producer: Joe Kaufmann.
Cast: George Raft, Coleen Gray, Enzo Staiola, Charles Goldner.
I'll Get You for This was the rather odd title for the film Warner's put me to work on while Peter Dukelow built the water tank for

Hornblower. Silly title or not, at least it meant I'd be having a nice holiday in San Remo. Set in a gambling casino and with Hollywood legend George Raft in the lead role, I suspected the film would have a strong gangster-theme running through it. I flew from Northolt airport in a noisy turbo-prop Viking and landed at Nice airport after an interminably long flight during which I developed a painful ear-ache. As I stepped off the plane feeling the worse for wear, I observed a respectable-looking Frenchman urinating in the gutter while his lady friend looked on. No doubt about it, I was in France. I felt tempted to try this French custom but the call of nature was not strong enough. I was then whisked off in a chauffeur-driven car to the set in San Remo, where I met the Production Manager, Ernie Holding, a rather heartless sort of chap, and the Art Director Fred Pewsey, who didn't seem very concerned about anything other than socialising. I knew then this wasn't going to be a top notch project.

Unconcerned, I quickly set to work hiring helpers and an interpreter who knew the town well. There was a scene where George Raft had to come out of a casino and scatter US dollar bills to the crowds – why, I don't know, but I guess it's because it was an American movie. I had plenty of prop money which I brought from Teddington along with the big rubber stamp to make them. Unfortunately, as the director decided to re-shoot the scene throughout the night, I wasn't able to retrieve enough of the damn bills. I sat in the street on an upturned box, trying to keep up with Raft's puzzling desire to reduce San Remo's debt by frantically stamping up more bills. Two *carabinieri*, who had been peering over my shoulder for an uncomfortably long time, became worried about my counterfeiting skills and was told to cease my activities forthwith. As we couldn't stop shooting I came up with a solution, which was to stamp one side of the bills the wrong way up. All was smiles as they congratulated each other for having solved the problem. The officers were then each handed a fistful of my wonky bills from my inexhaustible supply before walking off into the night. Whether they thought they had made a killing is not recorded, but at least I got them off my back.

Maybe as a result of this episode, I gained a reputation among the crew as an excellent trouble-shooter. While having a drink with Fred, the Art Director, at the hotel's terrace the following evening, he explained that the Director had asked him to put a scary looking tree on a certain location, high up on a rocky outcrop in the mountains and accessible only from a narrow, twisty track with hairpin bends. He casually asked if I wouldn't mind taking the tree to the top of the mountain and plant it myself the next day. I suspected he had forgotten to do it himself, and as I didn't fancy doing the job I turned him down. I explained that the truck would not be able to get to the top, but he was too deep in thought about the bollocking Newman would give him to listen to me. Feeling sorry for him (and shamelessly giving in to emotional blackmail), I promised that a scary tree would be planted on the exact place the next day. He instantly cheered up, no doubt relieved that he had passed the hot potato onto this poor sap.

Early the following morning I went with some of my crew and an American power wagon with an A-frame mounted on it to look for a suitable tree. Driving along we soon realised there were hardly any trees in the area and we were on the verge of giving up when we stumbled upon a gnarled old olive tree that seemed ideal for the job of scary prop. It showed very few signs of life so we cut it at ground level, which was no mean task as it was like sawing through iron. Looking and no doubt acting like guilty schoolchildren, we made off with the tree and safely delivered it to its new site where we were going to shoot the scene. Feeling smug about another job well done, I soon forgot about the entire episode.

But a few days later, while browsing through the pages of a local newspaper, my jaw fell open upon seeing a cartoon of a wild man with long hair striding from peak to peak on a mountain road, swinging an axe over his head, with trees flying in all directions. I put two and two together – it was me. The caption underneath read, "The mad man!". Apparently, the old tree was so ancient that the local church considered it a holy relic. Clearly, the tree was at least as old as Jesus Christ himself and chopping it down had been a major faux pas on our part. To make amends Holding made a generous donation to the local church, while I adopted a more pragmatic view arguing that, by appearing in the film, many more people would now get to enjoy seeing the relic. I don't think my comments went down too well. We shot another scene later on in the mountains in a dilapidated town, which had apparently been levelled by a powerful earthquake some eighty years before. Part of it fell into the deep gorge below and the town's main street finished, literally, at the edge of the precipice. During the scene the leading lady, played by Coleen Gray, had to run in panic through the ruins. But due to the way the scene was being shot it would have to be Gray, and not a double, on screen. It was going to be tricky to shoot because we had the precipice to contend with. It was decided that I would step out of the shadows and catch her just before the long drop. She was game and trusted me to get the job done safely. We rehearsed the scene on our own and found a way to do it. The trick when someone is running towards you at full speed is not to stand in front, as you can get knocked down flat, but to stand a little out of line to catch the person and bring them to you with one arm stretched out whilst wrapping them into a pirouette with the other. We practiced the move a few times and I'm glad to say we never missed once. Newman then instructed her to shoot off like a bat out of hell down the sloping main street and I grabbed her first time.

George Raft had kept a discreet presence for most of the shoot but one incident more than made up for it. One evening during a lull in filming a few of us, including Raft, got together for a few drinks and some banter. As the night wore on the laughter got louder and the boasts about sexual exploits more improbable, until George suddenly stood up and said, "I'm going to show you guys how I got to be a success," whereupon he undid his trouser buttons and laid his ample member on the table. He was quite right – it was obvious why he had been a success. It also put a swift end to some of the unlikely claims which had peppered the conversation up to that point, most notably from the Italian bright sparks who shut up altogether on witnessing George's hidden talent.

After we finished filming in San Remo we returned to Teddington to resume shooting, and I was reminded once more why the unions got up my nose. A union member slithered next to me and asked me to demonstrate how I had painted a door on the exterior of a cave. Not satisfied with the explanation, I was hauled up before the works committee and charged with violating my job description. Since I wasn't employed as a painter I knew I had to think of something quick, or face the sack. Standing before my accusers with a totally straight face, I told them I had used a broom instead of a paint brush and water with vegetable dye instead of paint. I failed to add that I had also painted the entire cliff, but it didn't seem the right moment to mention it. I could have sworn I heard some of the union leaders grinding their teeth in disappointment at not being able to throw me out, but there was little they could do. I got away with a fine, which I promptly got the accounts department to pay for.

With Hornblower in the can we resumed the run of the mill at Teddington, but it was not enough for me; there wasn't enough income and I couldn't do any overtime, so I got an evening job working six days a week, including Saturday afternoons, for a girlie review at the Hippodrome Theatre in the West End. It meant dashing to the theatre from the studio to do a twice nightly performance and a Saturday matinee. The show was the Folies Bergère and I had the rather unusual and, it has to be said, not entirely unpleasant job of lifting nude girls up on top of a pedestal, where they had to stand motionless like statues. Actually, that was all they were allowed to do. Censorship laws being what they were at the time meant that naked girls were not allowed to move for fear of getting the predominantly male audience too excited. But that was too boring a way to spend a night, so I devised a way of making things more interesting by making them giggle just before they went on. When the curtain dropped and there was a gap for us to change the set in between scenes I told them jokes while they stood still, desperately trying not to crack up. I guessed they were the main reason why men came, although they weren't always on. I judged my cues to lift them or bring them down to perfection, and instead of waiting in the wings for the cue to catch them I'd pop out to the White Bear pub across the road. My pint was usually waiting for me, topped up and ready. I couldn't do that on Saturdays as I had to be ready to fight off the drunken football fans who tried to invade the stage. The dancing girls got paid about half of what a nude starlet got, so I made a bit of extra cash by hiring some of them to work below stage for a little business I had set up, making paper-maché props for shop window displays and nightclubs, the highlight of which was a trick prop car I built for the Palladium.

My set dressing skills didn't go unnoticed and not long after that I was invited to a large dust covered office and offered the job of West End Property Master at the Moss Empire. I was to be in charge of all the main theatres, including the Hippodrome, the Palladium and the Prince of Wales. I distinctly remember being told that it would be a job for life and that I'd be getting a pension. My face dropped. The prospect of doing the same thing year after year horrified me and I couldn't get out fast enough. With my theatrical career at an end *The Crimson Pirate* came to the rescue. And not before time.

CHAPTER 3

Playing at pirates

The Crimson Pirate – US / UK (1952)
Director: Robert Siodmak. Writer: Roland Kibbee. Producer: Norman Deming, Harold Hecht and Burt Lancaster. Music: William Alwyn.
Cast: Burt Lancaster, Eva Bartok, Nick Cravat, Torin Thatcher, James Hayter.

The Crimson Pirate was in fact Burt Lancaster – in every sense. It was his film and his company produced it under his wife Norma's name. But it had big studio backing, nonetheless, and Gerry Blattner employed me as property master. I read the first draft of the script and felt it would need rewrites in the form of added action scenes, so I gathered many of the props we had previously used for Hornblower, including cannons and much of the ships' dressing, in case they were needed. We packed it all in crates and had it shipped out to Italy where most of the film was to be shot. Warners' had an old hull which had started life as a New Foundland cod fisher many years before. It had been made to look like a galleon and was to become our star pirate boat for the long shots at sea for the Hornblower movie.

At Teddington, Peter Dukelow made a lot of prefabricated parts that were to be sent out with the ship to the island of Ischia in the Bay of Naples. I quickly flew out from what was then the tiny airport of Heathrow to Rome to organise everything. The journey was long and once I arrived I was taken by car to Naples and from there by ferry to Ischia. When I arrived the set was virtually deserted and I realised I was one of the early birds. Curious to discover the state the old cod fisher was in, I rushed to the port where it was moored. It was not a pretty sight. Looking quite beat up, the old boat would need a lot of care and attention if it was to pass muster as the Crimson Pirate's flagship. A much smaller pirate boat, also to be used in the film, was tied alongside it and I got stuck in almost immediately to make both of them look right. Soon afterwards the crates arrived from the UK along with some of the construction men and art crew.

Although I had a plush hotel room to stay at, I chose to sleep at the port for most of the time we were filming; it was to become a lifelong habit during shoots. I preferred being alone on the boat, sleeping under the stars and wearing only shorts and a bandana on my head, in keeping with the job. If the role of devil-may-care pirate was beginning to rub off on me, I was not the only one. At the port I met an old man who despite being Italian spoke English with a heavy gangster-like accent. At the time I thought it was a habit he must have acquired from watching Hollywood movies. He came in useful whenever I encountered any local difficulties and would often help me. More mysterious sea dog than pirate, he kept to himself and asked for nothing in return. But he gradually opened up and spoke a bit about his life. It turned out he was an American and boasted he had been a close confidant of well-known mafia gang leaders, including Lucky Luciano, the legendary New York mobster. He never once told me he had been a member of the mafia himself, but later casually mentioned that he had been deported from the US. I recalled that Luciano had also been deported, but I never probed further and he never said anything more about the subject. I began to think my imagination was running away with me.

Meanwhile, the old boat was getting top heavy with all the additions so we filled its bottom with gravel to keep it from turning turtle, but because the old hull didn't look good we put steel cables all around it to ensure it didn't burst its belly. We went on a sort of sea trial to Naples, and as we approached the harbour a mass of warships and aircraft carriers converged all across the bay: the US sixth fleet had arrived. There was no movement anywhere under the hot sun, but as our little galleon passed seemingly unnoticed between them I decided to play a little joke and ran up the skull and crossbones flag. They pretended not to see us. I then fired two of the cannons, but still there was no response – I couldn't even see a lone sailor on any deck. They had probably been tracking us all the way down from Ischia and thought we were no more than a bunch of crazies from Hollywood. They weren't far off from the truth. We must have been quite mad to sail in this bucket of planks because apart from the keel and anything below the water line the decks, including the new additions, sprung so many leaks that no amount of corking kept the water out. There was also a huge fire risk on board as everyone smoked and threw their fag ends all over the deck. Of course, we had no life boats or fire extinguishers, and below the hold there were only a few life belts. To make matters worse, we sailed out to sea and out of sight of land desperately overloaded with all the shooting crew and filming equipment, including the landlubbing sailors. We tempted fate for months, yet we never had a fire or any other accident.

Burt Lancaster arrived early with his script writer, who stayed almost throughout the entire shoot. I'm not sure why he bothered turning up, as most of the script was made up as we went along.

Burt, who was very much an athlete and had at one time been a circus acrobat, was joined by a chap from his circus days called Nick Cravat. He was a lifelong friend, and although Burt had hit the jackpot in Hollywood (he was clever, good looking and a natural when it came to acting) he did not abandon his one-time circus buddy and had a part written in for him in the film. Evidently, it needed to be relatively easy as Cravat spoke with a heavy Brooklyn accent which was not quite right for his role as a pirate, so it was decided to create a character who was a mute; an acting device he would later use to great effect in most of the other films he appeared in.

Eva Bartok, a Hungarian actress who later made her name with English high society by having a much publicised affair with the Marquess of Milford Haven, was the romantic lead. She was a pleasant enough girl who just played her part and kept a low profile on the set, but she was definitely not very good with boats (I always found it difficult to load her up the side of the ship). The baddies were played by Torin Thatcher and James Hayter, an actor I didn't care for. He was a pompous and boastful little man who later went on to find fame of sorts as a pompous and boastful little salesman in *Are You Being Served?* Later on he found a niche doing pompous voice-overs for TV cake ads. I guess he effectively cornered that market.

Filming on location was obviously not as comfortable an experience back then as it later became with the advent of catering departments, but I like to think I was a bit of a pioneer here, too. During the morning out at sea I would make a rough count of those on board and radio back to the production office to arrange the lunch boxes. These were later sent out by speed boat, but I always ordered a lot more to hand out to a group of hungry children who milled around the port. All this enabled me to commit my own personal act of piracy. Below the main deck, in a false gun deck in the corner, I installed some big galvanised iron bath tubs which I filled with big ice blocks and generous stocks of *Birra Peroni* from the wholesaler. Every morning, when I was loading the drinking water, the crates of beer bottles were kept in a safe place. At the same time I would load big bars of ice into the bath tubs below the decks along with pre-cooled beer. At fifty liras a bottle I made a tidy profit by selling them to anyone on board for double the price – all on credit – to be collected at the end of the week. I made a fortune which I shared with Slimy Slim and Sid, the acting barman. There was so much paper money I had to press it down in a treasure chest to lock it. I then persuaded the production office that a bottle of beer should be offered with the lunch boxes every day. That way I could use the speed boat to get fresh supplies and more ice. Many times at the end of the day, when we shot a bit late, the producer Harold Hecht asked me to give everyone a bottle of beer and to put it on his tab. Soon I had to get a bigger treasure chest, and when Peter Dukelow came out for two weeks I gave him armfuls of cash. Slimy Slim was the unfortunate nickname we gave the tea boy who also had the unpleasant job of swabbing up vomit from the deck kindly left behind by seasick 'pirates', and to occasionally clean the two latrines which were located far below the stern. It required the use of a hand-operated pump to evacuate which not everybody did, and no wonder.

I recall a particularly memorable moment when standing on deck with my cockney prop man Sid, Eva Bartok came and coyly mentioned to him that the loo was full, to which he replied, "What you want me to do? Bleeding well stamp it down for you?" I suddenly remembered I was urgently needed at the other end of the ship. At sea, one of Harold Hecht's tasks was to intercede between Burt and the Director Robert Siodmak, who often fell out over how to shoot scenes. When they couldn't agree on something and there was a stalemate, Robert would go off in a huff and sit in his director's chair by the ship's bow, while Burt would take his and sit right up against the stern rail. That was the cue for Harold to do some shuttle diplomacy, hurrying back and forth the length of the crowded deck. It was usually a good time for my makeshift pub to come to the rescue and sooth frayed nerves.

Burt was a man of many talents and was one of the most energetic people I ever met. The only time I ever saw him sit down was for one of these confrontations, which were nevertheless totally good-hearted. He always seemed happy and smiled a lot, on and off camera, and I became a good enough friend to point out the fact to him. His response was typical. "These teeth cost me a lot of money and I'm going to get my money's worth out of them."

Most of the pirate crew were stunt men and about four of them were mates of his from Los Angeles, but nobody ever stood in to do Burt's stunts. He was also amazingly strong, and I recall one scene in which Burt and his pirates had to crawl, hand over hand, along a tow rope connecting two moving ships. We shot it for real and Burt was the only one able to cover the entire course. He could swing like Tarzan from mast to mast one handed, his sword held far out in the other one to land perfectly on his target, grinning broadly all the way. For my part, I had the pride and pleasure of organising many of his tricks, following his own carefully laid out plans.

We previously rigged and tested back at the dock side the night before. The temptation to have a go myself was too great and sometimes I would try a swing or two. By that time, I slept most of the time in the sails at night and had a piece of split hose fitted around a tight rope to a belaying pin below, which allowed me to descend quickly onto the deck. I'd often remain there during filming as it gave me a complete view of all the action. Inevitably, it also gave me time to wonder at my good luck, hundreds of miles away from a depressed, post-war Britain and getting paid for the privilege of playing at being a pirate and splashing about in the Mediterranean.

Some of our work which involved the boat close to land was shot on the far side of the island at a place called San Angelo. It was a small settlement where hot springs bubbled up from under the sea within yards of the sandy beach. It was pretty safe anchorage, and if I didn't need the ship back at port that night I was happy to leave it there. Returning to the island in one of the small boats I surveyed the huge dark cliffs above us. It was thrilling enough watching the big red sun sinking into the horizon, painting the sea and the sky with changing colours, but the group of about fifty young Neapolitan men accompanying me and breaking into song with their fine tenor voices was truly remarkable. The combination of their voices, the closeness of the cliffs trapping the sound and the fine setting was pure romance – better than any opera – and the memory of it thrills me to this day. During my long career I experienced moments which made the hair on the back of my neck literally stand on end, and this was the first.

Ischia, like the other islands in the Bay of Naples, is a volcanic relic and its peak is called Monte Epomeo. I rented one of the few trucks on the island and the driver invited me to eat with his family one Sunday afternoon, high up on the mountain. I gladly accepted, thinking that the view alone would make the trip worth the effort. It was a grinding drive up the hill with the old truck, until we reached a small plain with a few olive trees and his whitewashed cottage. His extended family greeted me with all the formality of a town hall official as we sat at a table under the trees. In deference to my being a foreigner I was served a slab of undercooked beef – I hated to think what the humble locals ate. My host kept filling my glass with wine that was kept in a cement-lined well and drawn out by a bucket on a rope. By the time we set off back home late in the evening we were all truly tanked up. As we clattered down in the truck to the bottom of the hill along awkward hairpin bends, I became ever more aware of the large quantities of wine my generous host had consumed. For some unfathomable reason, every so often he'd reach for a tap which he turned on when he encountered a particularly tight bend and then turned off along the straight. He explained that the tap was fixed to a copper tube which passed from the petrol tank on the cab roof, as if that made any more sense. I smiled blankly at him and began to think that the impressive views below me would be my last.

Back on the film we set about shooting one of the scenes which required a spectacular trick with a hot air balloon, Burt, and about five of his men. The balloon had to fly out to sea and pass over the big galleon where the remainder of Burt's men, hanging from a huge net bag on the mast, were being kept as prisoners. The stunt involved transferring the pirates from the balloon to the mast head by means of a rope, which they used to clamber down in order to free their mates. This was not done from the safety of dry land but for real in long shot, to include the balloon, the boat and the sea. Russell Sherman, a skilled special effects man from LA, built the balloon on a rigid frame and built a high steel tower on a high point ashore. He then placed a similar tower on top of a ruined monastery on a peninsula, fixing a tight wire between them. A wheeled skate, which could be moved back and forth by a motorised winch, was perched on top of it. Another wire was secured to the balloon with a pulley wheel, so that it could be raised and lowered as the situation required. The tight wire was out of camera frame, and all the ship had to do was to position itself while seemingly under sail. It all worked like a dream. It was as real as you could get and far more believable than today's computer animated graphics and blue screen backgrounds.

But if *The Crimson Pirate* was one of the films I had the most fun working on, it was mostly due to Burt Lancaster. An incident during our stay in Italy may have given the producers a big headache, but it also showed that Burt had a big heart. While taking a walk on his own up a steep cobbled road during a break in filming, he came upon a mule trying to haul a huge barrel on a heavy two wheeled cart up the hill. The poor animal, unable to pull the load, collapsed on its knees while two locals laid into it with heavy sticks. Incensed by what he saw, Burt angrily grabbed the sticks and threw them away, but as he turned his attention to the mule one of the peasants went for him. It was a bad decision. Burt knocked him out with a single blow while the other wisely backed away, just as a small crowd started to gather. The mule was freed by Burt but the two men soon returned with the Carabinieri and had him arrested.

Meanwhile, word quickly spread on the set about what had happened, and Harold Hecht was sent to bail Burt out. A liberal sprinkling of Liras secured his release but Burt would not leave until he was assured that the two men would be charged with unnecessary cruelty. He also insisted to Hecht to make sure the punishment was meted out. They didn't come much better than Burt Lancaster. Shortly after returning to Teddington, however, I came back to earth with a bump. We were told Warner Brothers had sold the studios to a new commercial television company and that we would have to move out within two weeks. We didn't have much time to dwell on the news. The prop room had huge amounts of stuff, worth many millions of pounds in today's money, which took fleets of trucks to clear out. Other studios swooped down on Teddington like vultures to pick the bones, buying and loading up with as many props as they could. Rental houses came too, but as the deadline approached it was still not being loaded quickly enough and we were faced with the thoroughly unpleasant task of having to destroy the rest. Windows were taken out on each floor, pushed out and burnt in piles along the river bank, including a unique collection of a room-full of rare posters on theatre, shipping, railways and commercial advertising. It was a sad end to what had been part of the country's artistic heritage, but we did as we were told. If we had wanted anything I suppose we could have helped ourselves, but I took nothing, not even one of the century-old books. When Warner suggested I go to Elstree as their property master I declined, but fortunately for me His Majesty O'Keefe's paradise beckoned.

CHAPTER 4

A visit to paradise

His Majesty O'Keefe – UK. 1954 (filmed between 1952-53) 91 minutes. Technicolor. Warner / Norma Productions.
Director: Byron Haskin. Writers: Borden Chase, James Hill, from the novel by Lawrence Kingman and Gerald Green. Photographer: Otto Heller. Music: Robert Farnon.
Cast: Burt Lancaster, Joan Rice, André Morel, Abraham Sofaer, Archie Savage, Benson Fong, Tessa Prendergast, Lloyd Berrell, Charles Horvath.

His Majesty O'Keefe was none other than Burt Lancaster, fresh from his role as mast-swinging pirate. Gerry Blattner gave me a wad of travellers' cheques, a plane ticket, and sent me to Los Angeles to meet Burt at Burbank Studios. I flew from Heathrow airport in a BOAC Boeing Stratocruiser, a large aircraft for the period but which still had to stop off to refuel at Shannon, New Foundland, and New York. To while away the time I got chatting with the steward who told me that this would be his last journey before retiring to run a pub in Ruislip. It gave us a good reason to spend most of the journey toasting to our future with champagne in a tiny bar located just below a tiny spiral staircase near the aircraft's landing gear. Needless to say, the flight to New York proved to be a long but painless journey.

When we landed I checked into the Sheraton Hotel, and as it was late in the afternoon I went out on the town. Not far away, I saw a bar displaying a sign I knew well: Guinness. I went in and had a few drinks with the natives, and by the time I got to the hotel – much later – I was starving. The room service menu looked appetising and included the grand-sounding 'Rib of Beef'; an almost unheard of delicacy in ration-hit Britain. When the waiter brought the meal up to my room I thought he had slaughtered a steer in the lobby and served me half of it on a plate. Nice though it was, most of it was still there when I woke up the next morning. I ventured further into the Manhattan jungle the next day and while in Broadway I came across a restaurant belonging to boxing legend

66

Jack Dempsey. It may have been an elegant diner but the gruff waiter who stuck the à la carte menu under my nose reminded me I was in New York. He returned barely a minute later to suggest I "speed it up, bud". By now I'd had my fill and was looking forward to the final stage of my journey.

Next day I took a plane to Los Angeles, and as we flew above tinsel town it was already evening. A sea of light lit the sprawling city below, quite unlike anything I had ever seen before. It was my first sight of Hollywood. I checked into the Roosevelt Hotel on Sunset Strip and early the following morning I went straight to Burbank to ask for Burt at the studio gates. As I waited, I recalled the last time I had stood at the gates of a large film studio almost eight years earlier. Back then, it had been under very different circumstances. Now I was about to be greeted like an old friend by one of Hollywood's biggest stars and shoot another film with him. It was a hard life, but somebody had to do it. I was snapped out of my momentary stupor by the sight of a familiar figure, bounding towards me and flashing that famous toothy grin of his.

After a tour of the studio, Burt handed me a copy of the script and I noted some interesting anecdotes. Yap is an island in the South Pacific where instead of paper money they have stones, which aren't in fact used to purchase anything. They're simply a symbolic sign of prosperity and standing in society. Looking like millstones, they range from a foot to five feet in diameter and are leant outside one's hut to show how rich a person is. The basis for the story centred on the expeditions that were organised to the neighbouring island from where the rock for the stone money was quarried. O'Keefe is a trader who discovers the use the natives have for the stones and decides to make himself rich by using dynamite to blow the rock, hence the name His Majesty O'Keefe, the King of Yap. The story was probably apocryphal, and even if there had been someone with that name I very much doubt he would have been as altruistic as Burt Lancaster's character.

Our Director, Byron Haskin, popularly known as 'Bunny', was a Hollywood film-maker of the old school. Tough but kind, he was a large gentleman who never got flustered during the making of a film but had a clause in his contract which banned him from taking a drop of alcohol. He had such an acute problem that he brought along with him his loving – and equally large – wife, Dot, to keep an eye on him. I was used to working with Americans and never had a

67

problem with them, but the Art Director hired for the film didn't inspire me one bit. I took one look at all the junk stored in the prop room and said that I wouldn't use it for a school pantomime. The remark didn't go down too well and I instantly made myself unpopular with some of the crew. In their eyes I was an impertinent Limey telling the greatest studio in the world that they were nothing but rank amateurs. I didn't delve any further but their antiquated building methods, using wooden scaffold poles lashed together with rope, also left a lot to be desired. Back in England, Peter Dukelow had been using tubular scaffolding with quick-fit couplings ever since I started working in films, but I wasn't encouraged to make any suggestions. The cosy club atmosphere, with its cliquey set up, was very negative, so I kept away from the studio for most of the time and did the next best thing, which was to have a beer. I spotted Burt's old sidekick, Nick Cravat, hanging about outside the gate at lunchtime as there was no place for him in the film. He looked a bit of a spare part, and feeling sorry for him I took him for a hot beef sandwich, which he proceeded to wolf down. By chance, we met up with the man in charge of the film's special effects, Lee Zavitz, who also happened to enjoy the odd night out. We painted the town, and I remember waking up in the Silver Grill at the Hollywood Roosevelt with a massive hangover before flying out to Fiji early the next morning. En route we stopped in San Francisco, and in the city by the bay we sat at Fisherman's Wharf to eat big succulent king crab. I didn't say anything but I guessed their rather large size was due to the fact they were being well fed by the outflow from Alcatraz prison island, just off shore. This all-expenses trip was beginning to look more like all fun and no work. We eventually arrived on the main island of Fiji, one of more than three hundred that make up the archipelago, which at that time was still a Crown colony. We drove for hours on the island's only road, a stony path inaptly named the Queen's Road. It was a bone-shaking, half a day's ride along the coastline to the capital Suva but before that, a bit more than half way along that road, was our location.

Fantastic Fiji

The journey finished at a place called Dueba. We were to start filming at the mouth of a broad river which flowed down all the way from the jungle highlands of the interior. Fiji has some intriguing secrets, not least the line which divides the dry and wet sides of the island. This meteorological quirk is caused when the prevailing winds carrying rainwater sweep across one side of the island, leaving it green and lush. The other half does not enjoy the same amount of rainfall due to the high mountain range dividing the island, which makes it generally drier and quite barren. The island was populated by Indians who had been brought over by the British to grow sugar on the dry side of the island where most of them lived and by a number of Chinese who mostly traded in Suva. But the ones who really stood out for me were the mixed race, and exotically beautiful, Chinese girls who were very popular around the port area.

Close by was a rest house where we lived and turned into a base for the film crew. We also built a large, covered studio stage for the interior and main sets, including the big native village which I was responsible for. The chief of Dueba, a man called Ratu Lala, got his people to help me. While the men were busy cutting building materials in the jungle to later float down the river, the girls sat cross-legged on the site, platting the leaves. Further back, the older women were allocated a different job making string and matting. It all seemed terribly well organised and needed very little of my own input. There was one danger, though. Whenever I walked too close to the girls, who were platting, they would suddenly reach out, introduce their hand inside the loose legs of my shorts, have a grab, and throw themselves on the ground in fits of laughter. I kept a safe distance…most of the time. They always wore a single hibiscus in their bushy hair, which glistened with coconut oil, and it was said that depending on which side of the head they wore the flower it let the men know if they were available or not. I had the suspicion that this quaint custom actually referred to the natives of Samoa and not Fiji, but I have to confess I never bothered to find out which side was which – I never asked.

Socialising with the locals inevitably also meant drinking Kava – Fiji's national drink fermented from the Yaqona root plant – which was said to produce a feeling of elation combined with fits of giggles to anyone who drank it. Many times during the course of the film I was obliged to attend the Kava ceremony which went on for hours. Despite what you may have heard, it was not the best drink in the world and tasted more like mouthwash. However, the mandatory sitting, cross-legged, was the most trying part of the entire ceremony, as it made one's legs go numb, which I suspect was the real reason why one couldn't stand up afterwards. I concluded that the only reason they went to the trouble of concocting such a foul brew was because alcohol was rationed. It was such a hot issue with the authorities that Fijians needed a licence to drink. This was linked to a points system, but not everyone got a licence, and those who did automatically got struck off if they used up their points tally.

To make life more bearable I built a one-room Fijian hut on the beach just under the coconut trees. It was exactly like the ones in the village, only this one was customised for my own personal use. I spent a lot of my evenings there, sitting quietly and looking over the lapping sea whilst savouring a drink. Surprisingly, it wasn't whiskey but pink champagne. There was a lot of it in the bar we had built and I decided that it was the right stuff to drink on a moonlit beach, under the gently swaying palmtree leaves. One evening, as I was sitting back enjoying a tipple after a long day's shoot, I heard a rustling sound amongst the canoes on the beach. I went to investigate and was startled by a figure that suddenly popped up from behind one of the rafts. It was Joan Rice, one of J. Arthur Rank's stable of young starlets and one of the film's leading ladies, in the company of a strapping young Fijian man. Looking flustered she coyly turned to me. "I hope you don't think there's anything wrong about us being here," she said, scurrying away with her chaperone.

Like all good pirate movies there should have been a parrot, but for O'Keefe they forgot to add one in. I set about changing that – the problem was finding one. Although Fiji is full of parrots, no one ever thought of keeping them as pets, so it was virtually impossible to get hold of one. After doing a little investigating I managed to find one that was kept by one of the New Zealand families working for the Government. They were very attached to the bird and at first refused to lend me their feathered friend, but after resorting to all my diplomacy and charm they agreed. His starring role came soon afterwards, perched on one of Joan's shoulders and looking happy as Larry. When not required for a scene I kept it in a cage in my hotel room but sadly one day, whilst I was out filming, the European office girls foolishly decided to give it and its cage a shower. Not long afterwards it caught pneumonia and died. Strange though it may seem, one of the hardest and most unpleasant things I ever had to do was to go back to the family and explain what had happened to their treasured pet.

Part of the film was set in old Hong Kong but as we did not have the budget to fly there I got some old sepia photos of the place and dressed some streets in Suva with Chinese signs and dirt roads. By adding around fifteen specially-built rickshaws, the illusion was complete. But as the canoes we needed could not be built in Fiji, we turned instead to the natives living on the Takaloa islands who had a reputation for building the best hollow-log, outrigger canoes. The order went out to construct forty paddle canoes, ten sailing canoes and a big Fijian war canoe, all of which were to be delivered by an island trading boat within three months. The war canoe was built in the authentic way and made from two gigantic trees, about forty to fifty foot long, hollowed out into two huge hulls and decked catamaran style with towering prows and stems that were later decorated with exotic seashells.

Much of my work required me to know many of the European and New Zealand businessmen who were on the island, but it still came as a surprise when they made me an honorary member of the exclusive The Lion's Club, otherwise known as the island's Old Boys' network. I saw it as an opportunity to make some useful contacts – and to do a little business of my own, of course – and when I was asked to give a talk at a dinner in front of local businessmen at the island's most luxurious hotel I gladly accepted. The Grand Pacific Hotel had a colonial grandeur to it, and as it was to be a formal occasion, I was told the restaurant would be closed off to the other guests. But as I stood up to start my speech, Burt and a couple of his friends burst through the door unannounced. As he tried to make his way towards a dinner table he was intercepted by a poker-faced waiter who politely told him that this was a private meeting. He was then quickly ushered into a smaller room, much to his disgust. Next day, Burt strode towards me clearly still smarting from the incident the previous night. "Who's the star of the show?" he said looking totally bemused. It was an awkward moment and I knew I needed to smooth his ruffled feathers. I quickly reassured him that there was no danger of my upstaging him and that he was still unequivocally the star of the show. His broad smile returned. "Ok, we've got that figured," and with a wink he turned on his heels and walked off.

Yet, despite Burt's unquestionable charm, *His Majesty O'Keefe* failed to take off the way *The Crimson Pirate* had because he never got the chance to do all his acrobatic stuff and wasn't nearly as swashbuckling. That said, it was still very much a typical Hollywood production in many ways, and even came with a chorus line of hoola hoola girls and the obligatory fisticuffs. There was also the odd brawl with clubs which I made out of sponge rubber. But a more complex scene involving Burt and his men being chased by the great war canoe handed me a unique acting opportunity. The huge catamaran had twenty men in each hull, while the deck was crowded with fierce-looking warriors, all painted up and bearing down on Lancaster and his men. If you watch the film, while the warriors throw spears at the hero, a fierce-looking steersman, sporting a huge mane of black hair and a bone through the nose, stands high up on a little platform on the stern. That's me.

Having failed to scare the locals, I made sure I would at least make a big impression on film by dressing up as a native, put there so that I could follow the director's instructions about the precise movements of each boat. In the scene we had to get the large war canoe to come from the river and out into the open sea. It worked perfectly well during various reruns, until the Director became impatient with the time it was taking me to return to the start mark. This was because I had chosen the exact spot where there was the least amount of turbulence, or where the river met the force of the sea's waves. But Bunny had other concerns. "Turn the boat now!" he shouted impatiently through the megaphone from the camera platform rigged to the bow. I yelled back that it was dangerous water. "Do it now!" he retorted angrily. I did as instructed and, as I feared, water immediately began to flood one of the hulls. The extras – fearless warriors and experienced seafaring men, I'd been told – scrambled into the next hull in a panic. But that too began to take in water fast and before we could do anything the canoe capsized, losing the expensive Technicolor camera in the process. Bunny kept quiet after that, clever sod.

Despite the odd hiccup, life in Fiji was wonderful and I began to think seriously of making it my home. When I was told that I had been given a piece of their land at a big chief's Kava ceremony I was bowled over, as this was the greatest honour they could bestow on anyone. Fijians are proud and very protective of their land, even when it was the property of the Crown at the time. In return, I gave my friend Ratu Lala a fine pair of the biggest shoes I could find. When the film company later gave him a bicycle it was quite normal to see him cycling everywhere with the shoes tied to the handlebars, or carrying them for important occasions. He once proudly showed me around the museum in Suva where all the traditional Fijian gear was displayed, such as shark's tooth swords which were made of hard wood with pointed shark's teeth fixed along the edge.

There were also references to the Fijians' more sinister past, such as wooden forks which had been used for eating human flesh at celebration feasts. On more ordinary occasions the food was eaten without the utensil, not that the victims would have appreciated the difference. I was shown a glass case displaying the old curled sole of a European boot, which Lara explained was all that remained of a boiled missionary as it had been too tough to eat. A chill ran down through me as I suddenly remembered that I had often been invited to feasts by the locals. Fortunately, there hadn't been any clerics on the menu, although one suspects it was only because it was no longer allowed. Instead we had pig – a similar type of meat, nonetheless – which they wrapped in green leaves, buried in red-hot stones and then cooked whole for many hours. Fijian feasts were always crowned with a sensuous display from dancing girls in grass skirts, and like the food it was one hundred per cent natural, with no added ingredients.

As an alternative to sitting outside my beach hut drinking champagne, I occasionally jumped into a canoe and sailed far out to sea, until land became a mere smudge in the distance. Alone, with the moon as my only reference point, I slowly entered into a trance-like state, lulled by the rhythmic waves of the sea caressing the hull and the slap from the outrigger. The gentle rocking motion became strangely hypnotic, and I felt as though I were floating in space. Looking down, I saw the stars and the moon reflected on the empty sea – empty that is, save for my presence. It was easy to be seduced by this beautifully primitive world, and when I sailed back to shore I did so reluctantly, as it also meant returning to the artifice of everyday life. However enjoyable making films was, I never felt quite at peace as when I took refuge in my own mind, far from the din of a film set. I realised that once the film was complete I would be forced to choose between remaining on the island and returning to England. Being Property Master I was almost always the last to leave when filming ended, and as I only had a dour-faced accountant for company it made me even more depressed.

Pondering over my future, I sat in the moonlight under a palm tree to digest just how much of an impression Fiji had made on me.

Perhaps I had been beguiled; maybe the island had been too perfect, too idyllic to be real. With a heavy heart I gave up my dream of staying on in Fiji.

The following day I took a plane to Sidney. When I arrived I decided to check into a top hotel for a couple of days and go for a stroll under the sweltering sun, through crowded streets and surrounded by swarms of irritating flies. It felt as though someone were rubbing salt into the wounds. The following day – a Sunday– I got an unexpected call from none other than Bunny Haskin who had also checked into the hotel, minus wife. He invited me to have breakfast with him, but little did I realise that for him 'breakfast' meant slugging down a whole bottle of whiskey in record time. By the time I got to his room he was well and truly sozzled. Haskin was clearly getting even for all those weeks he had spent under his wife's thumb without a drink. He became quite cantankerous and soon subjected the hotel's staff to a tirade of abuse, who in turn – and rather surprisingly for Aussies – threatened to go on strike unless he apologise immediately. The whole episode did little to lighten my spirits, so I decided to move on. I bought a ticket to Rome, with a stop-over at the wonderfully decadent and colonial Raffles Hotel in Singapore. The last stop before Rome was some hell-hole in Africa that was as fly-ridden as Sydney and finally, after five days travelling, I arrived exhausted in Italy. Feeling rather glum I bought a ticket to London after reading about a wonderful new jet-powered passenger aircraft, the Comet. Two hours later I was back in England, still ruing my decision to turn my back on paradise.

CHAPTER 5

Londoners and our Girl Friday

Our Girl Friday (UK) 1953. 87 minutes. Renown Pictures. Eastmancolour.
Director and Writer: Noel Langley.
Cast: Kenneth More, Joan Collins, George Cole, Robertson Hare, Hermione Gingold, Walter Fitzgerald.

It took a while to settle back into the drudgery of daily life in London after the beguiling charms of the South Pacific, but the experience taught me a valuable lesson because I was determined never to return to working in a film studio. I was now freelance and realised I was probably the only person in the film world with such a job title. Predictably, I fell foul of the unions, who liked to keep full control of their members, and getting work became an uphill struggle. Before long I was broke, and with my back against the wall I decided to take any job that came my way, even if it meant working for that relatively new fangled gimmick: television. Despite my misgivings, I realised television was beginning to take off and I could sense the start of a new revolution in entertainment. I wasn't the only one. So-called TV studios began sprouting all over London and no building was too small or ramshackle for the task. Any building large enough to house a few cameras on a small set would do – one was even built in an old church in Marylebone.

Clearly, TV was here to stay. I accepted a number of jobs as Property Master, Set Dresser, or as a Special Effects Consultant for the new half-hour shows that were becoming all the rage. Each contract was a week or two long and didn't earn me much money, but it was a worthwhile experience. While on a job I met an Art Director called Don Chaffie, who had decided to go it alone despite being clearly short of cash. He later went on to direct Charlie's Angels in LA; a change of fortune that would drastically improve his financial situation, if not his status as film-maker. As we were in dire straits financially, we both took on a job for the National Gas Board to make a mind-numbing film about the history and growth of domestic gas. It was a far cry from swashbuckling pirates and naval battles, but I was running short of beer money. With very little help, we made the film at a warehouse in Wembley, which at one time had been used as a studio. Most of the big film companies kept an office near one end of Wardour Street in London's Soho district, and the majority of the studio workers congregated at a nearby pub called the Duke of Wellington, close to Shaftesbury Avenue. There was good camaraderie between us, even if you were unemployed or freelance – something which irked the unions – but it was accepted that any one of us could end up on the dole at any time, so buying a beer for a colleague who had hit on hard times was the norm, especially when one knew you could be sharing his fate the following week. Sometimes charity extended beyond booze to offer 'a cow's calf', which was the equivalent of half a pound. It was a unique employment agency, in fact, in as much as employment was supposed to be controlled either by the unions or the labour exchange.

Through my connections I got to hear that Renown Pictures, whose offices were just around the corner in Old Compton Street, were going to shoot a film called *Our Girl Friday* in the Spanish island of Majorca. Peter and I got hired to transform the Mediterranean location into a more exotic one on an empty beach in the northern part of the island. It was not Fiji, but it beat Shaftesbury Avenue hands down. When we arrived we realised we had Majorca all to ourselves. We painted the rocks with paler, coral colours and made huge pink seashells. We then planted palm trees along the top fringe. The entire film was little more than an overblown exercise in cheesy romanticism…and a perfect setting for a young and very nubile Joan Collins to display her charms. But the illusion of paradise was shattered when our workmen dug up a man's skeleton early on. We dutifully reported the discovery to the Spanish Civil Guard, but shortly afterwards another bloody body was discovered. The skeletons had been found standing up and we were told this could either have been a pirate cemetery or a dumping ground for the victims of pirates. By now the police were getting a bit edgy, so they told us to play somewhere else along the beach, which didn't please us one bit after all the preparatory work we had done. We resolved to keep quiet in future, even if it meant discovering a mass grave. As it turned out, we were spared any further unpleasant surprises.

Our Girl Friday was set around four castaways – three men and a girl – who are marooned on a desert island after escaping from a burning cruise ship on a small rowing boat. The lucky men sharing the island with twenty-year-old Joan were Kenneth Moore, George Cole and Robertson Hare. Of course, the character played by Joan escapes the sinking liner wearing only a bikini, which makes the three chaps' ordeal even more pant-stretchingly unbearable. Early on, the characters agree to build a shelter, but to do that they need to get the tools from the rowing boat which has capsized in fairly deep water. Lo and behold, the only one who can swim is Joan's character, which inevitably afforded more detailed views of her delectable anatomy. Although Joan could swim well on the surface, she was lousy at diving beneath the water, so for the underwater camera shots a stunt double was required. And that's where I came in. With a devotion that went beyond the call of duty, I volunteered to don a bikini, complete with padding and a well fastened wig, although I stopped short of shaving my legs, back, front…well, you get the idea.

We reset the boat in shallow water and got ready to shoot the close up. Joan was game enough for me to take her round the waist in the water, turn her upside down and push her head first into the boat to get a few seconds of her arriving at the boat's stern. We did this for a number of shots, not that I was complaining. Another little job involved Joan taking her bikini top off in a scene. In those days there were strict censorship rules, such as not being allowed to shoot a scene with two people on a bed. Needless to say, a girl baring her breasts was strictly forbidden, so directors had to resort to being a bit more imaginative and resourceful. In the scene in question, Joan had to turn with her back to the camera as she hung her bikini top from a twig. Beside her, a big cockatoo was to raise his crown and squawk at precisely the moment she turned to face him. All this had to be shot in one take. To ensure the bird came in on cue I got a thin bicycle spoke below the unsuspecting bird and aimed it just under his tail. Keeping an eye on the bird and another one on Joan I jabbed the cockatoo's backside at the exact moment she turned to face him. He squawked in surprise and even did a spot of improvisation by bending down as if trying to get a better view of Joan's charms. An actor could not have done it better. The shot was virtually problem-free and felt more like a holiday than work, since we spent much of our time swimming in the warm sea and mucking about on the beach. It was certainly a far cry from being shut up on a sound stage in a London studio.

The boys

All good things come to an end and I was back in London in 1953. Finding it impossible to settle down to a mundane life, I bought an old motor car and drove around Surrey and Sussex with the macaw on my shoulder, often sleeping on the back seat and living off the land. Fortunately —and before I completely lost the plot – I met Don Chaffey who asked me if I wanted to help make a children's film entitled *The Hop Dog* in Kent, starring a very young Richard Briars. The film told the story of East London's hop pickers and the families who worked picking the hop flowers for the breweries. I met the producer Ted Lloyd, a huge but kindly man who was making films on a shoestring for the Merryfield Film Foundation. They couldn't pay me the sort of salary I had grown accustomed to but I readily accepted as long as they paid my 'expenses' (the bar bill, that is). I also instructed them not to tell the unions.

Our first day's shooting began early in the morning, around 4.30a.m., on an empty train platform, facing the iron gates at London Bridge station and waiting for them to open. When they did, a tidal wave of men, women and children, all carrying everything from kitchen utensils to bedding and even rolls of linoleum floor covering, surged towards us. Evidently, East Enders viewed hop-picking as a bit of a holiday, perhaps because many of them had never seen so much as a tree or a blade of grass in their lives. An empty train stood with all its doors open, but within minutes it was packed-full of excited people, with kids jammed up against windows or hanging out of them, yelling and squealing like pigs released from their pens. They were all en route to the hop-fields on the outskirts of a small town called Goudhurst. When they arrived they stayed in very basic and sparsely furnished corrugated huts. The entire event was a snapshot of history as nowadays hop-picking is done by machines, which is a shame.

The look of happiness on the faces of all the people at London Bridge station was evidence of better times, when communities were close knit despite material shortages and low wages. There were two or three pubs in the village; one was the Eagle where the film crew stayed although, true to form, I went further afield to another village, far from the madding crowd. Every evening the families of the hop-pickers went into the pubs to spend their earnings, but as the pubs couldn't accommodate such huge numbers of people the crowds spilled onto the main street. A piano was brought out and a group of cockneys gave a rendition of songs I'd heard before as a child on paddle steamers with my dad. Every pub made sure it didn't lose a single glass by charging a shilling deposit on each one and painting the base with a different colour to represent a specific pub. While waiting for a prop to be delivered at the train station, a group of young boys – probably around twelve years of age – got out of the train carrying cardboard boxes. "'Ere Tarz!" they shouted excitedly at me (I had apparently earned the nickname of Tarzan), "Give us a hand wiv these boxes!" They piled them into my old car and then clung on the outside for dear life. When we reached the camp, they quickly unpacked the boxes to reveal hundreds of glasses. *Cockney guile*, I thought, as they would save a packet by not paying a deposit. But I underestimated the little rascals, who were about to outdo me with their entrepreneurial vision. From a smaller package came matching paint like that used by the pubs to differentiate each other's glasses. I asked how much they had paid for them.

"Tuppence each, Tarz."

"And the train fare?"

"Nuffink. We bunked on."

I figured they would make a five hundred per cent profit. I also concluded they would probably go far in life – maybe own an airline, or something similar. Many of the hop pickers eventually went back to the streets and slums of London's East End but we moved on with a group of child actors to Brighton. Some miles from the city, in a place called Hassocks, on top of a round green hill, a pair of windmills aptly named Jack and Jill dominated the skyline. Both are still protected by the National Trust and smoking was not allowed anywhere near them for obvious reasons. At the time they belonged to Henry Longhurst, a one-time famous golfer and English gentleman who gave us permission to film in one of the mills. It was going to be tricky as the windmill was to catch fire with the children still inside. Rather than resort to complicated and potentially hazardous pyrotechnics to achieve the effect of billowing fumes I used piped smoke, which I blew at the appropriate time and at the correct angle when given the cue by the director. Even so, a fire

79

department unit was on standby just in case I got over enthusiastic with the 'tobacco'. Unseen by anybody, I put some pyrotechnics in some steel barrels inside the mill to warm the atmosphere a little. Before shooting the scene the following day I left an associate to control the 'smoke machine' while I focused on setting off the fireworks from inside the mill. I should have planned it better. By the time the explosive mix was nicely cooking away, the acrid smoke had become so thick I fell back three floors down the mill's zig-zag stairwell, unable to see or breathe. Afterwards, I said nothing and neither did the Longhurst family, which was rather sporting of them.

There was an interesting footnote to the film. In 2004, while I was watching the BBC news, a report came on about an enthusiastic collector of memorabilia. He was an Englishman who happened to be in Chicago buying some old cans of film which somebody had recently scavenged from a rubbish skip in the street. To his surprise, he stumbled upon the original reels of *The Hop Dog*. Amazingly, the film had a special significance for him because he also came from Goudhurst and remembered it being made. The cost of such a poignant piece of heritage was the derisory sum of $30. Even before shooting had finished I was contacted by a film director called Vernon Sewell, who asked me if I was up for another job. He apparently wanted my help to create a huge explosion that would emulate an atomic mushroom cloud at sea. Sewell had been a commander in the Royal Navy and apparently knew all the right people at the Admiralty willing to sign off the 'Big-Bang' at a certain date and spot in the English Channel. He must have had the right connections because he also obtained a Scotland Yard permit for submarine-blasting gelatine to be collected and used for the task.

The whole operation sounded completely crazy but appealed to my sense of mischief. "Count me in," I said, and quickly set about designing and building a mortar from an old steam boiler that would float submerged with its mouth at water level. On the big day I picked up my very large package of explosives from somewhere in the Thames Estuary, and with the mortar anchored and the charge with its detonator in place, Vernon started to manoeuvre his yacht from a safe distance to photograph it. He had clearly thought of everything – except to check the shipping forecast. The wind suddenly came up and quickly gained strength, becoming a fierce squall in no time. With a storm-strength wind and mountainous waves threatening to swallow us whole, we had no choice but to sit it out at anchor. I tried to keep an eye on the bomb with binoculars but managed to lose sight of it. Desperately searching for the hazardous package, I spotted it in the wrong place, cresting a wave and heading for Brighton. At this point, I really felt we had totally buggered it up. Although there was no immediate danger of it sinking as I had attached floating rings to it, no one fancied calling the emergency services to warn them that a bomb would shortly be sailing under Brighton Pier. With great difficulty the crew lowered a motor boat with Sewell and I in it. It was a wild ride, but we managed to catch up with the rogue bomb. With enormous difficulty we attached a line to the device and started to tow it back to the yacht. Then disaster struck and the tow line got tangled in the propeller. I was now beginning to panic somewhat and went over the side to disentangle the rope, which I was able to do after a great deal of swearing and groping around. The journey back to the boat was twice as hard, but we eventually managed to lift the bomb on a davit and onto the boat where I set about diffusing it. To make matters worse the package burst open and all the sticks of jelly were swept away. Undaunted, we later came back for another go. As it was unlikely we would get another load of explosives, this time I decided to wrap explosive cord around bottles of industrial propane. It worked a treat and we got a huge explosion with water vapour. Live and learn, as they say. It was only much later, in the safety of dry land, that Sewell – he of Royal Navy commander fame – confessed that he didn't know how to swim, reasoning that it was better that way. I could have drowned him.

The street kids

Driving back to London I realised that as I was extremely short of finance, there was no alternative but to call on my financial advisor at the Duke of Wellington pub. It was holiday time and as the union was unable to supply a suitable man they got me to fill in for a series being made for TV at an old studio in Southall. It was a film about a detective starring Boris Karloff, the legendary British actor who shot to stardom as Frankenstein's creature in the 1931 film. Although Karloff was a good actor and an extremely polite man to boot, I found the entire set up really dull. To break the monotony one lunchtime on my return from my usual pint at the local, I passed a fishmonger's shop and noticed a tank of live eels. A deliciously cruel idea suddenly flashed through my mind. I bought the biggest eel in the shop and took it back to the studio. Taking advantage that everyone was still in the canteen, I went onto the empty stage where I spotted the huge bed in which Karloff would be filming his next scene. I placed the slimy and still wriggling creature under the bed covers and attached a fishing line to it, which I then threaded to the back of the stage and waited for the crew to return. I didn't have long to wait. An unsuspecting Karloff pulled back the bedding and got in. I quickly reeled in my catch and the slimy eel shot out of the bed and across the stage to the cries of "Snake!". Poor old Boris jumped out of his skin and nearly fainted – so much for being the master of horror. My little peccadillo was not discovered and I was asked to stay on permanently, which did not appeal to me one bit, but as offers were rather thin on the ground I decided to see the project through. I was invited to the end of shoot party but declined. I always saw parties as an excuse for people who may not have got on together during filming to get sloshed and then wreck their cars on their way home. As I was leaving, I passed the open door of the stage and peered in. An enormous iced cake dominated a long buffet table, itself creaking under the weight of food. I suddenly remembered that we had been filming in Southall; a poor, forgotten working class neighbourhood trying to claw itself out of the misery of post-war rationing. There really wasn't much to think about. I grabbed the cake and placed it in my car, drove out of the studio gates and down the road. Within seconds, I came across a bunch of bedraggled kids playing football just up ahead. I screeched to a halt, got out and handed the cake to them. Their jaws dropped in surprise and they gratefully accepted my gift. I went to work the following day feeling thoroughly pleased with my selfless act. But my joy was short-lived. I was met by a glum-looking film crew who told me that some heartless cad had stolen Boris Karloff's birthday cake moments before he was meant to cut it. Poor old Karloff. Something tells me he didn't have many fond memories of his time in Southall.

My salvation came in the form of a phone call from Rome. The studio manager, Frank Kelly, rushed on stage to tell me that Gerry Blattner wanted to speak to me on the phone. An excited Gerry instructed me to fly urgently to Rome as they were going to make a blockbuster. I thanked Frank and told him to have a drink with the money he owed me. I left the very next day.

CHAPTER 6

Let's Build a Pyramid

Land of the Pharaohs – US 1955. Warnercolour/Cinemascope.
**Director: Howard Hawks. Writers: William Faulkner, Harry
Kurnitz. H. Jack Bloom. Photography: E.E. Games. Music:
Dimitri Tiomkin.**
**Cast: Jack Hawkins, Joan Collins, Alexis Minotis, James
Robertson Justice, Sidney Chaplin.**

I walked into Gerry Blattner's Rome office in Cine Citta and was
told Warner Brothers were about to produce two big films: *Helen of
Troy* and *Land of the Pharaohs*, using a new medium called
Cinemascope. I got hired as Property Master on *Pharaohs*, which
didn't sound as grand and meant I wouldn't get to build a giant
wooden horse, but beggars can't be choosers (ah well, it would just
have to be a pyramid). Gerry introduced me to the director, Howard
Hawks, who impressed me immediately. A quietly spoken man,
Hawks knew exactly what he wanted and wasted no time in telling
me he was going to make a mammoth production ("not yet written,"
he added helpfully) on location in Egypt by the pyramids, using ten
thousand extras to build the Cheops pyramid of Giza. I started
doing some research in Rome as well as ordering the construction of
twenty chariots, but on reading the first draft of the script I was
horrified to discover that there weren't any chariots in the film, so I
quickly sold the lot to another big American film that needed them.

I flew to Cairo shortly afterwards and drove through the desert
in a taxi to get to my hotel. If I had any doubts about Egypt's
grandeur they were laid to rest during the journey. We passed
beneath the shadow of the Great Pyramid, sharply outlined in the
moonlight, and as we left it behind the moon seemed to swell. I
took it as a good omen. When we arrived, I checked into the Meena
House Hotel close by which, although run-down, still showed signs
of its former glory. It had been a favourite hunting ground of the
British during colonial times, and in its heyday horses were kept for
the officers to ride on. I was impressed by the big stable yard with its
two great iron-studded wooden doors, and with the help of the

film's accountant I rented the whole place as my prop room. I then set about employing the best artisans, had electricity installed, and bought tools and machinery. Soon, the property-making department was up and running and humming with activity. There was only one problem. Every so often, the workers would roll out a little mat and kneel on it to pray. It made me wonder how a production line could ever work in Egypt. I was given carte blanche to go anywhere and I visited the museums where I photographed, measured, and handled every exhibit. Entire villages were hired, each churning out different props in huge numbers from clay pots to woven baskets and tools. I became so well known that I must have been invited by the locals to drink petal tea hundreds of times.

When the script eventually arrived I was relieved to discover that I had correctly anticipated the types of props that would be needed. I was ready to play the game of 'let's build a pyramid'. More and more people started to arrive on the set, including a pretentious French Art Director by the name of Alexandre Trauner; a short man whose most notable feature was the small sausage dog he always kept by his side. It wasn't long before we had a big falling out. Trauner presented me with a large drawing of a litter on which the pharaoh would be carried by some fifty pall bearers. He asked me to build the thing, but I quickly realised the design was severely flawed and would not support the weight of the pharaoh and his entourage of slave girls. I took it upon myself to make a few but all-important modifications before presenting it to him.

On the day, he turned up as if about to inaugurate a shopping centre. He stared at the finished product and walked slowly around it, carefully inspecting every inch with his dog in tow. He suddenly stopped in his tracks. "But izit like ze drawing?" he enquired.

"No," I replied with a deadpan expression.

Outraged by my insolence he demanded to know why, and I explained the drawing's shortcomings. It was too much for him. His features scrunched up like a used paper bag and he launched into a typically Gallic tirade, most of which I thankfully failed to understand. In between the spluttering, I understood he wanted his elaborate sketch back. I raised my eyebrows and shrugged my shoulders, which only served to infuriate him further. He stormed out, bleating that Mr Hawks would hear about my arrogance.

He found an unsympathetic Hawks practicing golf in the desert. "Tomorrow Alex, tomorrow," he replied nonchalantly. When things calmed down a bit Hawks later checked the litter himself and he asked me about the significance of the drawing.

"It was no bloody good, Howard. If the men got tired and put it down slightly out of sync, it could break its back. Then you'd be waiting under the hot sun for me to fix it while Alex sat at the bar with a cool daiquiri." My explanation had the desired effect.

A few days later Hawks called me over to the hotel bar with writer Faulkner and a special effects man. "Can you guys build me a set? Otherwise, we'll never get this movie off the ground." He then poured a trickle of beer along the bar top. "That's the River Nile, right? Perhaps a couple of miles," he said, staring intently. He then placed the bottle at one end. "That's the camera. All along this bank of the river there will be cranes lifting stones onto the boats." He wanted a few thousand extras playing slaves to drag the rocks from the quarry. "Can you do it?" he asked, gazing deep into my eyes. Don and I looked at each other and nodded our heads, trying hard to exude a look of calm assurance. "I want to shoot it two weeks from now. I guess we will also need a couple of hundred falookas. Do it in Aswan where the real quarries are," he added, almost as an afterthought. I swallowed hard, relieved he hadn't asked us to throw in the quarry as well.

We dashed back to the workshop and frantically ordered a fleet of trucks to transport all our tools and equipment to Aswan in a convoy that same evening. With our top men, we boarded the night train, which also happened to be transporting a troupe of luscious slave girls to Luxor for another MGM film being made at the same time, called *The Valley of the Kings*. I began to wonder whether I'd chosen the right film to work on. We arrived in Aswan early in the morning and I set about finding an appropriate site, while Don went to the Aswan Dam Company to convince them to lend us two large barges equipped with cranes, which he intended to adapt to carry two high-pressure water pumps. I soon had an army of people working under me, building sledges and fake rocks, cutting, preparing and putting in place palm tree trunks for the cranes which the special effects expert, an American called Don, would lift from his barge and plant upright. They patiently awaited our orders squatted in groups of one hundred every morning, while each group was allocated a master to whom you paid the equivalent of about two shillings and sixpence a day. It seemed odd that this motley crew – many of whom were children and cripples – were supposed to be portraying slaves from a bygone age. The irony was not lost on me. All the hard work made me rather thirsty, but my fondness for beer soon brought me in direct confrontation with an executive who had been sent from LA, ostensibly to check up on the start day. In reality, he was doing little more than snoop on us. He then committed that fatal error of suggesting that we shouldn't really be drinking on the job. Striding up to me during a break, he eyed my beer, while ignoring the vast set we had just built.

"We don't drink beer when we're working," he remarked loftily.

"You may not, but we do – especially me."

Hawks got to hear about our exchange and was adamant my supply of beer should not be cut off at any cost. "Eddie, you shall have your beer. What would you like?"

I pushed my luck. "Forty bottles of Stella a day," I replied with a big grin. The next day the production office let me know that forty bottles of Stella had been allocated to the property department on a daily basis. I knew there was something about Howard I liked.

The quarries of red granite used by the ancient Egyptians to cover and polish the pyramids were located at Aswan. Traces of the once great Egyptian civilisation were still visible for all to see and before me lay an unfinished obelisk which experts believed was the world's biggest. More importantly, I was able to see with my own eyes the ingenious methods used by the Ancient Egyptians to cut the rock. Rows of shallow, rectangular-shaped depressions were made into which slaves drove hard wedges of dry wood, hammered in and soaked with water. These would then split the rock along a line. Brilliant though the technique was, it still didn't explain how they managed to transport thousands of tons of rocks to the site of the pyramids. Even more mysterious (and a bigger problem for the Egyptian engineers than building the pyramids themselves) was the method used to stand the rocks on their ends. By contrast, my rocks were only props, made merely of fibreglass or softboard. Yet these presented a problem too, as they had to appear to be heavy for the hundreds of extras who pulled on the sledges we had made for them. I came upon an easy solution by simply turning the sledges upside down, so the more the extras pulled; the more the sledges dug into the sand.

We got back to Cairo pleased with all our hard work, but we were in for a shock. Alex had been back to his old tricks again. For some obscure reason known only to himself, Trauner had taken thousands of the long spears I had made, and which we had sent to the studio, and removed all the bright glitter on the tips. It was a petty gesture, but if the aim had been to get a reaction out of me, he succeeded. I commandeered a fleet of trucks with some of my men and headed for the studio. We loaded up all the spears and brought them back to my prop room where we had the tips restored to their former, glittery state. For good measure, I added pennants to a few, like streamers. I often did this to add a focal point of interest to the top part of a frame. Much later, while sitting in the cinema during the scene in which the pharaoh's triumphant procession was crossing the desert, Hawks said in a loud voice and within earshot of Alex, "It's a good thing those spears glint in the sunlight, otherwise we would have had a forest of sticks crossing the desert!" He was absolutely right, of course.

Before leaving Aswan, my young interpreter took me far south one night to see a strange festival. He made me dress in Arab clothes and told me to remain in the shadows as not many Westerners had witnessed what I was about to see. Stretching across the horizon as far as the eye could see there was a long line of fires beside which an army of drummers knelt, striking an incessant beat, with the entire row playing in unison. At the same time, on the far side, I could see a column of men dressed in white robes, swaying violently as one, with their heads almost touching the ground. Each held a dagger with which they made stabbing moves – some actually going as far as wounding themselves – and if one fell, another would jump in to close the gap. It was an eerie sight. As we slipped away I asked what it was about. He said it could have been a wedding and the men could have been drinking *booza*, an alcoholic drink made from fermented bread. It suddenly dawned on me where the word 'booze' must have come from.

The combination of the desert and the blistering heat made filming extremely difficult, particularly when there was a lull in shooting, as the actors and the crew found it hard to relax. To improve morale, I did my utmost to liven things up. In one of the processions, Jack Hawkins, who played the pharaoh, was hitched up on a litter under the melting hot sun, wearing a golden helmet and trying to look as regal as the difficult circumstances would allow. To increase his already considerable discomfort I called Jack through a megaphone during a break. He craned his neck in my direction, and far in the distance, at the tail end of the procession, he saw me raising an ice-cold bottle of beer.

"Cheers!" I shouted as I poured the golden brew onto the hot sand.

He shook his fist at me, yelling, "Bastard!" for all he was worth. Poor sod. Casting the suave Jack Hawkins as the pharaoh might have seemed inapt, but he was such a great actor that he got away with it.

I was by now quite close to Hawks, who admitted to me that he was having problems casting the slave girl who was meant to seduce Jack Hawkins' pharaoh. I suggested Joan Collins, recalling the effect she'd had on the set of *Our Girl Friday*. He said nothing at the time, but shortly afterwards we moved to Rome to view the rushes. A large crowd had milled together at the theatre entrance as we arrived and I suddenly spotted Joan Collins.

"I see you've been made the chief slave," I said as I approached her.

"Not likely," she replied, "I'm the bloody Queen!"

After dealing with sandstorms which sandblasted the paint off vehicles, we concluded our desert adventure and returned to Rome for the interior shots. The city was a different proposition altogether. The noisy Vespa scooters and Fiat Topolinos which buzzed incessantly through the busy streets were too much to bear after the serenity of the desert, and with my head about to burst from the noise I retreated to the nearby seaside town of Ostia, where I rented an apartment. Joan, her family and friends, and the make-up chiefs must have thought the same because they also rented flats nearby. At the time Joan was trying to dump her then husband, an unpleasant lowlife and bit-part actor called Maxwell Reed, who had a small part in Warner Brothers' other film, *Helen of Troy*, which was also being filmed in Rome. Their often violent relationship worried Blattner and knowing that I got on well with the family, he decided to appoint me as Joan's chaperone.

We then got down to the serious business of filming, and the first set we were due to build in Rome was a temple with massive columns and huge stone statues depicting various Gods.

We were shooting for the best part of a week when we were suddenly ordered to stop by the print laboratories in Los Angeles. To our astonishment we were told by the technicians viewing the rushes that the set had a startling pink hue. A Technicolor consultant flew over to sort the mess out. A baffled Alex, when told of the colour disaster, replied, "But I have not used ze pink, I have only used ze red and ze white!" The guy really was a genius. At least, as my job entailed dealing with so many different film-making aspects, I was able to forget about Trauner's bungling. A scene in the film had the slave throwing herself onto a snake to protect the young prince and required a close up shot with a real-live snake – a cobra, to be precise. It had to be a fair-sized reptile, but as we couldn't find an appropriate specimen in Rome I phoned a friend who worked as a curator at London Zoo and asked him to help me out. Shortly afterwards, Reg flew over with two fine cobras smuggled in a suitcase. When the time came to film the scene he milked the fangs of one of the snakes and got me to hold its mouth shut while he put two surgical stitches to keep it closed; a method few would approve of now but which resulted in no long-term ill effects to the animal. It was a shame we didn't do the same thing with Trauner – although he was to come unstuck shortly afterwards.

In one of the scenes Jack Hawkins' character has to wrestle a bull in a ring like a Portuguese bull-fighter to demonstrate his manliness and invincibility as pharaoh. We imported two of the famous black bulls from Portugal with their three handlers, not quite sure what to expect. When the day came the bulls arrived in a pen, while a nervous camera crew sat in the middle of the arena enclosed within the safety of a heavy duty timber cabin with slits to photograph the scene. But in their never ending quest to get noticed, Trauner's Art Department decided to build a large sphinx especially for the scene, which they placed on the opposite end of the ring from where the bull was to emerge. When Hawks shouted "Action!" and the gate was opened the bull charged out, stopped dead in the centre of the ring and glared at us, angrily pawing the ground and flaring his nostrils. He then spotted the sphinx. To our amazement, he went straight for it, head down. The horns went deep, and the naughty bull – which I instantly took a liking to – raised his head, no doubt as surprised as the rest of us to find the thing impaled on its horns. The bull eventually shook the absurd figure off while a bemused Hawks instructed the handlers to put the enraged animal back in its pen...and to get rid of the sphinx. It seemed as though Alex had finally learnt his lesson. The bull, however, felt he had more to say on the matter, and the second time he decided to charge the timber cabin containing the camera crew. The men inside were shaken by the experience, and the cabin fared little better as the bull managed to crush the side of it. We kept at it for ages, and the bull (who was now well into the swing of things) was taken in and out of the pen so many times that the camera crew became complacent and abandoned the safety of the cabin to watch. It turned out to be a big mistake. The bull spotted the crew next time round and charged towards them like a steam locomotive. The startled men stampeded back in the box and slammed the door shut, leaving the hapless camera operator, who had been slowed down by the baggy and totally inappropriate English shorts he was wearing, to face the bull's wrath. He started running round the cabin desperately trying to avoid the bull's sharp horns. I would be lying if I said I wasn't having a great time watching this and for a moment it seemed as though we were making a Marx Brothers' film. The chap tried to out-guess the bull's next move by peering around each corner, while the enraged animal chased him with a relentless determination until, finally, the door opened and the man shot inside the cabin.

After all the work, the pyramids, the desert, the huge crowd scenes, and the improvised bull runs, shooting finally came to an end. I found I was back where I started, getting rid of props instead of looking for them, and sharing my loneliness with the chief accountant who suggested we go home together on a boat through the French canals. Gerry asked me and Peter Dukelow, whose work on *Helen of Troy* had ended at the same time, to stay on in Rome on full pay with expenses for a holiday in gratitude for our help. The offer was just too good to pass. Peter and I had a great time, and for a number of weeks we did nothing but party and stuff ourselves silly on lobster thermidor and Champagne, after which we decided to return to London and reality, and for some Aberdeen Angus and beer.

CHAPTER 7

Heaven and Hell

Back at the Duke of Wellington, I was soon looking for work again after spending the little bit of money the taxman had left me. Although not much was happening, Terry Hunter – the production manager on *The Crimson Pirate* and now chief of Páthe – asked me if I wanted to go to Yemen on a job. It turned out the Government was planning on shooting a propaganda film for the army, and as it would involve a lot of explosions and mayhem, I was asked to give advice on special effects. I naively accepted, thinking it would be interesting as I hadn't been to Yemen before. I can't remember how I got there but I came to my senses when I woke up in a hot, dry hell-hole called Aden.

Shortly afterwards, I was transported to an even fouler shit-pit far to the north and in the desert. I looked around and realised I was in a small army camp, surrounded by layers of barbed wire, a few dusty tents, and a line of field guns ominously placed facing out towards the foothills. A batman who brought me food, drink, and a small amount of water to clean myself, advised me not to walk about in the camp unless nature called and I had no option but to use the cramped latrine. There was no way out except through the heavily guarded, barbed wire gate. Why they bothered with the heavy security is anyone's guess, as no one would have been crazy enough to venture into the vast desert alone.

To keep myself sane – and vent some of my anger and frustration – I turned my attention to blowing up trucks, simulating rocket hits from dive bombers, and bombarding a desert fort to oblivion; a job that would keep me busy for a few weeks and help pass the time. It was just up my street, although I wondered why the army weren't doing the job themselves. It seems they not only wanted realism but a good slice of spectacle to keep the troops and the MOD happy as well. The army was used to destroying heavy gear with Semtex, but the top brass were keen on using an explosive which would also produce an impressive firework display, and that's where I came in. I told the officer what I'd need and, to my surprise, he was most obliging. Every day, as we ventured out to play our little war games, I was escorted at all times by a squad of four armed soldiers, who sometimes took pot-shots at something I couldn't even see. One night, a couple of field guns were fired and I was almost catapulted through the tent roof. After three weeks of this I was ready for the funny farm, but to my immense relief I was told my contract had come to an end and I would be going back to London. When I returned, bewildered and out of sorts, I hot-footed it to the Intrepid Fox where I let Hunter know in no uncertain terms that we would definitely, and for the rest of time, no longer remain on speaking terms. It must have been bad, because I even refused to have a drink with him. Later, alone in a quiet and secluded part of the pub, I proposed a toast to all those poor sods who'd been left behind in Satan's hell-hole.

A glimpse of heaven

Thankfully, my next job was far removed from the latrine of Aden. After doing some TV work in London, I flew to Fiji and on to Samoa to make a picture called *Pacific Destiny*, based on a book by Sir Arthur Grimble about his experiences as Commissioner for the Queen's territories. The director, Wolf Rilla, was joined by Freddie Francis as cinematographer and a young Nicolas Roeg as his assistant, both of whom would eventually become film directors in their own right.

My base on the outskirts of the capital, Apia, was Aggie Gray's; a famous timber rest house which had been frequented by thousands of US military personnel during the war. One of the accompanying buildings had been built by American soldiers using only empty beer bottles, while the whole enterprise was run by girls, Aggie, and her lively live-in-lover. They were a happy bunch, but to be honest they didn't have to try too hard because Samoa was very much a happy place, anyway. They still kept their traditional ways, including the characteristic long houses, which were raised above the ground and occupied by an extended family. I discovered that young women were allowed and, indeed, encouraged to have children out of wedlock as it made a family wealthier. It was an interesting anecdote which I have to confess I never put to the test. Then again, gaining an insight into the way of life of local people was almost impossible because Samoan society cautiously guarded its customs and would not allow foreigners to enter the villages without the headman's permission – and that was never given. Samoans also had an ingenious and ecologically-minded sewage system which solved the problem of effluent and food in one fell swoop. In certain places, tall coconut trees had been felled out to sea, creating an improvised gangplank. At the end, they built a lavatory containing up to three open toilets facing the shore, while on the roof a man often squatted with a spear, ready to skewer any fish attracted by the waste. Talk about recycling. According to local legend, a group of Samoan women sitting on a certain rock on the shoreline could entice a tame shark to come close and frolic with them in a trance-like ritual. That was introduced into the script and I was instructed to find a tame shark. I had my work cut out, as this was not like getting a parrot or a monkey to do a party trick, so I decided to build one. I searched my childhood memories for inspiration and remembered a little toy snake I once made out of short, bevelled segments of wood. I then made a hole through which I threaded a tight cord. It was a rudimentary plaything but it gave me the idea to do the same thing with the shark. I had the entire thing carved from iron wood by the islanders, who were skilled craftsmen, and I covered the make-believe shark with a sponge rubber skin, similar to that used in diving suits. It looked convincing enough and the locals had a lot of fun learning how to operate the thing like a puppet, which they did by pulling it back and forth with lines, each move thoroughly rehearsed beforehand. It worked a treat and when we finished shooting we left it with the natives. Who knows, maybe it's still there.

In Samoa, I found out that bars were rare and alcohol was controlled by a points system similar to that adopted in Fiji. Only those whose behaviour was deemed good enough were allowed a certain amount of points. This called for drastic action. Everybody in the film crew was allowed the maximum, and I kept most of mine…for use at a native bar. By the time we left I figured Aggie could have built another house using the empty beer bottles left over by the crew.

One evening, we watched a small motor cruiser quickly head off to sea. It caused surprise among the locals, not least because the American owner of the boat had been banned from leaving until he paid his bills, including the port duty. It was said that he had somehow talked his way into starting up a ferry service around the nearby islands as a means of helping to pay back his debts. It was a commendable idea but unfortunately it didn't work out as neither he nor his eighteen passengers were ever seen again. A huge but ultimately fruitless search was launched, in which the services of the New Zealand Air Force were called upon in a desperate bid to find the boat and its occupants – or their remains. Three weeks later, the craft was found drifting near Fiji minus crew and passengers. It was intact, save for the expected damage following weeks of buffeting from the waves. Everyone instantly drew a parallel with the *Mary Celeste* mystery. It looked as if everyone had just got up from the dining table and stepped overboard. The incident kicked up a lot of interest from afar and whilst I was there, Robin Maugham – who was a close relative of Somerset's – came to write a story about it, but it proved too much of a task for him and he eventually gave up on the idea.

Following my experiences with Joan Collins years before, I was called in once again to step into the leading lady's considerably slimmer shoes as a stunt double. I was beginning to wonder if directors were starting to view my rather stocky physique with an altogether more sensuous eye. I convinced myself that from a long distance, and under certain circumstances, the audience would fail to detect that it was yours truly and not a curvaceous female film star on the screen. Susan Stevens, who like Joan Collins had been groomed for stardom by the J. Arthur Rank organisation, was my screen doppelganger. Stevens's character was to land ashore aboard a long boat in the middle of crashing waves. This was the cue for my entrance. I stepped into the breach wearing a long, white, flowing period dress, a parasol and a wide hat, but out of camera shot I also decided to don a pair of flippers, just in case things got too hairy. Of course, it had the crew falling about in hysterics, but I felt a moment's humiliation would be a reasonable price to pay for the sake of safety. I sat on the bow with the oarsmen from the Gilbert Islands, who were said to be the best in their trade. At the stern was the coxswain with the rudder, while the camera team stood by on the beach. We got ready beyond the reef where the steamer lay and the boys waited for a 'biggie' to carry us over the coral reef. It didn't take long. The next wave came rushing above the exposed coral, with us riding nose down and tail up. As I was at the bow I got a bird's eye view of the coral rushing up to greet me. Everybody thought it was a great take, except for the photographer who thought we could improve on it. "One more for luck," he suggested, although I suspected he was covering his arse in case he got the stop number wrong in the camera. The second time round a giant curling wave caught us all unawares, slewing the boat broadside and tossing it like a piece of driftwood. The wave broke over us, smashing the boat on the coral reef and tossing everyone overboard, except me. I instinctively ducked down and stayed in the boat until it came to a halt in the lagoon. Gasping for breath and hindered by layers of female clothing, I struggled to reach shallower water. Helped by the flippers, I eventually made it virtually unscathed, although the same could not be said for the nine islanders, some of whom were seriously injured. I ended up with fourteen cuts on my legs, all caused by the coral. To add insult to injury, the photographer decided that the first shot had been much better after all, rendering our near suicidal ride over the waves a pointless waste of time.

After a few days I could see that my wounds were not healing, and much to my disgust I turned to the set doctor for advice. She gave my legs a cursory inspection, frowning and tut-tutting in typical medical fashion. Her diagnosis was simple and suggested I rush to the local hospital as fast as my injured legs could take me, so that I could be treated with a new wonder drug called penicillin. I went grudgingly and when I saw the nurse (an imposing Samoan battleaxe) it seemed my worst fears about local quacks were confirmed. She hovered threateningly over me, frowning at my wounds as though I had personally been responsible for the lamentable state of my legs. Then she started to work on me. I discovered that her technique for applying an injection was limited to two, equally brutal methods. One consisted in raising the syringe high over her head and plunging it as hard as she could on the patient's trembling buttocks. The other method (presumably viewed as a more advanced form of skewering) was simply to rest the needle on the chosen spot and to lean on it until it broke through the skin. I helpfully suggested to the doctor that perhaps the needles were blunt; a remark that didn't amuse the medic one bit and she curtly told me to mind my own business. It was a pity they couldn't mind theirs with mine. Having experienced health care the Samoan way, I told the nurse I would be more than happy to inject myself in future. After a few days, I knew something still wasn't right as my leg looked like a piece of Swiss cheese and smelt almost as bad. I then remembered someone telling me that coral was actually alive, and the grim realisation dawned on me that the critters were trying to bore deeper into me with the sole objective of feasting on the calcium in my bones. I decided to kill the little buggers before they ate me whole. I got one of Aggie's girls to pour scalding hot water down one of the holes whilst I gritted my teeth and scrubbed the area with a toothbrush. I underwent the same harrowing experience with the remaining thirteen holes and increased the agony by pouring a quantity of hydrogen peroxide for good measure. The whole mixture bubbled nicely and my home-made remedy eventually paid off. I made a complete recovery – and all without a Samoan nurse in sight. But the experience left a few scars. Even now I can detect little dents in my shins – a small price to pay for not becoming a coral garden.

CHAPTER 8

A Fateful Bridge

The Bridge on the River Kwai – UK/US 1957. 161 minutes.
Technicolour/Cinemascope. Columbia.
Producer: Sam Spiegel. Director: David Lean. Writers: Carl
Foreman, Pierre Boulle, Michael Wilson (unofficially David
Lean and Michel Wilson). Photographer: Jack Hildyard.
Music: Malcolm Arnold.
Cast: Alec Guinness, William Holden, Jack Hawkins, Sessue
Katayama, James Donald, Geoffrey Horne, Andre Morell,
Percy Herbert.

Soon after arriving in London I got a message to meet film producer
Sam Spiegel at his office in Mayfair. Although I had never met him,
he was known as a tough negotiator and I knew I would need to
have all my wits about me if I was to get the job. Born in 1901 in
what was the Austro-Hungarian Empire, Spiegel fled Germany
when Hitler rose to power, and like many of his peers ended up in
the US, where he quickly established himself as one of Hollywood's
top producers. The driving force behind such classics as *On the
Waterfront* and *The African Queen*, Spiegel knew about success as much
as anyone else. He was vastly experienced, erudite, a known
womaniser and at the top of his game – no pun intended.

On the day of the appointment, I went for a walk in Green Park
to clear my head, thinking about our encounter and wondering what
to expect. As my philosophy was always to get to meetings on time I
was in his Dover Street office a minute early. I wasn't made to wait
long. Puffing away on a fat cigar behind a vast old desk that almost
filled the room sat Spiegel, flanked by two of his cronies who stood
impassively in a thick fog of cigar smoke. Determined to make a
point and not feel intimidated, I strode forward and offered my
hand just out of his reach, so that he was forced to rise a little from
his 'throne' to shake it. Without standing on ceremony, I quickly
grabbed a chair and sat down to face him. Spiegel's cigar drooped
slightly, but he quickly recovered his composure and offered me a
large Havana cigar from an even larger box, which I declined, as I

didn't smoke. Under the circumstances, I was convinced I had made the right impression. I listened intently as he told me about a film he was going to make in Ceylon. David Lean was to direct it and he had me down as Property Master. We did the deal in no time and before I knew it I was flying to Colombo, feeling quite smug with myself.

No sooner had I landed than I was told I was also being employed as a special effects man, which effectively meant that I would be doing two jobs for the price of one. Spiegel – the cunning old dog – had outsmarted me and got me on the cheap. I also learned that I would not be meeting Lean for some time as he was hiding away behind closed doors, working on the script with writer Mike Wilson in a nearby hotel. The film company in the meantime supplied me with a tasteless big white Chevrolet with matching white seat covers and a local boy as chauffeur. It looked like something straight out of a gangster movie, and just about as discreet. The nature of my job required me to search high and low for props, but being driven around in a flash Chevrolet was not the most subtle way of going about it. The problem was that Sam had banned the purchase of vehicles during the shoot. Despite his strict instructions I decided that I would not be driven around like some creaky remunerated ambassador. Searching around the area I found an old beaten up bus in a local yard which had been taken out of service and was slowly rotting away. I decided to buy it, thinking it would make an excellent mobile prop room. I wasn't being awkward for the sake of it, but word soon got round about what I'd done and I got a message from the production manager Cecil Ford, who was none too pleased about my purchase. "Sam has heard that you've bought a bus against his direct orders and he is very angry," It said. I replied with an equally blunt message: "you'd better fire me, then".

I was never fired, of course, but the incident wasn't forgotten. Right towards the end of the film we were doing that last helicopter shot over the remains of the collapsed bridge. Sam was supposed to be catching an aeroplane later that day, but David had made him wait until the very last moment while I dressed the set in the hope he would miss his flight, such was David's mischievous sense of humour. It was hot and dirty, I was beginning to flake, and it didn't help that the camera in the helicopter kept shooting the same scene over and over again. Eventually David was pleased with what he had and as I staggered over the bank feeling hot, tired and sweaty, I saw

Sam lumbering towards me. "My boy," he puffed, "you must be very thirsty."

I waited expectantly for some cool refreshment – like a beer, for instance. Instead, Sam thrust a paper cup filled with warm water into my hand. "Thanks Sam," I said dejectedly.

"About the bus," he muttered sheepishly. "You were right and I was wrong." I'm convinced that was the first and only time in his life he admitted to being wrong. He remembered the bus incident throughout the entire time we had been making the film, even with all the problems we had been faced with. It almost made up for the disappointment of not getting a cold beer.

Before we started filming, I was told David would be visiting the prop room. Despite all the highs and lows we would experience together in the coming years, our very first encounter was short and relatively uneventful. But we hit it off immediately. As he was about to leave, he turned round and commented that seeing the props had helped to shape his imagination. It was a great start.

The original story by Pierre Boulle had been toyed with as a film script by several people, and when the picture became a huge success afterwards many of them started claiming they had written it. The list of names was surprisingly long and included Carl Foreman, Norman Spencer, and Mike Wilson. The truth is, though, that the final script had been constructed by Lean with the help of Wilson, whose input in the dialogues had been invaluable. David always maintained it had been his script, but his efforts were seldom recognised in the film industry, and when the film won an Oscar for Best Adapted Screenplay, David was never mentioned; something which deeply upset him and caused friction between himself and Spiegel. It turned out that Sam had somehow fixed it so that Boulle, Wilson and Foreman got the credit. Personally, I was more interested in David getting the Best Film Oscar, and although he never walked away with one, cinemagoers gave him the best possible accolade a Director could receive by flocking to see the movie. Whatever their feelings about each other, the truth was that Sam was a great Producer and David a great Director. There was a frisson between the two and it was evident to anyone who knew them that they would produce something special together, whether they would openly admit to it or not.

We were told to start shooting in the prisoner-of-war camp, which had been built by my old friend Peter Dukelow in a jungle clearing not far from Colombo with an army of technicians, actors and film crew. Shortly before the first day of shooting, a cry of "Snake!" rang out from the small canteen. As the cooks scattered in all directions I ran into the kitchen wielding a large shovel and came face to face with a huge cobra. My back hairs stood on end, I took a deep breath and struck out at it as it slithered towards me. By sheer bad luck, I only managed to cut off part of its tail, which had the effect of infuriating the hapless creature even further. It thrashed around and suddenly reared up, dilating its neck in the classic pose. It turned towards me and just as it was about to strike, I knocked its head for six. I cautiously moved towards the still serpent and realised I had decapitated it, venom droplets clearly visible on its fangs. It suddenly occurred to me that its skin would make a nice belt. As the commotion died down and everyone could see the danger had passed, a small crowd gathered round me to view my handywork. A corpulent English canteen lady peered over my shoulder. "I wonder how I can get its skin off," I innocently enquired.

"Give it to me," she said. She then picked up the lifeless reptile and, hooking the thumbs at the top end, yanked the skin off in one quick motion. The sight of the portly, middle-class English lady with the flaccid snake skin in one hand and the writhing, slimy, white body in the other will probably haunt me for the rest of my days. Much to my shame I never made the belt, and for some odd reason the native workers avoided me for months after the incident. Maybe I'd killed a relative of theirs. Shortly afterwards, we attended a celebration to mark Buddha's birthday. Perahana, as it's called, attracts thousands of devotees, and a relic – a tooth – is paraded through the streets, accompanied by hundreds of dancers and musicians, and colourfully-adorned elephants. People gathered from all over Ceylon in Kandy for the festivities days before and lined the route in improvised tents. David rented a number of rooms at the Queen's Hotel for the crew to view what for us would be a unique event. It was a nice touch. Just as we were due to start filming at the camp, David and his chief cameraman, Jack Hildyard, paid a quick visit and gave us the thumbs up for our efforts. I observed as David stood for ages, peering out of the little window of the hut, from where one could see the ghastly corrugated iron-dog kennel used by the Japanese to bake their prisoners and in which Colonel Nicholson – played by Alec Guinness – was to be punished.

David turned to me, still deep in thought. "Eddie, hang a beautiful white orchid in this window," he said. I'd just had my first lesson from a master film-maker. The stark contrast between beauty and ugliness became one of David's trademarks. He believed scenes evoking man's inhumanity to man would be far more compelling if the brutality was shown within the context of a beautiful setting. In this scene he did it by framing the hut and placing an orchid in the foreground. He would later introduce this device to great effect in many of his films, as in the scene in *Doctor Zhivago* where the teenage soldiers are mowed down by a machine gun in a field of bright, red poppies. It was this painstaking attention to detail which made David stand head and shoulders above his peers. As he was about to get into his car he paused, and narrowing his eyes, added, "Do you see the biggest tree at the far end of the camp in the jungle? Can you make it into a Flame of the Forest tree? It will add depth to the shot." I wasn't quite sure how I would get around that one, bearing in mind that I was being asked to decorate a giant tree in full blossom and we only had two days before shooting started.

"No problem, David," I nodded dutifully. It was not all plain sailing, however. We heard that Guinness and David had had a big falling out over how Colonel Nicholson should be portrayed. There was talk at one stage that David was considering replacing Guinness in the role because he was hell-bent on giving his character a comic slant. In the end, sense prevailed and David got his way. But it also said a lot about the quality of Guinness' acting that he was willing and able to re-invent the role to fit the Director's vision. Not many actors can do this, which is why they become typecast. Sessue Hayakawa, a Japanese actor from the silent days who had been cast as the camp's Colonel, took longer to sort out. When he first arrived on the set he strolled into the POW camp wearing a silk kimono, with his personal secretary trailing two steps behind and carrying only those pages of the script in which he appeared – he evidently hadn't even bothered to read the rest. With such an arrogant attitude he inevitably became a juicy target for David, who systematically set out to break him down and squeeze the character out of him. In the scene where he loses the psychological battle with Colonel Nicholson after he refuses a tin of corned beef and a bottle of 'Scottish Medicine' that's been offered to him, Colonel Saito has to slump on his bunk bed in tears of frustration, humiliated at having been defeated by the obstinate and resolute Nicholson.

What few people know is that David forced Hayakawa to repeat the scene over and over again, clearly unsatisfied with his performance until he finally threw in the towel, but not without first adding a withering remark. "All right, print it. It's not that good, but I suppose that's the best you can do." A week or so later he told me he was going to re-shoot the entire scene in the hut. He rounded on Sessue mercilessly. "It's all your fault, you were terrible and you have cost the company a lot of money, and now Alec has to play his part all over again." It sounded like a terribly harsh thing to say, but David knew what he was doing. Sessue immediately shed the last bit of haughty pomposity and placed himself fully in David's hands. When Sessue's character pleads and cajoles in between tears it's for real. He could just as easily have been pleading to David for mercy. David was like that; as far as he was concerned, actors were only props.

A scene in the cramped 'oven' had Colonel Nicholson stubbornly refusing to agree to have his officers work with the men, which was not permitted under the rules of the Geneva Convention. The doctor, played by James Donald, knows that Nicholson is prepared to die rather than give in, and yet his task is to convince him to do the exact opposite, hence the awkward but heart rending scene. We shot the scene for real in the blistering heat to which I added heat shimmer below the camera lens. Unfortunately, David was not too impressed with the trial runs, and despite instructing Donald on how to play the scene, it was clear he wasn't getting it – much to David's irritation, who interpreted it as a sign of obstinacy. "He's trying to resist me, I'll crucify him," he muttered under his breath. We rehearsed the scene over and over again. James, who was beginning to fade under the sweltering heat, asked me for something to kneel on as his knees were not in the picture. "No!" David hissed, trying all manner of ploys to get a performance out of Donald. First, he suggested doing a take, knowing that there was no film in the camera. About forty false takes later, Donald almost broke down sobbing with frustration, which is exactly what David wanted. His pleading suddenly became real and David quietly instructed the cameraman to put a reel of film in. It all seemed unnecessarily harsh – almost sadistic – but in the end David got the scene the way he wanted it.

Kwai's famous Colonel Bogie march was a huge success in its own right, and much of that is due to the fact that the entire crew and cast whistled the tune in unison as the bedraggled prisoners marched into the prison camp. My back hairs actually stood on end and we all felt a tremendous sense of pride, certain we were witnessing something special. Another little-known fact is that the emaciated look of many of the prisoners was not down to the skills of the make-up department. Although most of the main actors were westerners, many of the extras were in fact beggars we picked up from the streets of Colombo. In many cases, they were no more than skin and bones, and we even had quite a few of them sprayed white by the make-up department in an attempt to hide their tan. It was perhaps not the most ethical way to obtain extras, but these were different times and most people had been hardened by the still-recent memory of war. To get to the camp, the prisoners had to march through the jungle in what David felt would be a necessary but boring scene. I sensed his edginess, and as he mulled over what to do next I joined him on a clearing under the shade of a large tree.

On the trunk I noticed a beautiful butterfly, gently fluttering its wings. I casually made a suggestion. "What if I cut a sort of narrow gap on the skyline and below it, like an arsehole with prisoners in it?" He smiled and agreed to try it out. With my gang and a few tools we spent hours felling trees under the hot sun, cutting myself badly in the process and ending up with a small hole in my head caused by a falling sapling. Caked with blood and dirt, I squashed a piece of lifebuoy soap in the gap and strode over to David, who was still sitting in his chair under the tree, soaking up the sun. I noticed the butterfly had gone, and that the unit had been playing cricket while we'd been slaughtering ourselves clearing trees and bushes. For a brief moment, the only sounds in the jungle were the cheers of the men in the distance and a bat hitting the ball.

David woke me from my momentary stupor. "I think when we do the scene of the punishment parade with the prisoners standing all day in the hot sun, we should have butterflies around them," he casually remarked.

I made a mental note and pointed to the skyline. "What do you think?" I asked.

He squinted, got up and walked towards the area we'd cleared and close to where I'd just been standing moments before. I followed a little distance back. Looking through the frames of his hands, he suddenly sprang to life. "Get the camera over here and the prisoners up there in that gap." Looking through the lens he then

103

instructed me to mark out the leaves that should be removed. When it was done he stepped back and asked me to look through the camera. It worked; we now had a sort of tunnel to the skyline. "That has saved us days of shots of men slashing around with machetes in the jungle," he said. I suddenly remembered the San Remo newspaper and the picture of the madman chopping down the trees. Maybe they had been right, after all.

We did something similar but in reverse later on in the film using bamboo, during the scene in which the young Canadian commando cannot bring himself to kill a young Japanese soldier with his knife. As the soldier ploughs through the jungle, David wanted the bamboo stems to get gradually thicker and to change colour accordingly; from a very pale hue, to a darker gold, yellow and green, and finally to a sombre black – all close together "like prison bars", as David described it. There, the two young men come face to face. The tense stand-off is shattered as a ruthless Jack Hawkins lunges with his knife and swiftly stabs the young Japanese soldier. The following scene, in which thousands of startled flying foxes scatter from the tree tops, was interesting for different reasons. The film crew stood at the ready to film the bats, but when I fired the gun all hell broke loose. The startled bats suddenly flew wing tip to wing tip, virtually blocking out the sunlight; their membranous wings glowing red in the sun in an eerie spectacle. As we watched in a trance-like state, we were suddenly given a rude awakening as a steady trickle of a liquid – which at first we thought was rain - splashed our clothes and faces. We then realised the hot, sticky and foul-smelling substance was in fact urine; we were being pissed on by the panic-stricken bats. The moral of the story is, if you see thousands of sleeping flying foxes in the forest, whatever you do, don't wake them up.

When we finished shooting in Colombo we moved to Kitulgala, where the two bridges were being built. One was supposed to be the proper one, built by the British prisoners, while the other was meant to be the partly completed failure, built with Japanese supervision and sabotaged by the Brits. Both were built under the guidance of Peter Dukelow with a team of well-trained elephants. I chose to camp in a rest house deep in the jungle alongside a small track. Although it was somewhat dilapidated and full of bugs, it was quiet and restful, and in the evenings I could relax on the porch with my glass of malt whilst listening to the murmur of chatty frogs. It occurred to me that sitting in the jungle at night was a rare privilege, but being part of a crowd in a noisy, smoke-filled bar in London was not.

David and I became close friends round about this time and he felt relaxed enough to confide in me about his personal life. He would often flash past me on the road in his beloved Aston Martin, which he told me had been the only thing he had managed to salvage from his divorce after leaving England in a hurry. That, and other tax-related problems, meant he was broke. But David's generosity to those close to him was at the root of his money problems. One weekend, when David wasn't due to come to Colombo, he told me that I was to go to his suite at the Mount Livinia Hotel to eat and drink as much I liked, and to charge the whole lot to his account. "Take my dressing gown! Play my gramophone records!" he enthused over the phone. I looked at them; the military marches and a few old dance bands, including Noel Coward's 'Mad Dogs and Englishmen', which seemed highly appropriate under the circumstances. Were we simply just grown up boys, playing an eccentric game with hoards of cash? I wondered.

I still had my chauffeur-driven Chevrolet; a hideous car with two torpedoes for mascots that made the damned thing look more like a grounded spacecraft. The chauffeur was somewhat better looking, but driving to Colombo one day I noticed he was stepping on the gas a little bit too hard, which was not a wise thing to do as the locals had a habit of driving down the middle of the narrow roads. Understandably concerned, I asked him to slow down, but his reasoning left me speechless. "We must go hurry up to Colombo, masa – we are running out of petrol!" When I told Peter about this, he smiled and recounted a similar incident in which he had stopped in a jungle rest house for a beer. Before going in, he instructed his driver to turn the car around in readiness to leave. He was enjoying the drink when the driver came in looking highly agitated.

"Mr Peter...sir...your car."

"Yes? What about it?"

"Mr Peter, sir...wheels on top."

Unsure what he meant, Peter went out to investigate. He was quite right; the wheels were on top because the car was upside down in a ditch. He sighed and went back in for another beer. The kamikaze driving of the locals was no more than a source of amusement to us, until one of the crew was killed in a car crash.

One day the Second Assistant Director, Johnny Kerrison, who was driving to work with the chief make-up man and a German stand-in, came to a brow of a hill too fast just as a truck was coming the other way – in the middle of the road, of course. He tried to avoid it, but the car clipped the side of the truck and flew off the road and into a tree. Kerrison was killed outright and his passengers were seriously injured. We all heard the crash as we were unloading, causing us to stop dead in our tracks. David was the first one to react after a brief silence. "I think we should get on with it. Get the camera out." David showed his impatience with cool, ruthless efficiency on many occasions, particularly whenever an actor didn't rise to the occasion. A case in point involved a scene in which Jack Hawkins' character is meant to lob a grenade at a group of Japanese soldiers, massacring the lot. They weren't rehearsing long when David, looking thoroughly unimpressed, leant over to me and said, "Their acting's terrible. Make sure you knock them over with the explosion when we shoot the scene." After a few more tries – all equally as bad – David had had enough. He nodded to me, "This time, do it," and then quietly instructed the camera crew to roll. The Japanese actors evidently hadn't heard this and David, with a roguish smile, shouted "One more rehearsal, then!" The scene played as before, with the exception that my safe bomb, hidden in the branches of a bush, went off with an almighty bang, knocking the totally unsuspecting bunch to the ground. They must have been fairly convincing because David was happy enough with the result.

Bill Holden was indisputably the star of the film thanks to his good looks – which were a sure-fire box office draw – and his on-screen magnetism. But his charm was more than skin deep and he was, in fact, as good a man as you could ever wish to meet. During the making of the film we suddenly ran out of stuntmen. One had been sent home for bad behaviour and the other got injured, leaving us in a dilemma. In one sequence, commandoes Bill and Geoffrey Horne are meant to guide the tiny bamboo raft loaded with explosives down the river at night. Both actors' faces are blackened, and at one point the raft has to pass through the rapids between the rocks. Bill was keen to do the scene himself, but his insurance company had banned him from doing any dangerous stunts. As a quick solution he agreed for me to act as his double. And to my everlasting relief I was not asked to wear a bikini and simply had to add a bit of dirt on my face as camouflage. Needless to say, hanging on to the raft and trying to guide it between the rocks as we shot through the rapids was quite exciting. Insurance clause or not, Holden was a bit of a prankster and, helped in no small measure by his love of alcohol, often took situations to the limit. As he got on well with Jack Hawkins (who was also known to like a drink or two) it wasn't long before they were both involved in a bit of mischief.

One evening in the crew bar located close to the bridge, they got hold of a large number of paper balloons which looked a bit like Chinese lanterns. God knows how they got their hands on them, but they came up with the novel idea of lighting them up. The heat from the wax flames caused the flimsy paper balloons to rise and drift away, creating pretty patterns in the night sky. It just so happened that Sam Spiegel was paying one of his rare visits to the set when he stumbled upon the two pyromaniacs at work. Sam panicked, convinced that one would land on the bridge and burn it down. It was all the encouragement Bill and Jack needed and they set about lighting more balloons at an even faster rate. The bridge did not go up in flames but the incident must have done little for Sam's own physical and mental state. A major film producer like Sam needed to have nerves of steel, but every so often these would desert him. David told me that before filming began they had been looking for locations and on returning to their car after a long walk, David pulled up his trouser legs to look at his shins. "Vot are you doing, baby?" asked a puzzled Sam.

"Looking for leeches," David calmly replied as he undid the top of his trousers.

"Leeches?!" Sam shrieked.

"Yes, you know – blood suckers." Sam frantically pulled up his trouser legs while David continued. "Surely you know what they are: big black slugs that latch on to you and suck your blood."

Furiously inspecting his crotch, Sam suddenly let out a horrific scream. With his trousers down, he leapt from the car in terror. "Take it off! Take it off!" he screamed. There, next to his essential equipment, hung a big, bloated leech.

"Don't pull it off, Sam, otherwise it will leave its teeth and jaws in you. It has to be burned off." Sam was now beside himself with terror. Unfazed by all the commotion (and clearly savouring every moment) David took out a cigarette and lit it. "It will let go when I touch it with this," he said. Just as Sam was about to collapse in a heap, David leant over and applied the burning tip on the blood-filled leech, which instantly detached itself and fell to the ground. David then gave me a very lurid description of a red-faced Sam holding up his trousers and stamping furiously on the flattened leech, shouting abuse at it for all he was worth. Admittedly, leeches were a problem where we were, but we got used to them after a while and used soap to keep them at bay. Sam, who kept away from the jungle after his very personal encounter with one of the blood suckers, had himself made a pair of fine lace-up jungle boots as a safety precaution, although he did not say whether he had also ordered some sort of crotch protector. Of course, not everybody reacted in blind panic. In one scene, Jack Hawkins had to have leeches removed in the prescribed manner. I persuaded Jack to let me use real leeches (big fat ones which were called, rather disconcertingly, elephant leeches) by appealing to his ego and telling him that the ones seen on Humphrey Bogart in the *African Queen* were obviously prop ones. It worked.

Sometimes, if the film story has a factual background, a technical advisor, or someone with experience or knowledge on the subject, is employed. On Kwai we had an ex-army General called Peron, who had served in that theatre of war and was rumoured to have been with the famed Chindits, a special force that had been trained to operate behind Japanese lines. As a rule, I didn't care for these advisors who never did much except to make a comment every now and again in order to justify their presence and large wage packet. Peron never bothered me until one day at the bridge he asked me if he could see the two-inch mortar carriers where the bombs were kept. I told him it was authentic but that it was highly unlikely the audience would get to see it in the film, anyway. Disregarding my comments he asked to have it brought down for him to see. "If you want to see it, you'll just have to march up to the top of the hill. This is not the army, you know – we're only playing at being soldiers." I couldn't resist saying. He didn't bother me from then on. A far more interesting character was a huge Dutchman and former army officer by the name of Wyman who had been taken prisoner by the Japanese when Singapore fell. He was sent to the notorious Changi POW camp where he was put in charge of officers, very much like Colonel Nicholson in the film. Because he was so big, he became a target for the guards and received brutal treatment at the hands of the Japanese, who regularly tortured him in a variety of ways, including attaching electrodes to his private parts. He had been badly crippled as a result and needed the aid of two sticks to walk. When I met him, he was the head of the zoo in Colombo, which he ran with tender loving care. He also kept a room full of memorabilia from his war time experiences, which gave me the idea to ask him if he was willing to become the film's technical advisor.

"Will there be any Japanese on the set?" he asked nervously. I nodded. "I won't be able to do it, then. It's impossible for me to be around them. I won't even allow any Japanese into the zoo."

Wyman's scars were more than just skin deep and I felt sorry for him. But although his mind had been badly misused, he found solace in the zoo, which he never left, and in his animals, who loved him dearly. He then turned away and gave an order to one of the elephants. The large beast gently took me in its trunk and hauled me high up above its head, and with another instruction the elephant took me by the waist and lifted me sideways in its mouth. The demonstration not yet over, I was then told to lie still on the ground. The elephant moved menacingly forward and gingerly placed its foot on me, light as a feather. After another command the elephant stepped over me. Finally, Wyman put a coin on the ground and told the elephant to pick it up, which it did with the fine tip at the end of its trunk, handing it back to the large Dutchman with remarkable tenderness. These wonderful elephants actually built our bridge. Rolling, pushing and carrying up great tree trunks from the surrounding jungle, the gentle giants did all the work that would normally have been done by machines. They knew what to do and how to do it, and only needed a word from their mahouts who had a close bond with each of their animals. Nature wasn't always so kind. We almost had another tragedy on our hands when a man fell into the water after being shot in one of the scenes. By sheer bad luck he was caught in a vortex and unable to surface. My one and only prop man from London, an Irishman named Tommy, dived in with a rope to help. The problem was that Tommy had inexplicably forgotten that he couldn't swim. A local man who saw what was happening also dived in, but fared no better. Now there were three men struggling to reach the surface. Just as they were about to give up, the vortex miraculously sucked them all out of the bottom. The boys in the river brought them ashore and resuscitated them. The stuntman, who was in such a bad state that he had to be sent back to London, never fully recovered from his ordeal. Tommy came around, and the first thing the rascal demanded was a shot of brandy, knowing that I always kept a bottle handy in the bus, ostensibly for such occasions. David came over to me and said he had been sending me mental messages not to jump in.

"I got them," I said.

Years later, Tommy, who was a close friend of Peter Dukelow and also came from County Kildare, had been told by his doctor to quit drinking, something no self-respecting Irishman would ever seriously contemplate doing. While out on a pub crawl in Hammersmith Broadway, Tommy suddenly dropped dead after knocking back one last brandy. Dukelow looked down on him nonplussed and dryly remarked, "He hasn't paid for his round."

We were nearing the end of filming and the climax of the movie. But just before we were due to blow the bridge up, Jack Hawkins still had to shoot a scene in which his character has to fire a two-inch mortar. As the bombs fall, Colonel Nicholson is killed and his body falls on the plunger, causing the bridge to blow up. Surprisingly for a producer, Sam was interested in finding out just how dangerous it might be to blow a man up. Maybe he was thinking of his insurance. "There's no danger whatsoever, Sam. Come over and I'll show you myself." I placed the cone-shaped, heavy iron mortar shell leaning slightly away from the actor and just below the surface of the water. I made the 'bomb' myself, using black gunpowder in a paper bag rolled in black insulation tape – the more tape one used, the greater the force of the explosion – and inside this was the igniter. Simple. On top of the bomb I packed sawdust which I had pre-soaked for days in various colours. It was heavy in order to increase the pressure and, therefore, the potency of the bomb. It all looked pretty dramatic and dangerous but was utterly harmless, unless someone was actually foolish enough to sit on it. The aim, of course, was to throw up a lot of mud and pebbles high into the air. To show how safe it was I even stood on top of the 'bomb' and fired it. I then asked Sam to try it out for himself, but he declined, saying that it would make his clothes dirty. He may have been right.

The famous scene of the bridge blowing up and the train careering to its destruction was real, not a mock up. We only got one shot at it, understandably, as there wasn't enough time or money to build another bridge. Inside the carriages I had three hundred rubber Japanese soldiers placed with guns, in case the carriages burst open.

A demolition company from the UK came over to demolish the bridge following David's strict instructions. The explosion had to look real and last long enough to get sufficient footage.

There were many points to consider, not least the angle at which the train should fall. It was also made very clear that there should be no flames, smoke or far-fetched fireballs. In real life, when a building is brought down with explosives it collapses in almost slow motion instead of exploding in a hail of flame and debris (this is a point missed on many modern film directors who are invariably obsessed with creating ridiculous, computer-enhanced blasts). We positioned five cameras in five different points to give the editing crew a variety of angles to choose from. Each had a switch that triggered a light on a control panel, giving a signal to the director that the camera was running and the operator was safe. There was another light which the train driver had to operate when he jumped off at the crucial moment before the explosives were detonated. The main control panel was located at a safe distance from the main camera with David close by. At the far end of the bridge there was a long track, with an uphill gradient leading to a sand trap. This was intended to stop the unmanned train in the unlikely event that the bridge had not been blown up. Everybody in their places, the order was given to start the operation. Four lights came on and then the driver's. As the train came onto the bridge, David suddenly spotted that one of the lights had not been switched on and did not give the order to detonate. The train shot over the bridge at full speed, up the gradient and through the sand drag, collecting a big truck and a generator along the way. Peter and I were the first on the scene and found the steaming train sitting upright, its wheels dug deep in the jungle floor.

After a few minutes Sam turned up in his car. It was difficult to gauge his reaction, but he was either in deep shock or dead calm. I have to admit to feeling admiration for him as he uttered his first words to us. "My boys, how long before we get it ready again?" With all the right railway equipment and workers it didn't take long to slip some track under it and shunt it back. It wasn't all tickety-boo, though. After Sam left us, he marched back and summarily fired the camera operator who had failed to turn on his light switch, even though his camera had been running. He was an experienced and well-known operator, whom David knew and trusted. Unfazed by the poor man's blunder, David quietly reinstated him and took him out to dinner that same night. After the nerve-jangling experience, we were all even more wary of making any further mistakes.

To my surprise, David asked me to drive the train for the second attempt. Apparently, the driver had got cold feet about driving the thing. Relieved he would no longer be risking his life, he was more than happy to give me a crash course on how to drive the locomotive to oblivion. I had the light switch and the sandbag shelter on which I was to dive when I bailed out moved almost to the beginning of the bridge. This gave me a few more precious seconds to jam the throttle lever open once I had set the right speed. It also gave me a pretty good close up view of the bridge going down. Getting the timing right was a matter of life and death. Too late and I would end up in pieces amid tons of twisted wreckage at the bottom of the river; too early and we would ruin the shot. I set off inside the train, and this time I had a unique view from the driver's cabin, looking down on the river some thirty metres below as the bridge rushed up to meet me. The train picked up speed and I waited till the last possible moment before jamming the lever. I dived on the sandbags and watched as the train clattered by, followed by an almighty bang as the dynamite went off. In an instant, the bridge which had taken us eight months to construct collapsed in a twisted heap. Still breathless, I shook myself down and looked down below, feeling mixed emotions. I was relieved the operation had been a success but also felt a twinge of sadness at seeing all the destruction. We had one final 'special effects' scene in which the commandos were to set the explosive charges to the bridge support. We shot it during the day and filtered the lens to make it look like night time. Setting up the dynamite was fine and as I surfaced I saw David looking down on me, smiling. By the glint in his eye, I knew what he was thinking.

"Bloody millionaire's stuff!" I remarked – we *were* just grown up boys after all, playing games with loads of cash.

Many years later, while staying in a hotel in Westwood village in LA, I went for a drink in the bar and noticed a frail-looking man hunched on the chair at a corner table. He looked over and suddenly stood up and walked over to me. "You're Eddie," he said with a smile. Surprised that this man knew my name and curious as to who he was, I struggled to recognise him but I was saved my blushes. He thrust his hand out and introduced himself. "It's me, Bill Holden." I was shocked. The ravages of time and alcohol had sadly taken their toll on him, but I tried to not let it show on my face. I greeted him warmly and gave the impression that I had recognised him. What amazed me even more is that he knew who I was despite my hair having gone entirely white since I had last seen him. I never saw him again and was deeply saddened when I heard a few years later that he had died in such sad and lonely circumstances. The death of Burt Lancaster also affected me in a similar way. Both actors were larger than life individuals.

CHAPTER 9

The Vikings are coming

The Vikings (US) 1958. **Released by United Artists.**
Director: Richard Fleisher. Producer: Lee Katz. Writer: Calder Willingham. Photographer: Jack Cardiff Music: Mario Nascimbene.
Cast: Kirk Douglas, Tony Curtis, Ernest Borgnine, Janet Leigh, Alexander Knox, James Donald.

As we were wrapping up *The Bridge on the River Kwai*, I got a message from producer Lee Katz asking me if I wanted to work on a movie he was making about Vikings. Norse warriors sailing around the freezing North Sea in longships was a world away from the sticky heat of the jungle, so I took the job, thinking it would be a far better option than joining the dole queue at the Duke of Wellington pub. With *Kwai* finished, Sam chartered a plane to fly the whole crew home, but I was not on it. Instead, I flew first class to Copenhagen. I drew strange looks from the Danes as I strolled through the airport in my shorts and short-sleeved shirt, and was even more self-conscious when I checked into a very posh hotel. That was when it hit me that I was somewhere completely different; the change in the weather was a shock to the system, but Copenhagen was a clean and extremely pleasant city, especially after Colombo. The famed Tivoli gardens, the swish restaurants, the old-mime pantomime theatres and the Princess' golden coach, drawn by white ponies and escorted by guardsmen, acted like a soothing balm after the gruelling months spent in Ceylon. I counted about twenty-six different bars and restaurants, all of which enjoyed my custom. If this is how Vikings lived I'm surprised they turned to pillaging.

I immediately got started on my prop workshop and we were soon manufacturing all the gear Vikings normally used for their nefarious trips abroad, including swords, axes, helmets and pikes. Fortunately, this did not include the two long ships, as they had already been built and were being transported to Norway, where we planned to shoot the film. We had a good cast: Kirk Douglas was the film's driving force in much the same way Burt Lancaster had been in *The Crimson Pirate*, and with Tony Curtis and Janet Leigh he had strong support. Soon after I moved to Norway to the main location at Hardanger Fjord; a spectacular sight surrounded on three sides by distant, bleak mountains. To solve the problem of accommodation, Katz chartered an old, retired cruise ship: the famed *Stella Polaris*. It was a great idea, but it wasn't for me. I opted to stay with a fishing family in a cottage close to the shoreline. Every morning, a boat picked me up to join the film crew and later dropped me off in the evening, that way I could enjoy a nice home-cooked meal and bathe in a spring outside, and there was no better way to end the day than to watch the long sunsets at two o'clock in the morning.

Admittedly, not everyone was so lucky. For some strange reason, I could find no bars in the area. It was almost as if (horror of horrors) alcohol had been banned. In the only store I found in the area they sold everything from boat anchors to children's toys, but the only alcohol on offer was contained in those ridiculous liquor-filled chocolate bottles. I noticed how tough-looking fishermen would charge in to buy them by the box load after a hard day's slog, desperate for the droplets of whisky contained within. It was a very sad spectacle watching grown men fight over such toys. I, on the other hand, had come prepared and brought a couple of bottles of Scottish medicine along with me to sip while contemplating the lovely sunset, sitting with my feet up around midnight.

Along the shoreline we built a faithful reproduction of a fairly large Viking village, which I dressed in detail. The biggest building – a hall – was built back into the hillside. I prepared the interior to use as an on-site workshop and prop room, but in the meantime I had other designs. Every day I had boxes of fresh fish delivered, ostensibly as props for the film, but which were being put to far better use. I had decided to set up my own fish and chip shop – newspaper wrapping included. I boiled the fish in a big cauldron of fat at the back of the prop room and just as I had previously done with my bootleg beer enterprise, my new venture into the restaurant business became enormously popular with the crew, the only difference being that this time there was no charge.

Kirk and Tony, in their roles as beer-swilling, wench-pulling, village-sacking warriors, were due to shoot some pretty fierce sword fights between them. Since I would be needing some very strong, safe swords to work with I flew to England to get them made. In the early days of movies, swords were often made of stiff leather, laminated and stitched together, but these were heavy and snapped way too easily. I started making a lot of plastic swords just for display but found a better material normally used for making switchboards called Tufnel, which was light and tough, and could be cut and shaped without breaking or bending excessively. Unfortunately Tony and Kirk were a bit over-enthusiastic during their fight scenes and it was obvious that I would require something even sturdier and more resilient. So I went to a metal merchant in England and bought the highest quality Duralumin; an aluminium-based alloy containing copper and iron which was being used in the aircraft industry at the time. I got it in strips of about two inches wide and half an inch thick. From that I cut and milled the blades right through the hilt in order to remove any sharp points. The two halves of the hand grip were simply fixed to the blade. They were light and flexible, but also very stiff. If one thrust the point into a wooden floor the swords would stand upright and sway while keeping their shape. I made many, and the actors told me they were the best they had ever used. They became my standard stage sword for the rest of my career. I believe they use carbon fibre nowadays, but a prototype I tested some years ago failed to convince me about its superiority because, despite its unquestionable strength, carbon fibre tends to shatter, and a broken sword blade flying across the set could kill or maim someone. Indeed, I'd say they are far more dangerous than any of my mortar bombs.

The days were getting colder in Norway and it wasn't long before our tough-looking Vikings were grumbling about getting paid more. Lee Katz suspected something was afoot, so we quickly packed everything up and flew like the wind with our two boats to Germany (in huge trucks, that is) while the crew and actors filmed some scenes at a castle in Dinar in France with my swords. Soon we had a longship sitting on hydraulic rockers on a stage at the Bavaria Film Studios, at a place just outside Munich called Geiselgasteig. Life couldn't be easier, going to the studio in the morning, looking in at the stage where the longships were rocked surrounded by a fake mist, and dropping in at the bar, which had a big green lawn and a bevy of pretty young frauleins parading outside and waiting to be discovered. As we were in Munich I thought it would be a terrible shame if I didn't take advantage of the plethora of beer gardens which the city was famous for. But aside from the good beer there was little else to do. It was time for a change, so when an offer came to film in the Virgin Islands I took it like a shot.

From Vikings to Virgins

Our Virgin Island **(US) 1958   Released by British Lion Film Corporation**
Director: Pat Jackson.   Producer: Leon Clore and Grahame Tharp. Writers: Pat Jackson, Ring Lardner Jr. and Robb White. Cinematographer: Freddie Francis.
Cast: John Cassavetes, Virginia Maskell, Sidney Poitier, Isabel Dean, Colin Gordon, Ruby Dee.

After the Vikings, the virgins. I packed my bags and left the longships and the German beer far behind me to make a gentler and more relaxed movie in distinctly sunnier climes. *Our Virgin Island* was based on a novel by Pat Jackson about a young couple setting up home on a remote island. The picture boasted an excellent cast which included Sidney Poitier, John Cassavetes and a relatively unknown actress at the time, Virginia Maskell. When I met Jackson, who also happened to be directing the movie, he wasted no time in checking my credentials. "You *do* know how to sail a dinghy, don't you?" he probed. I didn't take the bait.

"Of course I do, Pat" I confidently replied. I was lying through my teeth, but by now I readily assumed that having no experience at something was not a sound reason for not doing it, and sailing a dinghy did not seem much of a challenge after blowing up bridges. But as soon as I read the script I could see why Jackson had been such a stickler about it. Among the main props they had listed a sailing dinghy, which I quickly purchased along with a small outboard motor I kept hidden under the stern, just in case. I then set about the task of mastering the complexities of dinghy sailing, such as they were, quietly and without any fuss. For a novice like me the fact that the area was virtually deserted considerably reduced the chances of my bumping into another craft, or of making an ass of myself in front of nosy crew members.

The Virgins were divided between the British and the Americans. The Yanks were far more sophisticated in every way and had plentiful supplies of everything, in contrast to the British who were quite happy to cling to a more old-fashioned, romantic view of

117

colonialism; a world in which 'making-do' was still the accepted doctrine. But the Americans' well-stocked supplies – which included a very convenient duty-free law – always won hands down as far as I was concerned. I happily admit I was spotted popping over to the Yankee side of the islands on more than one occasion. Inevitably, some Americans also raised a few eyebrows by doing things their own way and taking too many risks. One chap, an American who used to fly me between the British and American islands in a beaten up two-seater plane, had a cavalier attitude to safety. He had a habit of taking off from the curving beach with one wing tip close to the water while trying to get airborne before running out of sand. Sadly, not long after our crew moved out, the intrepid pilot was killed after crashing his flying bucket of bolts (perhaps a bit of sticky tape had come undone while trying to get airborne).

When cast and crew arrived they set up their base at a hotel and yacht club under construction on Beef Island. The two people who were building it were also constructing an airstrip, and one could not help but admire their remarkable enterprise. One of the men was a former Polish soldier who had been based in Scotland during the war. There he met a girl, got married and sailed around the world in an old ketch they bought after the war. They got as far as this group of islands and decided to stay. Slowly, they began to lay down roots and expand. When we arrived he was out every day, using an old bulldozer to level the ground for the airstrip, which I now believe is the airport. What was then the club house has now become a top-draw yacht and deep sea fisherman's resort. Not bad for an amateur couple. While the crew made themselves comfortable, I decided to make my home out of a wooden crate which had been used to ship a motor car to Roadtown. I had it landed on a deserted island beach from where I was picked up in the mornings and dropped off again after the day's work. And thanks to the plentiful supplies of tinned chicken and champagne which I'd purchased at the 'Duty-Free Virgins' (aka. 'the American end') I felt like an up-market Robinson Crusoe without a Man Friday. I never went far from the beach as the jungle was quite inaccessible, although in hindsight maybe I should have ventured further in. It turned out I was sharing my little beach retreat with some very peculiar creatures; huge and quite ferocious-looking land crabs that were attracted by my discarded food tins, the contents of which they viciously fought over at night. Fearing an encounter with the oversized claws of a ravenous

118

crustacean, I always made sure I threw the discarded tins a safe distance away. But land crabs weren't the only unwelcome visitors. One morning I was woken up by the sound of an earthquake. My box house was shaking so violently that I sprang out of bed in a panic. I rushed out and was suddenly confronted by a cow scratching itself against a corner of the box. How it came to be there I'll never know, and all my enquiries failed to come up with an answer. Maybe it was a good swimmer.

My recently acquired skill sailing dinghies was soon put to the test in a stunt that almost cost me my life. When Jackson asked me to stand in for Virginia for a hair-raising scene involving a dinghy in a storm, I recalled my earlier conversation with him and his insistence that I should be the on-set sailing expert. It was now all beginning to piece together. I began to suspect there was an unwritten agreement in Hollywood that I was to be hired for all the risky stunt scenes involving women at sea. To this day I can't quite put my finger on why, since I was far too hairy and stocky, and my bust size left a lot to be desired. On this occasion, the scene involved shooting some fraught scenes with the couple setting sail in the miniscule dinghy towards the main town's hospital, where a heavily pregnant Virginia is to give birth. To add to the drama, the scene unfolds just as a violent storm – what else – unleashes all its fury. It was agreed that the Director would stand in for Cassavetes while yours truly would step into Virginia's shoes, as it were. I took to the role with my usual aplomb and added weight in all the right places; we were fitted with the right wardrobe and waited for a real storm to whip up. Almost on cue the sky darkened over the horizon, while the camera crew scrambled to set up at a suitable high vantage point.

In the meantime, Pat and I set sail headlong into the ever strengthening wind, which soon hit us with such force that we almost capsized. It was then that I began to question the wisdom of volunteering for such a crazy stunt. As we struggled with the madly flapping sail, I realised of all the stupid and dangerous things I had done, this took some beating. We were suddenly lashed by heavy rain and a fierce wind. Looking like a demented Mother O'Reilly, I desperately fought with Pat to control the dinghy. With an oar each, we tried to head into the high waves, knowing that, without lifejackets, the smallest error would mean certain death. I frantically tore at the baby bag, whilst anxiously eyeing the jagged rocks looming menacingly close as we were mercilessly pounded by the waves. Suddenly, a small landing craft emerged from the thick rain to our rescue. Much to our embarrassment, the vessel, which had been left over by the Americans during the war and was being used by us to ship supplies in, was owned and skippered by a tough, elderly American lady and manned by two local lads. For all I cared, Mickey Mouse could have been at the helm. The feisty woman, whose name I sadly can't remember, showed superb seamanship as she manoeuvred her boat towards us, threw a line and towed us back to safety. When we staggered ashore the camera crew descended upon us, babbling on about having "some great stuff on film". I could have throttled them.

When we finally abandoned our Virgin Island I left my lovely car crate to the friendly cow whose only crime, after all, had been to scare the shit out of me in the middle of the night. The cow wasn't the only creature to inherit something used. I returned to the UK and to the Duke of Wellington Pub wearing a fine cashmere jersey generously given to me by Sidney Poitier after I'd remarked how good it looked. "It's yours," he smiled as he pulled it off and pulled it over my head.

19 years old and in the army... but not for long.

Watching O'Toole in action just before problems
started with the 'quicksand'.

Popping out for a drink...Peter O'Toole handing me a glass of water
during the famous quicksand scene in *Lawrence of Arabia*.

You want a dust storm, you got it – throwing sand
in Lawrence's face.

A mug's game – the crew trying to sweep the desert clean for *Lawrence*, prior to the next take.

Tooling up for *Lawrence*

The Aqaba set in *Lawrence of Arabia* – actually
a beach in Almería, Spain.

John Box and David on the Aqaba set.

Doctor Zhivago's Varykino frozen palace
– not a bad piece of work, that.

Dick Lester – a brilliant director who spent most of his time trying
to catch me out... the swine.

Dick Lester tries to sell me a joke – I'm not buying.

THE THREE MUSKETEERS
FILMING
1973

Looking tanned and happy on the set of
The Three Musketeers (1973).

In Budapest with the crew of *The Prince and the Pauper.*

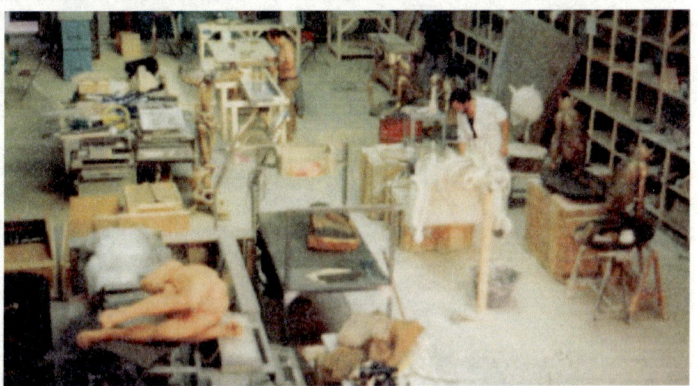
One of my workshops on a film set
– but don't ask where or when.

Me and a couple of stand-ins that never made it on set.

Put it over there! in Bora Bora.

The writer, the director and the dedicated maniac
– Robert Bolt, David and me in Tahiti.

Not what it looks – searching for Cook's anchor.

Gotcha! Shortly after lifting Cook's anchor from the seabed, and all under David's watchful eye.

David checking up on my offer of a location.

David loading his camera while on a flying safari over Kenya.

Stephanie Powers' pussycat.

Looking like two exhausted OAPs in Kew Gardens.

Taking a break while looking for locations on *Passage to India*

India's got talent – spot the erotic sculptures.

Set decorating on *Passage to India* – it was to be
David's last film.

Signing autographs in Spain for film buffs
– those other dedicated maniacs.

On stage receiving my lifetime achievement award in Spain -
December 2009 – it was aproud moment.

CHAPTER 10

Sand and Snow

Sea of Sand ('Desert Patrol' in the US) – UK (1958). 97 minutes. Tempean Films Ltd. Black and White. Director: Guy Green. Writer: Robert Westerby.
Cast: Richard Attenborough, Vincent Ball, Michael Craig, Barry Foster, Ray McAnally.

Counting the money I'd made after a job was usually a short exercise because I wasn't particularly good at saving and the taxes were high. After making three overlapping films, all non-stop and in every corner of the globe, it was impossible to feel settled anywhere. Where was home? I tried being philosophical about it and decided to call on the Duke of Wellington for a few bevies and to meet a few friends, knowing that another job would not be long in coming. When it did, however, I was horrified to discover that it was an offer to work in Libya at a desert location. I quickly turned it down, but the producers insisted, telling me that they were planning to make a movie called *Sea of Sand* about the North African campaign. That didn't make it any more appealing as I was not interested in working on a film about modern warfare. However, when they told me that Guy Green – a great friend who had been the chief lighting cameraman on *Hornblower* – was going to direct it, I quickly changed my mind. Although I agreed to work on the film – foolishly, as it turned out – I made it clear that as long as I kept my side of the bargain and set everything up first, they should not expect me to see it through to the end.

After my experience in Yemen, I wasn't looking forward to working within a million square kilometres of a desert. Despite careful planning, by the time I'd done my bit I was so crestfallen by the experience that I wished the movie had sunk without trace beneath the sand. Notwithstanding a professional cast, which included Richard Attenborough and Barry Foster, the film had a shoestring budget and we were forced to work with clapped out army vehicles left over from the war fourteen years earlier. The script had the desert patrol in constant movement, but I knew that if the vehicles had had a problem charging through the desert in World War Two it would be even harder to get them going again more than a decade later. With more time and money available I would have fitted new engines, but we had neither, so we had to make do with a lot of elbow grease and a bit of ingenuity. I spent most of my time marshalling a team of mechanics working all through the night in order to keep them running during the day.

The chosen location was far south of Tripoli, about two hours' drive along a straight desert road that was occasionally marked out by up-ended oil barrels. It was not a place you'd want to get lost in at night (or during the day, come to think of it). As one of the hottest places on earth, it was disturbing to think that anyone could spend any amount of time here and survive. We were amazed to discover that we were close to the actual location where the Desert Rats had attempted to hold off Rommel's army during a major retreat. Known as 'The Knightsbridge Box', the battle was named after the barracks in London which housed several units of the Guards. They managed to hold out for several days without food and water, but despite putting up a fierce fight they were all eventually killed after their ammunition ran out. Seeing how hot it got, theirs seemed a merciful ending.

Baking under the blistering hot sun, it was quite simply hell, and the only good memory I had of the place was in the tourist centre of Tripoli with the strong smell of jasmine and the groups of young beggar children who tried selling necklaces made from these flowers. I also made the mistake of living in the Arab quarter of Tripoli, which was overrun by thousands of barking mad scavenging dogs that kept me awake all night with their howling. With nerves frayed and bags under my eyes, the pooches kindly decided to stop their yelping only when the sun began to rise over the horizon…just as morning prayers started up at the mosque. To make matters worse, there were no creature comforts – certainly no air-conditioning – and not much of anything else. It was hot, filthy and fly-ridden, and it was fair to say that it was top of my 'don't-even-think-about-working-here-again' list. When I got a call from London with an offer to work in the Swiss Alps, I jumped at the chance faster than a kangaroo with its arse on fire. As if by a miracle, my mood suddenly changed; I was about to swap the hot, stinking shit-pit of Libya for the crisp, clean mountain air of Zermatt, at the foot of the Matterhorn.

Travelling by train from Zurich through countryside so sparklingly clean that it seemed as though someone had polished the mountain tops, the contrast could not have been greater; it was like jumping from a fiery hell into the Garden of Eden. As the countryside sped past I caught glimpses of lush green valleys and tumbling streams, and I suddenly felt good about my job once more. The railway station on the outskirts of the town was quite inaccessible and no motorised vehicles were allowed in, so when I arrived I was taken by horse-drawn carriage to my hotel. My first port of call was, naturally, the bar which coincidentally was where I had arranged to meet the director – Ken Annakin, also known within industry circles as 'Panickin' Annakin for reasons that would become clearer during the shoot. I knew Annakin from his early Warner days when he had directed a film there, but he didn't know me because I had only been a lowly prop man at the time. I wasn't sure why I was being asked to work on this picture. I was the odd-man out on a studio-based, Walt Disney production and I really didn't think I fitted in. *Third Man on the Mountain* was based on a true story about an Englishman called Edward Wymper, who had been the first man to reach the peak of the Matterhorn.

Annakin and I didn't get off to a good start. For some unfathomable reason, he seemed perturbed by the sight of my white mane of hair – perhaps it gave him the impression I was over the hill. But I shouldn't have been surprised by his prickliness. True to his namesake he was known for being an obsessive and rather neurotic director who made a mountain out of a molehill. As if to test me, and noticing that I was limping a bit, his first words were, "You do know that this film is about mountain climbing, don't you?" It sounded like a challenge. Ignoring his evident lack of confidence in me, I told him not to worry and that I would have everything organised once I'd read the script. Shifting uncomfortably in his seat, he then asked me to go to the top of a mountain known as The Rifflap, "to see if it is any good and whether we can get a crew up there".

The next day a mountain guide took me to the summit after a not inconsiderable effort on my part. I was awestruck at the breathtaking view before me and was in no doubt this would be an excellent location for filming. We got back by late afternoon and I was sitting in the bar enjoying a beer when an irate Annakin strode towards me, none too pleased to see me. "I thought I told you to investigate the top of the Rifflap!" he barked.

"Done that Ken," I said, with a trace of smugness. "The views are stunning – it'll be well worth getting a camera crew up there. Now sit down and have a drink." He declined. My composure seemed to have put his nose out of joint and he was in no mood to relax.

British actor Michael Rennie starred in the film alongside James McArthur, who would go on to find fame playing a police detective in *Hawaii Five-O* many years later. The female lead would be played by Janet Munro, who very sadly died years later at a very young age. They were all great actors and great to work with, but Herbert Lom, however, was badly miscast as the mountain guide. This was because the man suffered from vertigo so badly that he even had a problem climbing two rungs of a ladder. It wasn't the poor guy's fault, but it was a clear disadvantage, made doubly worse by the fact that he was a bit of a short-arse and Rennie, a tall man by any account, towered over him. To compensate for his lack of stature we came up with the unsophisticated solution of placing him on an apple box in the scenes where he had to stand next to Rennie, but even that made him nervous. It was a farcical situation to work under, but at least I was in good company as many of the crew really knew their stuff. I had worked with many of them before on *Hornblower* and felt reassured that the task ahead would be made easier.

Just before we started shooting, Walt Disney himself was scheduled to pay us a visit on location. To ensure it all ran smoothly, Annakin and various crew members gave the site a thorough inspection the day before in preparation for the great man's tour. To add a bit of excitement, Annakin arranged it so that Disney's arrival would coincide with the shooting of the first scene. It was agreed that we would have actor James McArthur bounding across a fast-running mountain stream, using a series of stepping stones which the studio construction department were to strategically place for him in between the boulders. I had my doubts about the charade because it was a fast moving stream and I was concerned that the stones would be dislodged but, uncharacteristically for me, I chose to be diplomatic and keep my mouth shut, seeing as I had been left out of the plan entirely. Nonetheless, and true to my philosophy that you should always be ready with a back-up plan, that same evening I had a tubular, steel ladder made which I took to the set as a precaution. I put it out of sight behind some rocks and said nothing. If I got it wrong and nothing happened no one would be any the wiser.

Next morning, Walt came on the set wearing a Tyrolean hat with lots of pin badges that made him look like a cross between a yodeller and General Montgomery. Everyone was in a party mood, except me. The construction crew started placing the stones where they were told, but it soon became clear that it wouldn't work because the stones either wouldn't balance or they rolled away by the force of the current. It was a farce. I walked up to Annakin and quietly suggested that I could fix it. In the trying circumstances – and in the absence of any better ideas – he agreed and loudly gave the order to let me get on with it. I sauntered over to the stream, surveying the situation with grave concern (I could also act when the situation required it). Looking like a surgeon about to perform a delicate operation, I frowned and instructed my crew to get the ladder, whose length just so happened to coincide with the width of the stream. It fell exactly right.

"Try putting the boulders in the rungs," I suggested. Within minutes the stepping stones were safely in position. James skipped across and the scene was in the can in no time.

I must admit I was half-expecting it when Walt Disney came up to me. "You're on my next film. Bill, fix it!" he told his European Chief, Bill Anderson. Suddenly, everyone wanted to be my friend, including our neurotic Director.

To while away the time in the hotel that same evening the crew made friends with a curious lodger which happened to be, rather appropriately as we were shooting a Disney film, a small and fearless mouse. The little creature ran along the tops of chairs, demanding to be fed peanuts by his captive human audience. One of 'Mickey's' fans was Janet, a Scottish actress who was also quite fearless. In one scene, she had to swing from a climbing rope high above a cliff. I told her that I would do the scene for the long shots, but she expressed surprise at the idea and happily volunteered to do it herself. Not only did she do the stunt like a natural but added an extra element of danger by swinging wildly like a pendulum, clearly enjoying every moment of it. I later found out that her parents had been circus performers in Glasgow.

In the film, the story recounted the fact that many mountaineers had unsuccessfully tried to climb the Matterhorn. A pretty little cemetery nearby, where almost all the headstones had English names, was testament to this. As in all films about climbers, we had to have the ubiquitous rock avalanche in one scene, so I had fake polystyrene boulders made in my prop shop. We sculptured the Styrofoam and shaped it at will with a blowtorch, being careful not to set it alight. It shrank and wrinkled nicely, forming a hard crystalline skin which took on the colour of stone. We also thrust six-inch nails into it to add weight. We prepared the rock fall, along with some dust, at the top of the mountain in a tent. But one night, a windstorm dispersed our 'rocks' all across the Alps. For days and weeks afterwards, excited tourists were seen returning to town with tales of a new geological find. They had carefully tied the rocks to the top of their backpacks to show the world their newly-found treasure, but I didn't have the heart to tell them that polystyrene was not a rock. If you happen to go on a hill-walking holiday in Zermatt and find a light-weight 'geological wonder', just remember that it's the property of Walt Disney Studios.

Once in London, I was back to work on a new project. I had a request to go to Canada where the BBC had given financial backing to a successful producer with offices and small studios in Toronto and Ottawa. He was going to make a series about the Royal Canadian Mounted Police, the Mounties. Canada had strict employment laws, and I was asked for a reference which David Lean gladly provided. I was not aware of the contents until weeks after arriving in the country. I was eventually shown a letter written by David that said, "You may borrow Eddie until I need him, as I will not start a film without him." It was a kind gesture and no doubt helped to convince producer Budge Crawley to employ me. I was given an apartment facing the parliament building; its 'Big Ben' was my timepiece from my window. Despite having just finished filming in the Alps, I wasn't prepared for the Canadian cold and living in forty degrees below zero. We were knee-deep in snow the entire time we were filming and had to resort to using dog-sledges, wearing snow shoes and very thick clothing. The camera – like ourselves – had to be heated and constantly put away to keep warm in between shots. We even had to stoke fires and electrical heaters under cars to ensure the engine blocks did not crack. I wore battery-heated gloves to keep my hands from freezing, while icicles formed around people's mouths and noses – the only parts of the body that were exposed. These were unpleasant and risky conditions to work in, and only the trained huskies seem to thrive in the snow.

In one episode, a scene called for a rabid fox to make an appearance. Not finding any available volunteers I turned to a charming dog called Shep that belonged to a family close by. He was about the size of a fox, and after a few hours in the make-up department, during which we applied vegetable dye and one of those awful fox furs with ears some women insist on wearing to this day, a new star for the film emerged. Shep was more than happy to play the role of demented fox, prancing around and teasing the tethered huskies, who regarded him with a mixture of curiosity and disdain. Away from the cameras, there wasn't much to shout about. In Ontario, public consumption of alcohol was banned on Sundays (when else could one enjoy a drink?) while Ottawa was a grim, depressing town, at least during the winter. There was little to take your mind off the dirty snow which piled up everywhere. There were no bars to hang around in except at the hotel, perhaps because women did not frequent them unless accompanied by a male partner. Even then, they could not go to the bar to order drinks. I had to do something.

Taking advantage of the police cars which we used as props in the film, I drove across the bridge to Quebec in a desperate search of liquid refreshment. I was in luck. Here, there were no absurd laws banning alcohol on a Sunday. I hit the jackpot when I discovered a large room attached to an hotel where wedding receptions were regularly held. Dressed smartly, I gate crashed at just about every wedding and drank as much as I wanted. I had a lot of fun speeding around in the cop cars, but the only time I agreed to be driven back to town proved a costly mistake. The road, as always, was frozen over and taking a bend we drifted into a car that was coming in the opposite direction. I had just enough time to remark "we're going to hit that car" before we did. We collided head-on, and as I was not wearing a seatbelt I ducked to avoid hitting the windscreen. I ended up fracturing my left foot, however, although I stubbornly refused to see a doctor about it. Instead, I got a pair of crutches and continued working, oblivious to the pain and discomfort. That was another costly mistake on my part and to this day, I suffer because of that.

Mercifully I got a letter from Basil Keys telling me that I would be required for a job on the movie *Swiss Family Robinson* to be filmed in England's Pinewood Studios. Unfortunately, this meant the crew would be subject to the usual absurd union rules which I had fought so hard against throughout my working life. There was no way I could agree to working under such conditions (not that I would be allowed to, anyway) so I wrote back thanking him…but added that I was satisfied where I was. Sometime later, I got a letter from the union telling me that as I had not paid my dues I was no longer a member. I promptly replied, pointing out that I had assiduously been paying my dues into the Shepperton branch. An evident ploy to get me on board had failed.

Refusing to take 'no' for an answer, Basil sent me another letter: "Walt insists that you work on the picture". I wrote back telling him that they could employ me as an 'advisor'; a term which would conveniently bypass union employment rules. Yet another letter arrived, this time telling me that I would be employed as a 'Special Effects Advisor'. By now, I'd grown so weary of all the friction with the unions that I almost turned the job down for good, but it was so bitterly cold in Ottawa that Tobago beckoned, and so I accepted. During the intervening period, the sun came out and suddenly it was spring. The snow melted, and the crocuses – which seemed to have been waiting to bud throughout winter – were everywhere. Little chipmunks stuck their heads out of the ground to stare excitedly all around as if to say: "Why, you're leaving us just as it's getting warmer." With some trepidation, I packed my bag and left in haste before I felt tempted to change my mind.

CHAPTER 11

Coconutty

Swiss Family Robinson (US) 1960. Director: Ken Annakin. 126 minutes. Walt Disney Pictures. Writers: Johann David Wyss, Lowell S Hawley.
Cast: John Mills, Dorothy McGuire, James MacArthur, Janet Munro, Sessue Hayakawa.

I had taken the bait and walked into a trap. We were in the Caribbean, but I found Tobago to be almost as dull as Ottawa at the height of winter. I checked into the Blue Haven Hotel, reputedly the best on the island, but soon found a chalet to rent instead as I was keen to get away from the hurly burly of filming. Lesser mortals – the other members of the crew – had to stay, rather ironically, at the Robinson Crusoe Hotel. The studio people had been busy building an expensive studio set and everything from offices, to workshops and a sound-stage were being constructed. As an 'advisor' I watched with passive interest, ruefully noting the extravagant waste of money.

Nothing, though, prepared me for what I was about to witness in the prop yard. Crew members were busily unpacking large, wooden crates sent over from England and filled with hundreds of rubber coconuts. I stood open jawed. Apparently, I was the only person on the set who realised we had been sent to an island where there were millions of the real, non-rubber variety. I said nothing, but a little while later I noticed they had been quietly repacked and hidden away. I later found out through the cost department that they had been made at an English rubber factory. They bounced around like footballs and if it had been up to me I would have given them away to the local children to use as such. Some clever clod decided instead to burn them in the dead of night.

The little episode was but a sideshow to the absurd chaos which, thanks to the unions, became the norm on the set of *Swiss Family Robinson*. I was to learn, at a price, that I was better off keeping my mouth shut by sticking to my role as advisor, while only occasionally offering to make the odd suggestion. But the union shop stewards among the crew chose to ignore me by spending more time filling out pointless timesheets for time and a half pay, double-time pay, tea breaks and even water money for getting wet. A simple, 'all-in' contract would have saved a lot of time and money, but that would have gone against the rules and their warped sense of logic.

Annakin wanted a stream that ran from the interior of the island to the beach moved so that it was closer to the headland. "You could do that, couldn't you?" he asked, more in hope than certainty. I thought he was joking at first, but no, he wasn't. I was thus promoted from advisor to civil engineer in one fell swoop. I blocked the stream off with sandbags and rerouted it through the trees. I wasn't sure why Annakin had given me this job, and then it occurred to me that he may have been thinking of the fracas in the Swiss Alps the last time he'd gotten construction 'experts' involved.

Weeks into shooting I witnessed some of Annakin's first panic attacks. A grip had to walk a few yards to pick up a tool he should have had at hand and Ken went spare, berating the man long after the little job had been done. "Ken, the job was done ten minutes ago – we could shoot now," I suggested. He gave me a cross look but managed to calm down – until the next 'crisis'.

A couple of special effects men from the Walt Disney studios in LA came over to do their thing, but after botching a few scenes it was obvious they were totally hopeless at their jobs, perhaps because they had never ventured out of a studio workshop in their lives. Before we began filming the scene, I got together with the second unit director, Yakima Canutt, of *Ben Hur* fame, who came for a week to advise Ken for the scene where the family escapes from the shipwreck in tubs. He told Ken to fit outboard motors hidden from view on each of the tubs, and the two special effects men quickly adapted the fibre glass vessels. The shipwreck had been built on some off-shore rocks and eventually all the tubs were looped together in a line with all the livestock, like a caravan. Unfortunately Yakima didn't stay on to see how the whole scene played out. Almost as soon as he left and the director shouted "Action!", all hell broke loose. The lines became entangled and took all morning to sort out, but despite trying all afternoon they could not shoot the scene.

"I can fix it, but I'll need three days," I suggested to Ken.

"Just do it," Annakin pleaded. Out came the engines and into the sea went two large anchors, each with heavy-duty steel-snatch, pulley blocks attached, more than one hundred yards apart. On the beach there were two more pulleys and a steel cable which passed through the blocks, forming a large rectangle. There, at one of the anchor points on the beach, a heavy-duty four-wheeled truck pulled the line to which the tubs were attached. We shot the scene in no time, and I figured I had earned my pay for the film there and then.

But of all the people in the crew, the most professional were the animal handlers brought in from the US. I learned how to grab a running ostrich and that a zebra could kick sideways – although I must confess I wasn't quite sure how useful that knowledge would be in the future. In one scene, a zebra was to sink in the swamp in the usual porridge mix, otherwise known as 'quicksand'. The zebra was placed in it, but the stripy one would not play ball and, struggling fiercely, managed to get out every time they tried to shoot the scene. That evening Annakin told me to 'fix it' once again, to which I replied that I would need two or three days to get it right. To be fair – and despite appearances – I quite liked Annakin and we got on well; he accepted my way of doing things and I understood and made allowances for his quirks. I had all the 'porridge' taken out and then I placed four pieces of iron tubing angled up a few yards away with cables threaded through it. At the bottom, I added a water pipe from a tank and a pump to fill the pit. The men then carefully guided the animal in and the mud put back. The zebra sank to its neck with no harm coming to the animal. I liked things to be in control and puppetry was a good method but not always easy with live animals – and almost impossible with monkeys, as you might guess. I was called upon to fix many little things but, if anything, it made things worse for me. I was virtually ignored by the crew and after a set-to with a couple of them I left and went to Trinidad for a while.

Embarrassingly, I later found that I had spent all my cash on the enormous bar-bill and didn't have enough for the air fare back – there weren't any credit cards at the time to bail one out of sticky situations – so I sailed to Liverpool, appropriately enough on a banana boat. It was grim. Take a tip – don't try it, you'll end up looking like an overripe fruit. When I got back it seemed like another depressing rerun: film over, back to dreary London and no cash – the tax man was always beating me to it. Since 1943, when I'd gone to Warners' looking for work and offering to dress their sets, I had never solicited for work. Yet here I was, out of pocket and facing an uncertain future. In those days, salaries were nowhere near as high as they are today and the astronomical wages now associated with the film industry came in about the time I left the business, although to be honest I never saved much, I never really tried. Now it looked as though I would really have to look for work. Just in the nick of time and before the storm clouds loomed ahead, I was called to Dover Street to Sam Spiegel's Horizon Films office. I arrived dead on time and brimming with self-confidence, unaware that I was about to embark on making one of the greatest films of all time.

CHAPTER 12

Camels Galore

Lawrence of Arabia. 1962. Great Britain. 221 minutes. Technicolor in Super Panavision 70. Columbia/Horizon Films. Producer: Sam Spiegel. Director: David Lean. Writer: Robert Bolt. Photographer: Frederick A Young. Music: Maurice Jarre.
Cast: Peter O'Toole, Omar Sharif, Jack Hawkins, Alec Guinness, Anthony Quinn, Donald Wolfit, Claude Rains, Anthony Quayle, Arthur Kennedy.
Oscars: Best Film, Best Director, Best Photography, Best Music, Best Editing, Best Colour, Art Direction and Set Decoration.

The next two-and-a-half years would be spent with Lawrence. It would be a pivotal point in the lives of many people who worked on the film, not least the stars themselves. Costing seventeen million dollars to make, *Lawrence of Arabia* consecrated Lean as one of the greatest film directors of all time and probably marked the greatest achievement of his career – at least in the critics' eyes. Of course, none of us had any inkling at the time that the film would be so important, or that it would be such a hit.

Sam Spiegel – using Columbia's money and distribution – was going to produce it, and with Robert Bolt writing the script and Freddie Young hired as the photographer, David knew he had the best men working under him. I was hired as the Property Master but John Bryant, the Production Designer, fell ill during the location recce and was ably replaced by John Box. John Palmer, who was in the hot seat of the manager's production office, recced for locations while Sam employed the services of a British diplomat, Anthony Nutting, to pave the way for the film crew in Arabia. His task was to get the full co-operation of King Hussein of Jordan, who was extremely helpful in every way, even down to offering the assistance of his Desert Patrol force. We started filming in Jordan and I soon left London for Amman. There I met Jerry O'Hara, who was hired as the First Assistant, and my old friend Peter Dukelow as the Construction Manager.

Yet, despite all the meticulous planning we encountered difficulties almost from the start. Bryant was soon forced to abandon through ill-health and O'Hara quit after falling out with Lean over an idea to shoot a big scene in Petra. It was decided that we should set up base in Jordan's only coastal town, Aqaba, which at the time was a small and rather squalid port. We built a tented camp, setting up prop workshops and plumbing. We imported caravans, to be used as make-up departments and production offices – anything, in fact, which needed air-conditioning. When all that was done, Peter built an entire complex – all under canvas – including a five-star restaurant. David was easy to spot in the circus-like camp; he was the one driving around in a flashy Rolls Royce while the rest of us got by in rugged four-wheel drive vehicles. We made hundreds of saddles, decorative rugs and tassels, as well as weapons and tribal flags which we aged by bleaching. I also built up a stock of the black, goat hair Bedouin tents, all hand-woven by the women over a number of years. They held a special significance for the local tribesmen and were handed down in the same way we in the west hand on a house. The tents were excellent whether in the blistering heat, or during cold nights and dust storms.

I liked the Bedouins a lot and got on well with them, which was just as well as we were living with them day in, day out. Before the actors began to arrive there was a hiatus, and to fight the boredom we provided our own entertainment in the form of a pet goat (a present from a grateful Bedouin to me), which developed a taste for liquor. Billy, as we had unimaginatively named him, promptly arrived at the bar at six o'clock every evening, waiting patiently for each of the twelve prop men to buy his round. "What will you have this time, Billy? A Grand Marnier?" He drank everything in sight and invariably got stone drunk. These were hard-drinking, hard-living prop men, but the goat – who took his place at a chair like the rest of us – could drink any of the guys under the table. Of course, for Billy to sit down at a table like a human was a challenge in itself – especially after a few drinks – and he ended up falling off most of the time, but then so did the rest of the crew. Not surprisingly he became everyone's friend (not that it would have been too hard a task after a few drinks). Inevitably, drink took its toll and Billy the alcoholic goat became Lawrence's third casualty after O'Hara and Bryant.

The crew and cast began steadily to arrive. I walked into the bar tent for a beer and at the far end spotted a sort of cowboy, wearing a hat and boots and sitting with his feet slumped on the low table top, quietly watching everyone entering and leaving. This was my first glimpse of a twenty-eight-year-old, Irish-born actor from Leeds who would go on to become a star thanks to Lawrence. David told me he had seen Peter O'Toole in a Shakespeare play and knew at once that he would be 'The One'. Much has been written about the subject, but O'Toole was unquestionably David's first choice for the role. Many other actors had been earmarked to play Lawrence, including Albert Finney (who was Spiegel's first choice) and Marlon Brando who, in my opinion, would have been quite dreadful (one only had to hear his woeful attempts at an English accent on the film *Mutiny on the Bounty* to know that he would have been totally unsuitable for the part). In contrast, O'Toole was made for the role, despite being considerably taller than the real Lawrence. We got on famously, too, not least because he also liked a drink or two. Peter was another example of how David tried not to stereotype actors in the lead role. O'Toole's Lawrence was a flawed hero; a man given to fits of megalomania one moment, and episodes of tortured self-doubt the next. But Peter was also a receptive actor, a quality which was well suited to David's obsessive hands-on approach. Peter himself rose to the challenge magnificently, becoming an expert and fearless camel rider at full charge – better even than many of the Arabs on the set.

Alec Guinness was cast as Feisal, the cunning prince who steers his people to victory with Lawrence's help. The last time I saw Guinness was when he played the bridge-building Colonel Nicholson on Kwai. David was an admirer of his, despite not always seeing eye to eye with him, and always tried to find a part for Alec ever since his remarkable Fagin in *Oliver Twist*. Whatever arguments they had over how to interpret a character these were invariably won hands down by David, anyway. In any case, Alec was a good enough actor to play the role whichever way the director wanted. Off stage, Alec kept quietly to himself. I did a lot of work with him over many years, but I can't say I ever really got to know him. He didn't mix with the crew and wasn't easy to approach, but it was a quality I admired in him because it mirrored much of my own behaviour. A total professional, he limited himself to doing his job just as I did mine. My old friend Jack Hawkins was also back, this time as General Allenby. He was as popular as ever with the crew, although I did notice that on this film he was a little less jovial in the bar at night without William Holden by his side.

Not all the casting was as trouble-free. In his insistence to get involved with every aspect of the movie, Sam had signed a French actor, Maurice Ronet, to play the part of Ali; a piece of casting which David firmly objected to. "For God's sake, he has blue eyes!" he complained. As always, David had made up his mind as to who should be playing the role, and in this case he was adamant that he wanted Omar Sharif. The problem was that Omar was virtually unknown in the west, despite being a star in his native Egypt, and this was a major obstacle for the publicity-conscious Sam, who was irked by what he perceived to be David's stubbornness. He had hired at great cost the French star and would now have to pay him off for doing no work at all. It was the last time Sam would attempt to cast an actor for a David Lean film and in future would limit himself to doing the deals. Without doubt David had made the right choice. Omar infused the role with humanity and a wisdom that was a perfect foil for O'Toole's combustible and unpredictable Lawrence. They both became good friends during filming and O'Toole even adopted a peculiar nickname for Omar, 'Cairo Fred'.

Behind the scenes, however, there were other concerns. The proximity of the Israel–Jordan border was a constant reminder to Sam that he was a Jew in an Arab country. Consequently, he spent most of his time on his luxury 500-ton yacht, *Malahne*, anchored just offshore from our beach. His fears were unfounded, though. King Hussein always made him feel welcome and not just for the money he was bringing in. He was captivated by the film's subject and also made close friends with some of the crew members. In fact, he later married Toni Gardiner, who was one of the English girls in the production office working as a switchboard operator. Anthony Quinn also fell in love during the making of the film, in his case with his dresser; an Italian girl called Jolanda Addolori, whom he went on to marry in 1966. Lawrence seemed to be casting a spell on the crew. I, on the other hand, had more pressing engagements – and not of the amorous kind. We made our beach camp in a pleasant resort and put a large anti-submarine net all around it to keep out the sharks. Sam, who was a different type of shark, moored outside the net, although I'm quite sure he still felt at home. We could not complain about our lifestyle, though. We had the best caterers cooking the best food and using ingredients which had been specially flown in from all around the world. I doubt if any one of us would have eaten any better in London.

Freddie Young, who was to photograph the movie, decided at David's insistence for the very best and used Technicolor Super Panavision 70. David always maintained that you ought to be able to take any single frame from any part of the film, put a picture frame around it, and hang it on the wall. Technicolor was just another tool to help him achieve that. Working with Lean for the second time also gave me a greater insight into the way he went about making films. During our time in the desert he refused to wear sunglasses, explaining that he needed to see a scene in its proper light, colour and detail, in the same way an audience would. "They don't see it through sunglasses," he remarked. As for myself, all I ever wore during my entire time in the desert were a pair of lightweight shorts and canvas shoes.

Filming in the desert posed other, more obvious problems, and we found that working non-stop for three weeks and resting for a few days afterwards was the best option. Sam hired a fleet of planes to ferry supplies, crew and props to and from our desert locations. One of the aircraft was a DC-3 Dakota, a trusty old workhorse which never let us down. It landed and took off anywhere, often so full that there was only standing room. Sometimes the plane would speed across the desert and take off with its door wide open like a London bus, usually to shouts of "Mind the Gap!" and "Shut that bloody door!". It wasn't as smooth as this all the time, though. During one of the many flights, a de Havilland Dove – a twin turbo-prop popular at the time – made a spectacular crash landing after the pilot forgot to deploy the landing gear. I watched it slide for about one kilometre through a cloud of sand and dust before coming to a halt. The aircraft door flung open and the film's doctor jumped out, wild-eyed. He suddenly turned to the crashed airplane and, camera in hand, started snapping away at a dazed Anthony Quinn who was climbing out of the stricken plane. Spiegel had barred the sale of unauthorised photos, so the Doc was making sure he got in quick before anyone spotted him. He was quite a character.

On one occasion, while playing a game of poker, a man rushed into the tent and pleaded with him to attend to a patient who, from the sound of things, was about to croak. Without bothering to look up the Doc replied, "I've got a good hand – God will take good care of him until I've played it." After winning his pot he sauntered off to resuscitate the man.

The news finally came in that we were to start filming in a remote and spectacular desert location which, as far as we could gather, was close to the Saudi Arabian border. David had spotted the place from a helicopter and was impressed by the startling pyramid-like rock formations, shaped by the winds over millions of years and towering above the vast, flat carpet of red sands. This was Jebel Tubeiq, where I was to take the first convoy of trucks and my prop men. But it wasn't easy to find. Today, thanks to GPS and satellite navigation systems it's a cinch to find any spot on the globe, but back then I had to work from a vaguely drawn map given to me by Hussein's Desert Patrol. It had a grid system which more or less coincided with numbers that had been marked out with stones. It was primitive but effective since they could be seen from miles away and did not get blown away by the frequent desert storms. The problem was that it didn't cover the entire distance and I had to work from aerial photographs to find the place. Having overcome that problem, a potentially disastrous incident almost brought shooting to a complete halt.

We were all loaded and ready to set off early the next morning when there was a meeting called by the shop steward members of the electrical union. When I went over to see what was brewing I was met by a hostile crowd who told me to leave because, as far as they were concerned, I was management. I pointed out that I had been a union member for longer than most of them, but my protests fell on deaf ears. Not wishing to inflame the situation any further I agreed to leave, although I did notice that Billy the goat, who I could confidently say was not a fully paid-up union member, had been allowed to stay. After a tense wait I was told that it had been decided that the convoy would not move until the company agreed to pay each person £12 extra for living in a tent. In a way, I felt they had every right to fight for a better deal (when in London they had been told about extra pay), but I was angry at the way they had gone about the whole thing and felt they were effectively holding us to ransom. I told them that if there was to be a strike the union would have to call it and that, until then, I would be the one giving the orders. I sounded off with a warning. "At five o'clock tomorrow morning when I blow a whistle the convoy moves out. Anybody not on it can report to the production office where their ticket back home will be waiting for them." There was a tense stand-off, and next morning I stood beside the line of trucks and drivers, the men's baggage still loaded from the previous day. Looking the part with my whistle, map and binoculars in hand, I glanced at my watch. Dead on five a steady stream of men made their way to the vehicles. I had called their bluff and couldn't help feeling a tad triumphant. With a sweep of my arm I blew the whistle and shouted, "Wagon's roll!", just like John Wayne. I jumped on my trusty Austin Gypsy steed and led the convoy out into the desert.

The incident did not go unnoticed by a very grateful Sam, who months later cornered me to show his gratitude. "My boy! I'll never forget what you've done for my movie! You must always work for me!" he said, with tears welling in his eyes.

"Just doing my job, Sam," I replied, a trifle embarrassed by this outpouring of emotion. He stepped back, arching his back for effect. "You stopped a strike!" he gushed. It was heady stuff, but I didn't work for him again until we made *Nicholas and Alexander* more than ten years later.

Despite the outcome, I understood the crew's dissatisfaction and could not blame them for trying to get a few extra pounds a week. We went on to develop a great sense of camaraderie and the experience did not alter the fact that we all felt as though we were an independent small nation, cut off from the rest of the world and living a unique adventure. We made good progress that day across the vast plains and laid camp for the night with all the trucks parked in a small group. The vast deserted area we chose was as flat as a billiard table. All the sand had been blown away to leave a surface of rounded stones a few inches deep. Our trucks were like flies in the middle, accompanied only by an eerie silence throughout the cold of night. It felt as though we had landed on another planet and were the only humans on it. I slept on the roof of a gigantic, cigar-shaped silver trailer left over by an American oil company, which I modified by removing the undercarriage and loading the body onto the biggest truck I could find. Even so, it overhung the tail by about six feet, so that it was best to drive up steep slopes backwards. In it, I kept the most important props as well as my office and work bench.

It may have appeared odd that I slept outside while the gear was kept inside, particularly as the desert became a very cold and seemingly hostile place at night, but I felt safer. Every so often I would hear unexplainable rustling sounds, but lying there on the roof of the trailer, looking up at millions of stars, and surrounded by nothing more than endless space, I was overwhelmed by a supreme feeling of tranquillity. I now understood how Lawrence must have felt when he described the cleansing effect the desert landscape and "the strength of heaven, so vast, so beautiful, so strong" had on him.

Before setting off the next day, I ventured off with my Zenith shortwave radio some distance away into the pre-dawn light to listen to the BBC World News Service. I didn't notice that the volume control was full on and as I switched on the radio the opening bars of the Colonel Bogey theme from *The Bridge on the River Kwai* rang out. It made my back hairs stand on end. I thought, *'if this isn't a good omen, I don't know what is'*. Just then the sun rose, bathing the stones in a warm red light. It was a dramatic backdrop and quite simply, perfect. Later that afternoon we organised an unusual lunch menu.

Everyone collected their supply of food rations from the catering department and flung it all in a big cauldron: eggs, bacon, baked beans, canned vegetables, salmon, bread, chicken; anything, in fact, that qualified as edible. They then boiled the mixture up and served the slop with a tipple of gin. Peter O'Toole's finely tuned nostrils alerted him to the fact that alcohol was being served and decided to join them. It didn't take long for the alcohol to take effect and shortly afterwards I spotted Peter and two prop men practicing swallow dives on the sand dunes from the roof of the truck. It was nothing out of the ordinary, though. Peter stayed up late most nights, living it up with the crew members – as long as you could keep up with him – but he was a consummate professional. Before dawn he'd be in the make-up chair with a cold tea bag over each eye for about fifteen minutes, then make-up Chief Charlie Parker would get to work on him. Bang on cue, Peter would come on set in full costume ready to mount his camel, charge into battle, or take any orders from David. He was one of the very few actors who could pull this off. One night, he staggered back to his wooden bungalow after another typical drinking spree. Too drunk to see the door knob in the dark, he punched a hole through door to get in and broke his hand. He didn't seem too bothered by the incident, though, and it certainly didn't dent his enthusiasm for drinking. During our long weekends off, Peter, Omar and General Peron (he of *The Bridge on the River Kwai* fame) often went to Beirut's famous café bars to swill Champagne by the bucket load, and would invariably end up dancing on the tables with the belly dancer. Yet they were all on parade first thing Monday morning, ready to shoot and without whiffing of alcohol.

A couple of days before we began shooting, David, Freddie and others left the Jebel Tubeiq camp to meet us some twelve miles away. We chose to film on a lip of a very high sand dune, so high in fact that we had to build a cable access to get the men and equipment to the top. Below us the trucks looked like little toys, and beyond that there was nothing but miles upon miles of spectacular desert. The scene would later show Peter and his guide riding on camels and reaching the summit to view the empty desert beneath them, while the camera showed that same angle from their P.O.V. ('point of view'). David was always keen to add a spectacular shot now and again in his films to ensure that the audience sat up and took notice during key moments – he called it 'the wow factor'– and in this shot he did it "to show those buggers in Columbia the kind of thing they were getting for their money". It was at times such as these that David would sit staring out into the distance for what seemed like hours. Most of the crew would grow restless, wondering why the hell he wasn't getting on with it, but I'd be wondering instead about what he was cooking up and trying to be one step ahead of him.

The sun which rose on the first day of shooting was blisteringly hot and did not let up for a single day during the following months in Jordan. But it was glorious and frightening at the same time. As the edge of the sun first appeared, it grew rapidly; a huge red disc dominating the entire horizon. To lighten the mood on the very first day for the opening shot of the film I came up with an idea. Living up to the stereotype of eccentric Englishman, I took a garden umbrella and laid a table and four chairs on an artificial lawn in front of my caravan. On it, I prepared a pot of tea and waited for David to drive up in his Rolls. "Care for tea on the lawn?" I asked in my best Queen's English. It was our way of showing that we were not going to be overawed by the enormity of the desert. As time went on the scenes got bigger, not in scale or background, but in the numbers of camels and actors deployed. To keep ahead of them during tracking shots we had a sort of portable railway built by a company called Wickham shipped out from England. The Wickham dolly incorporated a locomotive which towed a number of flatbed trucks along on a narrow train track for hundreds of yards at high speed. It was brilliant for shooting cavalry charges and the like.

The other stars began to trickle in. Anthony Quinn, who settled in quietly and without any fuss, was a true professional who would sit for hours on end in his heavy costume and huge false nose in between takes, waiting to be called for his next scene in the sweltering heat without so much as a grumble. The nose was another work of art which took so long to apply that Anthony decided it would be better if he kept it on for most of the time. Chief make-up man Charlie Parker became so concerned with the state of Quinn's fake conk that he would watch it through opera glasses as a scene was played out, fearing that it would either fall off during the action sequences or perhaps melt in the oven-like temperatures. Sometimes he called for a ladder to be leaned up against Quinn's camel, which Charlie then climbed, calling back down to his assistant for a brush if he felt it needed retouching. This was then handed to him like a nurse hands a scalpel to a surgeon. He was a perfectionist like David, but he couldn't control everything.

One day, to Charlie's amazement, his wife showed up in the desert. Melanie was a small, but well built and rather feisty Jewish lady whom Charlie called his child-bride, and judging by the amount of time the two spent arguing we figured she had come to keep an eye on him. The next morning, just as we were ready to start the day's shooting, I spotted Tony Quinn sitting at his chair in his costume minus prosthetic nose, evidently waiting for Charlie to start to work on him. David was getting irritated with the delay and quietly began to simmer under the early morning sun. Charlie eventually staggered onto the set with a pair of crutches, helped on by his assistants while he pointed sheepishly at a heavily bandaged foot. He claimed he had broken it during the night after tripping over one of the iron tent pegs, but we knew better. Heaven knows what Charlie had been up to, but it must have upset Melanie enough to want to throw a heavy object at him. A chair was arranged for him to sit next to Tony and another to put his foot on, but as he started to apply the false nose, a red-faced David stormed in. "You're late!" he snapped, jabbing his finger accusingly. Charlie pointed at his foot in a futile gesture, in the hope David would offer some sympathy. He didn't get any. "You can hop, can't you?" David snorted, and then marched out, although I did notice a faint trace of a smile on his lips, not that Charlie noticed.

The first of the big sets I built was Auda's camp, which only appears briefly in the finished movie, but was part of one of those 'wow' shots David insisted on. Spread out far beyond the great red plain of Wadi Rumm were the black Bedouin tents, an entire town where thousands of families lived with all their livestock. That's how it appears on film, but was in fact a carefully constructed set devised by John Box and myself to give the impression that it was far bigger than it really was. I climbed a high point from which we were to film the scene, and on top of a post we placed a cone-shaped box with an eye-hole at one end and a film screen-rectangle at the other. John had had this made to give a clear idea of what the camera would 'see' on the day, and when he was satisfied with the results he gave me a simple instruction to "fill it up" and promptly drove back to Aqaba several miles away. In total, it took me about three weeks to build a Bedouin camp and 'fill' an area more than three kilometres wide by one kilometre and a half deep.

To speed things up I lived on the site, adding around three hundred tents and a number of Bedouin tribes recruited by the Desert Patrol from hundreds of miles away. I arranged a council with tribal chiefs to do the work, an essential prerequisite if I was to avoid having warring tribes knocking ten bells out of each other. In fact, feuds between Arab tribes were common then just as they are now and the Desert Patrol gave me a list containing the names of tribes that were not on speaking terms. To avoid any unnecessary confrontations I placed the more quarrelsome tribes far apart at opposite ends of the camp. We also had to organise everyday tasks such as supplying water and grain and tending the sick. And just as in any town, women and girls were also giving birth at this time, a problem which needed our attention. I tried offering paid work for the young men, particularly as cleaning and sanitation was a priority in such a large camp. But that suggestion was dismissed outright by the men who viewed menial tasks as being beneath them.

In the middle of all this I got an unwelcome visit from Art Director John Stoll. In those days it was a long and difficult drive from Aqaba and he appeared in a substantial four-wheel drive vehicle driven by what seemed to be an escort of Jordanian bodyguards. The car stopped beside me and a man in full Arab regalia stepped out, preceded by a large cigar and an air of self-importance.

Stoll watched the activity for a short while. "It's big, isn't it ducky?" he remarked perceptively.

"Yes John, and it will be even bigger" I replied with some restraint. I didn't want him to miss a thing so I suggested that the best vantage point would be from the camera position up the hill, although he would have to climb a bit to get to it.

He reluctantly hauled his carcass up to the top and peered through the box. "Well, you seem to know what you're doing, ducky," he sighed, clearly overwhelmed by what he'd seen. "You'll know where to find me if you need me. I'm going for a gin and tonic." And with that he got back in the car and sped off back to Aqaba, never to return. Stoll later got an Oscar for Art Direction. John Box at least made more of an effort and came to look at my 'town planning arrangements' during the first week. Thankfully, I was left alone to get on with it for the following two. I must admit I felt that John Stoll's Oscar should have been mine, and John Box thought so too. But the fact is I wasn't in the right union and so it wasn't to be.

My set was finished and ready for shooting, but when I announced that I would be cutting back on paid labour it didn't go down at all well with the workers. They strode menacingly towards me, brandishing iron tent-pegs and a dark look that suggested they hadn't taken the news too well. I made a swift retreat to the back of my truck where I kept a four-foot piece of heavy rubber water hose for just such occasions. I then leapt from the van and waved it about like a mad dervish, which, I later pondered, would have been quite a familiar sight to them. It did the trick. They turned and fled in a blind panic. It was a technique I first adopted during the making of *Land of the Pharaohs* and which never failed. The second set I built – this time Prince Feisal's – was easier to lay out because the main wide shot did not cover such a large area and a substantial part of filming was done inside the set. Consequently, it also had a distinct feel of domesticity. By now I was very familiar with Bedouin customs and was often invited into their family tents for a spot of their thick black coffee. I still had to mind my manners because propriety required that you didn't acknowledge the presence of females.

In one scene we had to shoot the aerial attack on Feisal's camp using two biplanes which we had built and shipped out from England. As they flew over the length of the camp, their bombs dropped on the tents and the people. Guinness, who was mounted on a beautiful black horse, charged after them with his sword raised above his head and his robes trailing behind him. It was going to be another of those big shots that David specialised in. It began with a quiet domestic scene with the women, children and their donkeys at the well. Then, as the bombers dived from over the cliffs, the camera had to pan from the scene of domesticity and follow the progress of the planes until the violent denouement. David shouted "Action!" and the planes flew over as planned. Just then, an amorous donkey oblivious to the mayhem that was about to unfold, mounted his partner in close up, moving forward together and filling the frame for the entire shot. That was as far as we got. David turned to me red-faced. "Eddie! Can't you control your bloody donkeys?" I had no answer for that one but I sprang into action and swiftly removed the offending lovers. The scene was set up all over again – minus donkeys – and we got the shot, but it left me wondering that if we had wanted to get two donkeys bonking away like crazy in close-up it would probably have been impossible.

David's Rolls Royce – a Silver Cloud I – was one of three which we had in the desert. The other two were original Silver Ghost armoured cars we had shipped over from England along with mechanics from the factory in Crewe. They had been used in the desert during the Great War and were now doing it all over again for our movie. They were still in excellent shape and gave us no trouble. David drove his all across the desert as well, with the added bonus that his car had air conditioning. He was absolutely barmy about the marque and in one scene, when one of the armoured Rolls had to drive in close to the camera, David asked me to make sure that when the car stopped the famous RR letters on the polished hubcaps were the right way up.

A far bigger problem for me was keeping the desert clean. This was not an obsession with hygiene, but a necessary touch if we were to make the audience believe that this was virgin territory; that is, a vast unspoilt landscape. It was also a question of continuity. I would attempt to tape off the vital area for the day's work but, inevitably, it didn't stay taped up for long. It only required some stupid bugger to walk out on it, or for a paper cup to blow carelessly across it, to have to repair the damaged surface. As it turned out, it often had to be 'repaired' after each take, a task that required painstaking care as I would walk out onto the existing footprints and then walk backwards, filling them carefully with very gentle broom strokes – all this while trying to blend the surrounding sand. For the marks nearer the camera I used huge powder puffs on the end of long, thin canes to lightly add the finishing touch. If there were ripples in the sand, which tended to appear a lot, I'd use a hand-held fan or hairdryer while feeding small amounts of fine sand into the wind. If a larger area had been disturbed by camels I had clay tennis court harrows and brushes to tow back and forth. One of the worst culprits was the ubiquitous polystyrene cup, which would blow far out into the pristine set and lay there; an annoying white spot just waiting to be retrieved. There were also occasions when we painted the desert with dramatic streaks of colour. For that I used the big aero engine wind machines which we had imported from England. The method was simple but effective. We threw whole sackfuls of coloured powder into the wind, and these would stream out and settle neatly in lines across the desert. It's virtually unnoticeable on the film, but it created the desired effect. Up to this point I had been solely the prop man and exterior set dresser, but an incident was to change all that and launch me unexpectedly into special effects territory.

The scene in which Daud, one of the Arab boys, disappears into quicksand whilst his horrified friend and Lawrence look helplessly on was so awkward to film that it caused a major behind-the-scenes ruckus. David wanted the boy, played by John Dimech, to sink fairly quickly despite Lawrence's desperate efforts to reach out across the quicksand and help him. Cliff Richardson, who was in charge of the special effects, had prepared the sand by making the usual cereal grain mix, which we in the business called the 'porridge pit'. But it didn't work (shades of Tobago's Zebra). The mix he used was damp and had the consistency of mud, which in normal situations would have been perfect for creating the illusion of quicksand. But because of the heat the surface became lumpy and wouldn't photograph well for Freddie, who grew increasingly irate along with David. Cliff could see this and it set him off.

Almost in tears, he suddenly snapped, "I quit!" and stormed off.

David had no time for temper tantrums – unless they were his own — and shouted back, "Good! Bugger off! Eddie Fowlie, take over!"

I felt deeply embarrassed by the entire episode and the way David had gone about it. "I can't do that," I said quietly, "you'll get me into fucking trouble. Let me have a few minutes with him." I went over to a little tent Cliff had gone into and found him sobbing. "Come on now, Cliff. That was just a bit of a temper show out there but it'll all come right. It just needs a bit more patience and we'll get it. Come back out." I looked at him almost pleading and hoping to get him to reason.

"No. I am not going out. He's got to apologise first."

"Don't be daft. You know David won't do that, just come out and do it."

"No, no. I am not going," he said, sulking. I tried reasoning with him.

"David hasn't apologised to anyone in his life and I am damned sure he is not going to do it now in the middle of the desert."

"I am not going." he repeated, oblivious to my comments. It was no use. I now had to work out how this kid was going to be swallowed up by the sands of the desert. My idea was to dig a hole big enough for a wooden box to be lowered into the ground with me in it. We needed something on top that would allow the sand to sift gradually down. Then, once inside, I would pull at the boy's legs until he disappeared. I decided to place layers of sheet rubber (the type used in floor covering) with overlying segments cut out in a triangular shape and laid out like the shutter of a camera. It looked good, but I had to get it done there and then. The crew got ready to shoot and I got into the box. The lads put the rubber lid on and covered it with a thick layer of matching sand. I eased Johnnie's feet and continued to let him come through at the speed I knew David wanted; first the kid and then the headscarf. From under the ground we heard "cut!", followed by "get them out!". It was in the can and everyone was happy, except me. I should have felt contented but didn't. It had been a humiliating experience for Cliff in front of the entire crew. Fortunately, everything was forgotten the next day and he stayed on. In any case, the quicksand scene was just about the only bloody special effect in the entire film.

By now, we had got used to living in the desert. David had fallen in love with it and to my surprise so had I, despite my unpleasant experiences in Lybia and Egypt. But this was different. I remember a line in the script when Arthur Kennedy, who was playing the part of a newspaper reporter, asks Lawrence what he likes about the desert. "It's clean," he comments dryly. He meant that it was untouched by the hand of man. I suspect today's film stars would not be seen within a hundred miles of a desert and would insist on the best five-star accommodation after a day's shoot. Their loss. Sam and Columbia were by this stage getting worried about the film's soaring costs and it was decided that we should move the unit somewhere cheaper and easier to shoot. Everything was put on hold for a three-month break and the crew was laid off without pay, but I stayed on with a few others to do our last shot in Jordan. It was very much like our first; from a very high viewpoint and using a wide-angle lens on a 70mm Panavision camera. The vast, empty desert lay before us one last time, and in the distance, the tiny figures of two men could be seen riding across on camels.

I was standing alongside David watching the scene play out. He leant over. "Let them try *that* somewhere else," he said, before shouting: "Cut! Let's wrap it all up." Soon, almost everyone was gone except me. I stayed on in the empty beach camp with the Jordanian army for company. My job was to ensure that everything belonging to the movie was loaded onto a chartered ship and made ready for transportation to the new location. Inevitably, after the roller coaster of activity during so many months, the shock of being completely on my own suddenly hit me. Sharing my life with shadier elements of the Jordanian Army and having to check in and out past their sentry every day was no substitute for making films. Relief came before too long and I was told that the ship was to set sail.

Lawrence of Almería

Once on the ship I was able to take stock. They say moving home is one of the most traumatic experiences in one's life, so I can't imagine what moving an entire film unit would be like for most people. But here I was, on a chartered ship loaded with horses, tents, caravans, vehicles, camels, guns…and furniture. We steamed down the Gulf of Aqaba, up the Red Sea, through the Suez Canal, into the Mediterranean Sea and around the foot of Italy to dock in Naples – doing the exact reverse of what I had previously done for *The Crimson Pirate*. We then set off on our final destination: Almería, on

Spain's south-east coast and where a scout in Spain for Columbia Films had assured us we'd find a genuine desert. I oversaw the unloading at Almería's dockside and almost the entire dock area was filled with our stuff. Concerned that some light-fingered local would nab one of the props, I asked a couple of Civil Guard officers if it was safe to leave our property lying around. They looked surprised. I was told we needn't worry as no one was about to steal anything with the *Guardia Civil* around; this was Franco's Spain, after all. Almería was an old Moroccan seaport, and transport around the town was mostly done by horse. I sent our horses – including Tony Quinn's and a few others which I had brought with me – to be cared for at a stable. My next job was to scout the desert and the coastline to find a suitable place to build the town of Aqaba and other locations. I was joined in the task by Stoll; the same man who had visited Auda's camp for a few minutes and then vanished in a cloud of dust in his limo before taking refuge at the club bar. True to form, he spent most of his time nodding off in the back of the scout car as we drove through the province, mostly after having drunk a few glasses of Spanish wine which he seemed to take a special liking to. Observing a particularly attractive spot I woke him up to get some feedback.

Stirring from his slumber he totally failed to notice the scenery and eyed a girl on the side of the road instead. "She's lovely! She smiled at me!" he drooled and went back to sleep again.

We were in a very dry and poor part of Spain but it was blessed with some incredible scenery, including an arid desert and small volcanic hills. These had been weathered to form astonishing shapes, interspersed with deep ravines and dry riverbeds, called *ramblas* in Spanish, which had been formed by storm rain. It was along these that we drove, looking for locations which might be suitable for shooting some scenes. We didn't know it at the time but we were the first of many film crews to land in Almería and much later others would follow our lead, mostly to shoot Westerns. It became known as mini-Hollywood and remains a tourist attraction to this day.

The province of Almería has come a long way since then, attracting many retired Brits looking for a quiet life under the sun and developers keen to exploit the situation by clogging much of the coastline with luxury hotels. When we arrived there were none and the roads were mostly dirt tracks, but most importantly I learned that Almería has the most hours of sunshine on the continent. There were also impressive sand dunes located on the extreme south-eastern tip of the Iberian Peninsula, at a place called *Cabo de Gata*. There, we built a railway track for Lawrence to blow up. At a small fishing village to the east was a broad, dry riverbed coursing down between barren hills to end on a wide beach. We decided that this would be the perfect spot to build the town of Aqaba. The village was called Carboneras, and I was so impressed by it that I finally decided to settle down here. Between the village and the set I saw a strip of land covered in little blue flowers along the edge of a beach. On the headland beyond it, the rock formation on a hill – at least in profile – looked exactly like MGM's lion. I interpreted this as another good omen, so I bought the land shortly afterwards. Forty-eight years later I am still here, so it can't have been that bad a choice.

Meanwhile, John Box had been doing his own research and found his Damascus and his Cairo in Seville. When he arrived in Almería sometime later he agreed that the beach in Carboneras would be the ideal site for the town of Aqaba. In no time at all Peter Dukelow got down to building the mock town and grading the wide riverbed for the charge of the Arab army. In the meantime, we moved to Seville where the crew had gathered once again to restart filming. There, I had to live in an hotel but made sure that it was far from where the main unit were staying. I don't know how it has changed over the years, but back then film units could become pretty rowdy. At one of the hotels where it was required to wear a tie to dine, one of our riggers staggered out of an elevator and across the crowded foyer and into another set of lifts. Perhaps he was making his way to his room to get dressed (I say this because he was wearing nothing but a pair of shoes and a smart tie). And in Seville's very best hotel, the Alfonso XIII where O'Toole was staying, he and another member of the film unit unsuccessfully tried to get two horses through the hotel's revolving doors and into the lobby. They had better luck with the swing doors of two taxi carriages, which they unhitched in order to hold a chariot race around the town. The feat was all the more remarkable as they did it without getting caught or arrested for being drunk and disorderly. I suspect Franco never got to hear about this, or the ensuing diplomatic incident would have given rise to newspaper headlines about the piratical English getting up to their old tricks again.

In Seville we shot all of what was meant to be Cairo in the movie, except for one scene involving a palm tree-lined street with a streetcar running along it. We filmed this in the city of Almería, which we achieved by putting down the track ourselves and importing the tram. The famous Alcázar in Seville is where we filmed the officer's mess in the scene where Lawrence and the Arab boy trudge back after their trek across the desert and demand a glass of lemonade.

Just before shooting the scene David asked me to look through the camera viewfinder. "Got it," I said, having twigged it at once.

"The flowers," David nodded, "do something about it." At the back of the bar, I spotted a big picture of a cavalry charge entitled *The Charge of the Scot Greys*. It was a good choice, but we felt the tall glass vase with flowers placed on a shelf below clashed with the painting, so I dashed out into the streets to look for something different. Twenty minutes later I returned with my spoils. I took down the vase and replaced it with a long, low cut glass bowl shaped like a boat. Spilling out of it and trailing down was a blood red bougainvillea. David made no comment but instructed the film crew to get ready to shoot. I'd gotten used to last minute changes and often anticipated David's flashes of inspiration by having a back-up plan. I was always ready to supply anything, no matter what. After David had the scene in the can he came over to me. "I liked the blood," he said. Appreciating the important little details, the subtle touches that would burrow into people's minds, was one of the many things I learned from David.

We moved on, still with a bloody theme in mind. The lovely ancient palace in the narrow streets of Seville, the Casa de Pilatos, is where we shot the tense scene in which Allenby sees the blood seeping through the back of Lawrence's jacket. It was a difficult scene for the actors to shoot as we were filming on a balcony, very much in public. Somewhere nearby in the high narrow streets an ardent cockerel kept up its incessant crowing and it became impossible to continue shooting the scene. David turned to me in frustration. "Eddie, keep that bird quiet." I knew the pesky bird would be on the rooftops as all the livestock was kept up there, so I clambered over the tops of the houses, blindly at first, until I found the culprit in a wire mesh. I quickly wrung its neck and left in cash more than its value beside it. Back on set I found them shooting, and afterwards David came over to me. "What happened to the chicken?" he asked.

"Got himself strangled," I replied.

Many other scenes were shot in the magnificent Plaza de España and other fine Moorish buildings. That done, we returned to Almería in March 1962 to shoot the Aqaba battle scene in Carboneras, where Peter had been busy building the entire mock town. As we were on a tight budget, we took time to shoot other scenes elsewhere to give him more time to get everything finalised and ready. One of the most memorable of these involved the railway track explosion across the *Cabo de Gata* sand dunes. The state railway company, *Renfe*, helped us a lot and when it was ready I had the sand dunes 'virginised' with the help of three hundred gypsies hired for the job. On screen it looked perfect; off screen it was a different story. Some of the horses which were loaded on the ill-fated train made for the hills after the explosion and were never seen again – at least, not by us. Today, the sand dunes have all but disappeared, blown away not by explosives but by strong winds from Africa.

The script also called for a number of scenes in a pleasant oasis, unfortunately there weren't any in Almería, so we built one. We created a nice pool, around which we planted tall date-palms loaded into big trucks from some distance away. This turned out to be so successful that it is still flourishing more than forty years later and has now become a popular picnic spot for the locals. Switching deserts from Jordan to Spain also required some inventive solutions, such as matching the colour of the sand at Wadi Rumm by bringing in truck loads of red-coloured earth to spread on the surface.

We also worked on the scene where Lawrence and the Arab boy reach the Suez Canal in Almería. The set was imaginatively entitled the 'ruins of Suez' and consisted of a group of dilapidated huts, beaten by the blowing wind and sand, and standing eerily abandoned in the desert. Just then, at the sound of a ship's siren, there's the magnificent view over the high sand bank of the top of the funnel of a passing White Star ship (which was later superimposed). That was done nowhere near the sea and a petrol station now stands on the site. At another place nearby we built the Damascus hospital where a horrified Lawrence witnesses the dead and dying at first hand. Not that I underestimated Peter O'Toole's acting talents, but I went the extra mile by buying carcasses at a local slaughterhouse to add a certain rotting ambience. I strategically placed entrails under the hot sun for days, close to where Peter would be walking. I then spattered cow dung on the walls and obtained rotting fish from a fish market in Almería to scatter behind the set. The flies did the rest. When he did the scene, O'Toole almost puked his guts out.

At Peter Dukelow's Aqaba, with its white buildings and minarets, we placed the Turkish army camp just behind the huge coastal defence guns that pointed out to sea and which left the rear of the town vulnerable to attack from inland. Behind that, along the riverbed and back into the hills, we gathered and housed hundreds of camels and Tuareg riders which we had brought over by ship from Morocco. But even this wasn't enough, so we added hundreds of fine horses and their riders from all over Andalusia. This was Auda's Arab army which charged into the camp and the town, and without a stunt double in sight. The scene, which lasted for only a few minutes, tracked one end of the dry riverbed, past the town, and out to the edge of the sea where we 'parked' some large ships. It took a few days to shoot and afterwards the set was destroyed. Today, there is a bridge across what had been the location for Aqaba, in addition to a huge, half-finished hotel which lies abandoned. The irony is that, at the time, we couldn't find a single hotel anywhere, not even in the capital, so I made do with a Bedouin tent, which I moved to wherever we worked. On one occasion, we were shooting on a dried up riverbed between hills. Unbeknown to us there was a heavy rainstorm, but the first thing I knew about it was when a wall of water rushed in. Within seconds we were five feet deep in water. There was a mad scramble to save everything and we almost drowned in the process, but it taught us a lesson not to be fooled into thinking that it was safe to camp in the *ramblas*.

When we finished shooting in Spain, we loaded every prop and moved it, lock, stock and barrel, to Morocco. There the king agreed to loan much of his army out to us as extras to represent the Turkish forces. We crossed the Atlas Mountains to the edge of the Sahara to Ouarzazate, an Arab town of mainly mud brick construction, but which at least had one decent hotel. Because of the high spirits of my prop men I set up a camp for them with all the props outside the town. Following tradition, I moved into a one-room mud hut well away from everybody. But I wasn't alone. At night, I heard the patter of tiny feet, scurrying across the floor. I lit the oil lamp and discovered to my horror that hundreds of cockroaches had decided to keep me company. The floor was carpeted with them and some, no doubt looking to make themselves more comfortable, joined me in bed. I jumped out as if my arse was on fire, only to hear the sickening crunch as I stepped on some of my unwelcome guests. I tried to stop them crawling into my bed by standing the legs of the bed in film cans filled with water. It wasn't very successful as the pesky pests were good swimmers. There was only one solution. I got hold of a cat which seemed to enjoy crunching away on them like a snack. That lasted for a while until the bloated mog had its fill and began vomiting the half-digested insects everywhere. I decided to adopt a more conciliatory approach, which was to live and let live – it was their town, after all.

I was then able to vent my frustration by getting on with the job of killing Turks, or rather to stage the scene in which the Turkish army gets slaughtered. The scene starts with a small, coloured piece of fine cloth – like a girl's silk scarf – drifting across the desert, gently blown by the soft breeze. The camera pans to the edge of the destroyed village where we see scores of girls who have been raped by the Turkish army, lying dead or dying in grotesque poses. I dressed that set using local girls, their clothing torn aside and bearing their blood-stained legs. We had each girl carefully positioned, draped upon piles of bricks. It was like a Goya painting, except we were using real people. I did the same with the men by tying them to posts with their guts spilling out, but this proved to be too much for David, who decided not to include it all in the final scene.

He focused instead on the anger and outrage felt by Lawrence and his men, particularly Tafas; one of Lawrence's top men whose village it is. When they witness the destruction wrought upon their village by the Turkish army, who are seen marching slowly away in the distance, they decide to charge at them on hearing the order "No prisoners!" The image of Lawrence with the bloody dagger in his hand is memorable for many reasons, not least because it marks a turning point in his character. The bodies of the Turkish soldiers were spread out in a great swathe, curving away from the camera's point of view and into the distant horizon. To add depth we also filmed the sun just behind the low clouds, while fingers of sunlight shone through the grey darkness beyond. It took me most of the day to dress the set carefully with the wreckage from the battle and the people all carefully laid out. Earlier on, David had asked me out of curiosity what the medium-sized tank truck which I had on standby was for.

"That's where I keep the blood for the blood bath," I replied with an impish grin. It contained blood-red oil which I added to the scene by the bucketload to glint in the low backlight. We used some two thousand soldiers to stand in for the Turkish army. What's more, they hadn't just been told to lie down on the ground. They had all been carefully positioned to create the shape. Those furthest away were spread further apart, like the tents in Auda's Wadi Rumm camp. Scenes like that will probably never be set dressed that way ever again. I don't think you can create art – and this was art – with the aid of computers. You don't paint a Van Gogh with computer software. It's all about brushstrokes, subtly applied and forcing the viewer to stand back and think. But you can't really draw emotions by using silly computer effects. All they do is to generate excitement; it's like watching an empty firework display. The whole point of making films is to draw emotions out of people. I always think that if at the end of a film you've got to turn away from whoever you're with to wipe away a tear you've done a good job because you've got inside their head.

It had all been very intense, and to break the tension I went for a drink with Peter O'Toole on our day off. I'd been told it was the main street, but for the life of me it looked more like a fly-blown dirt track. All was dead quiet apart from the sound of bloated bluebottles buzzing around our ears. We were sizzling under the midday heat, quietly sipping our drinks when we suddenly heard loud shouting in the distance. We looked up, and coming towards us was a group of bandaged Turkish soldiers mounted on donkeys and waving their swords about like madmen. Fearing that the real Turkish army had got wind that we were making some sort of anti-Turkish propaganda film, we jumped up ready to flee for our lives. Then I realised I was staring at my prop men. It seems they had taken the uniforms from my spare dummies and the donkeys and saddles from my compound, all of which were kept far from the town. The animals were charging about in circles, and judging by the way the men were flopping about on the saddles they were not very good at riding donkeys. One Tommy Raeburn was desperately clinging on, his saddle having slipped underneath the beast. It didn't take long to reach the conclusion that they were all pissed out of their heads. Things were about to get worse. They began shouting at an invisible Arab army by waving their swords and challenging them to come out and fight, presumably from one of the mud huts. They then spotted us, and rode into the bar…on their donkeys. To their eternal credit, the long-suffering asses (the animals, not the men) were totally unruffled by the behaviour of their loutish riders and stood silent, casually crapping by the bar to their hearts content. Despite their loud curses, I don't think the prop department would have stood a cat in hell's chance of taking on the skilful swordsmen of the Moroccan army. Their swashbuckling commander, whom I knew well, could open a bottle of champagne with a swift swing of his sword, and I was sure he would just as easily have lobbed their heads off if he'd been tempted. Fortunately for them, the Moroccan soldiers were a good bunch, although I had a few nasty moments when trying to take props back from a few of them. The trick, I quickly learned, was to square up to them like a crazy man. It had the desired effect and they quickly backed off.

The film was all in the can and once again I was the last man to leave; as I was left in charge to pack everything up. I bought one of the trailer caravans and an Austin Gypsy, and drove over the Atlas Mountains to Marrakech (interesting) and on to Casablanca (boring) and Tangier, where I camped right outside a posh hotel for a week. Afterwards, I shipped my vehicle and caravan to Gibraltar before driving back along the tortured roads of Spain's southern coast to the plot on the beach I had bought in Carboneras. There, I took a well-earned rest, living in my caravan and thinking about the last two years of my life with Lawrence.

Some years later O'Toole asked me to meet Jack Hawkins and himself at a pub called The Ship, close to Shepperton Studios in London. Before we arrived, Peter pulled me to one side and told me Jack was feeling depressed. Following an operation for throat cancer, which had left him without his wonderful voice, he had been forced to learn to speak again through a hole in his throat. Although saddened by the news I was determined not to show it. I was in the bar when they came in, and after a few emotional hugs Jack tried to talk. It was an awkward moment for him and then I suddenly noticed a round metal object which hung from his neck to cover the hole. "I'm told they've created a short cut for the brandy, Jack. Is that it?" I joked. It broke the ice and we relived some of the great moments we enjoyed filming Lawrence.

CHAPTER 13

Jungleslavia

The Long Ships (UK / Yugoslavia 1964). 126 minutes Technicolor. Columbia/Warwick.
Director: Jack Cardiff. Writers: Berkely Mather, Beverly Cross, from a novel by Frans G Bengtsson. Photographer: Christopher Challis. Music: Dusan Radic.
Cast: Richard Widmark, Sidney Poitier, Russ Tamblyn, Rosanna Schiaffino, Oscar Homolka, Colin Blakely.

While living in my trailer by the sea in Carboneras I got busy erecting a wall around me in what were my first tentative steps at building a proper home. More convinced than ever that I was in Spain to stay, I took to the task with as much enthusiasm as when working on a film set. But when a call came from the studios asking me if I wanted to take part in another film about Vikings, I didn't need asking twice; I hooked the trailer up and eagerly set off for Yugoslavia. In those days roads were bad everywhere but one had considerably more fun getting from A to B. I drove north and into southern France, eastwards through northern Italy to Trieste, and finally to Zagreb and Belgrade, where the Avala Film Studios were located. Perhaps if I had thought about it better I would have realised that *The Long Ships* was too silly a story to make into a film and turned back home right there and then. It didn't help that it was going to be co-produced with the Yugoslavians, who were under Tito's Communist regime at the time and had some odd business ideas, to say the least. To his credit, Richard Widmark, who was to star in the lead role, made the most of what little he had to work with. He was one of those old Hollywood pros who just got on with the job without any fuss. As for me, it was a pleasure to work with Sidney Poitier, who cheerily announced to anyone who would listen that the movie was a going to be a disaster even before we got started.

The omens, admittedly, were bad. Belgrade was a miserable place. Everyone seemed terribly unhappy, except for the people who were dead drunk – and there were plenty of those lying around on the streets. The film was supposed to be a combined effort between Warwick Films and Avala Films, with the latter paying for the sets and everything to do with Yugoslavia. In return, Avala would get a share of the hard currency market.

Producer Irvin Allen thought he would be getting a movie on the cheap, while the Yugoslavs thought they'd be ripping off a bunch of decadent capitalists. In effect what we had was an uncomfortable marriage between the East and the West, with everyone deeply suspicious of everyone else. In a sense, the commies were good at their jobs because everything I spent had to be approved by the works' committee first. Being a co-operative run by workers they thought they were all equal and acted with a ridiculous air of self-importance. Representatives of every branch of the commune (little more than glorified shop stewards) needed to be consulted at every stage. I couldn't buy anything without presenting a list first, which they would then discuss at length in order to decide whether or not they would pay for it.

I was saddled with a very officious and dour blonde girl with spectacles to act as my interpreter. I smelled a rat and made sure I didn't make any condescending remarks about 'commies' in front of her, but she wasn't easily duped and tagged along wherever I went on 'official' business. Unfortunately she understood that to mean virtually any transaction, including the buying of a box of matches, and even that had to be Okayed by the committee. I knew then that it was going to be a hard slog, but I hatched a cunning plan. Having had quite a lot of experience making lists, I simply drew up an enormously long inventory of every bloody thing I would need; might need; might not need…plus a lot of complete bullshit thrown in for good measure. Not surprisingly, this didn't make me very popular with the committee, who viewed me not just as a decadent westerner but possibly a spy who was perhaps hatching a sinister plot to sabotage the film. They were right about my being a westerner – admittedly a trifle decadent – but as for sabotaging the film, they certainly didn't need my help as they were doing an excellent job of it themselves.

While no one questioned their bureaucratic ineptitude, painstakingly honed over years of tyrannical communist rule, when it came to making films they were definitely clueless. To make matters worse, I couldn't find any comfort in my work. The film's plot was just about as absurd as it could get, at least for a movie made in the early 1960s, although perhaps not if it had been made today. *The Long Ships* was loosely based on Vikings, but that was as close as the script got to being historically accurate. It tells the unlikely story of two men, one a Viking, the other a Moor, and their obsessive quest to find a bloody great golden bell. It was a multi-purpose bell at that, as aside from ringing, it would have to roll down a hill and plunge into the sea at some stage. The only saving grace was the film's two stars: Widmark, who stuck his tongue firmly in his cheek to give a solid performance, and the always stoical Poitier.

Having set up a prop room, I went to a place called Limski Fjord on the Adriatic Coast near Pula where they were building the Viking village. Irving Allen had already bought our old Viking boats with Columbia's money and they were on their way from Munich. However, I knew enough about them, including the draught, to know that many parts of the fjord were not deep enough for the vessels. The art department who had chosen this location were totally unaware of this rather important point, and when I told them we would have to dredge the bottom of the fjord if they wanted to sail a Viking ship across it I became very unpopular, yet again. They were killing the messenger and couldn't see beyond their noses but we went ahead anyway.

When I got back to Belgrade I found out that the designer, Colonel Zoran Zorchich, had been whingeing about me to the committee and claiming I had damaged their props. He was referring to a lot of Viking helmets the 'brothers' had made – all out of the same mould, as it happens – some of which I had added horns to. My crime had been to go ahead without first asking the committee for permission. I'd had enough, so I went looking for him and found him skulking in a corridor. I squared up to him and instructed him to stay out of the prop room "or else". To make doubly sure nothing had been lost in the translation, I thumped his chest. He went scurrying off to his superiors to lick his wounds, and shortly afterwards I was told to appear before the top dogs. I was met by stern-faced apparatchiks who eyed me up and down contemptuously. If I was on a hiding to nothing, I thought, I might as well go out with a bang. I took a deep breath and told my nervous translator to translate every single word, delivered staccato-like as if speaking to idiots. "You-think-you-are-God, but-I-think-you-are-full-of-shit." It wasn't exactly Shakespeare, but I made my point and left before they could recover from my brief but accurate summation. I suspected there would be repercussions of sorts and soon afterwards a horrified Allen called a meeting in which he issued strict instructions to the crew that "they should all show more respect towards their Yugoslavian hosts". It was a bit rich as Allen himself showed little respect for anything or anyone, except perhaps racehorses. I took absolutely no notice, although I began to wonder whether the secret police had got to hear about the latest incident and were thinking about paying me a visit in the middle of the night.

Fed up with all the goings on, and feeling strangely homesick for Blighty, I decided to pay a courtesy visit to the British Embassy. When I told them I was part of a film crew in charge of a major movie they went all starry eyed and welcomed the British crew members at their very nice and, it has to be said, remarkably cheap bar. It was predictably a big success with all the film crew, who made full use of the excellent bar service, and the embassy staff, who in turn must have enjoyed the novelty of rubbing shoulders with 'real movie people'.

It was all going rather well until everyone decided to gather together with the diplomats and their bingo-playing wives. I was at one end of the semi-circular bar and our Australian First Assistant Director, 'Bluey' Hill, was at the other, looking thoroughly bored at how this bunch of starchy poms were whiling the evening away. I noticed a glint in his eye as he chose a quiet moment between the calls of 'Bingo!' to shout across to me in his best Australian accent, "Oi, Eddie, I've gotta go. I've got this little girl waiting for me back at the Metropole who's just dying to suck me cock!" The gasps from all round the room suggested the diplomats' wives and, come to think of it, some of the diplomats, found Bluey's description a little too blue. All our privileges were immediately withdrawn and we were summarily booted out. I was not with Bluey later on at the hotel when he reputedly marched up to the gypsy violin orchestra and demanded to hear a rendition of Waltzing Matilda with him on vocals. The ensemble were baffled by the request, pointing out that they couldn't join in with their instruments, to which he responded by taking a bow, taking his member out and adding, "Play it on this, then!" Whether he gave a memorable performance on it is not recorded.

It wasn't all fun, though, because we still had to make a truly god-awful film. It was early spring and we went to shoot at the Viking village in Zagreb where it was snowing hard. I crossed the

Dolomites in my Austin Gypsy with my caravan in tow in the worst blizzard I had ever seen. When I got down to the other side I was confronted by two very agitated and bemused policemen, apparently surprised at the sight of this crazed foreigner who'd had the temerity to cross when the pass had been closed to everyone else. Waving me on I came to rest near Reijka, just north of Pula and near the fjord where our village was.

No sooner had I recovered from the trip than I was faced with a new problem. Some clever clod at the studio apparently thought it would be a good idea to bring over a huge Danish chap to teach the actors how to row a Viking ship. Among his other tricks was a lesson on how to bring the boat to a dead stop by applying the equivalent of 'reverse thrust' on the oars. This would come in handy in the scene where the Viking kings had to stand at the end of the jetty to greet the returning marauders. The long ship was to sail down the fjords at full speed and come to a juddering stop, with its figurehead inches away from the king's nose, eyeball to eyeball. That was the idea, anyway, but I'd had enough experience to know that one should always plan for the unexpected when shooting a complicated scene, particularly one as badly managed as this. The thought did cross my mind that we could end up with an out-of-control ship sailing straight on and taking out the entire cast. Perhaps the big Dane suspected it too because he conveniently called in sick the day of the stunt. I wasn't surprised, but Jack Cardiff refused to postpone shooting and asked me to take charge. I replied I would only accept the job if we did things my way, as I would need time to arrange the stunt. Since there weren't any spare Viking naval experts lining up to volunteer, he readily agreed. I buried my anchor at the side of the fjord in the middle of the main road and ran a wire cable through the rings on the boat's keel – all properly built prop boats had them. I then fixed the wire to the bow stem post. The length of the steel rope had to be precise; not long, just a couple of hundred yards. The boat wouldn't have to travel very far to get up to speed; a quick rev of its engine would suffice. We shot the scene without a hitch and wrapped it up for the day.

Next morning, the sick Dane made a miraculous recovery but the sod didn't even buy me a drink for having bailed him out. Things didn't change for the better, either. The works' committee once again raised objections to a request of mine and were puzzled as to why I had asked for a large piece of firm cheese to be delivered to the special effects department. My intention was to shape a torso out of it and to use it to thrust a bloodied sword all the way through and out the other end. I had the cheese sculpted like a belly, which was then hollowed out and filled with tomato ketchup. It worked a treat, and a grateful works' committee devoured it afterwards. The same thing could not be said about the prop golden bell. Carved from a solid block of polystyrene, it was about three metres in diameter and four metres high, and when finished was covered inside and out in marine canvas, which was gilded by a machine we had sent over from England. Because of the difficulty in getting it over the Montenegro Mountains I decided to have another one built on the spot, using the same techniques and artisans. But the dreaded works' committee stuck their oar in once again and refused to approve my idea. This time they said it was the turn of other workers to build the bell. I was my usual diplomatic self, told them where to shove it and left. However, it wasn't long before they reviewed their decision, deliberated a while and unanimously agreed that I was right, after all.

The original workforce were reinstated, I hitched up my caravan and drove over the Montenegro Mountains to Budva, close to the Albanian border. At a beach close by we shot the crazy scenes of the bell mowing people down and hurtling over a cliff face and into the water. Regrettably they also forgot to cut the scene out where the ill-fated bell is seen floating on the water like a piece of balsa wood. When I was told afterwards that I would not be needed for the retakes in Belgrade I was relieved beyond words. I jumped in my caravan and drove like mad along the Adriatic coast in case they changed their minds. Despite driving over some of the most difficult and hair-raising roads – including crossing a narrow wooden bridge over a deep ravine without side rails – I felt a free man once again.

Somewhere north of Dubrovnik, however, I was forced to stop in a remote area when the towing-hook broke. As I stepped out of the car I noticed a peasant walking towards with me in the company of two little girls, who watched me silently for some time. Suddenly everything was clear in my mind and I knew what I should do. On a large piece of card I wrote my passport number, my name and details, along with the caravan's licence number and a signed note which said: "This caravan and contents are a gift, freely given by me, without any money or payment asked in exchange," and placed it in the peasant's hands. As capital investment was not allowed in

177

Yugoslavia, it took me some time to make the poor man understand what I was trying to do. I showed him inside what had until now been my home, and after some frantic sign language I handed him my keys. As I drove away I looked in my rear-view mirror and saw him crying inconsolably, while the little girls happily waved goodbye. That was without doubt my fondest memory of Yugoslavia and I was happy to be leaving the wretched country behind. My only hope is that the peasant did not bump into the dreaded works' committee. "Is that yours? Wait a minute comrade, I'm sure I've seen that caravan somewhere before!"

CHAPTER 14

The snowmaker in summer

Doctor Zhivago, 1965. Metrocolor / Panavision 70. MGM. Producer: Carlo Ponti. Director: David Lean. Writer: Robert Bolt, from the novel by Boris Pasternak. Photography: Frederick A. Young. Music: Maurice Jarre. Special Effects: Eddie Fowlie.

Cast: Omar Sharif, Julie Christie, Rod Steiger, Alec Guinness, Rita Tunshingham, Ralph Richardson, Tom Courtney, Geraldine Chaplin, Siobham McKenna, Adrienne Corri.

Oscars: Best Script, Best Music, Best Cinematography.

Oscar Nominations: David Lean for Best Picture, Tom Courtney for Best Supporting Actor.

Once in London I went straight to Shepperton Studios, where we built a replica of the long ship on rockers. I thought that would be the end of my sorry involvement in the film, but I was hounded all the way back to England by some of the top dogs from Belgrade, who unexpectedly showed up at the studio to see how their grand project was progressing. Before succumbing to the temptation of grabbing a twelve-bore and using it on the group I bumped into David, who told me that he was thinking of doing a film based on Boris Pasternak's novel, *Doctor Zhivago*. "What do you think about Yugoslavia as a location for this Russian subject?" he asked.

I didn't need to mull over the answer for long – I took a deep breath and let rip. "Great scenery, but in every other sense it's a hopeless place. The system is rotten to the core; the protocol is impossible to wade through; and the people don't work well. There's no way you could make a major movie there." I couldn't resist letting the Yugoslav entourage at Shepperton know about our little exchange. Their faces turned an appropriate shade of red and they suddenly changed their tune.

"No! We admire your work, Mr Fowlie, you're welcome in our country any time!" gushed one of the officials. I can't deny feeling a little smug, but on reflection I didn't want to be solely responsible for scuppering the entire project, so I approached David and

179

suggested he go to Yugoslavia and see for himself. He went with John Box to Belgrade but returned soon afterwards looking disappointed – he evidently had drawn the same conclusions as me. Having finished my work I hooked up my Austin Gypsy to my 'new' caravan and set off on a tour of France and Spain for a long break, my first proper holiday in many years. It was the summer of 1963, and things couldn't be better; I'd found a permanent home and it looked as though I would be working with David again. Sure enough, I got a call from him shortly after arriving. He made it clear his happy experience in Spain with *Lawrence of Arabia* had persuaded him to do *Doctor Zhivago* there as well. He instructed me to shoot off to Madrid to look for possible locations and that same evening I drove straight to a spot where I'd been to once before on a caravan trip. I thought the move further north would make a pleasant change from the heat of the south for at least a few months, but I should have known by now that with a David Lean film it was never a few months. If *Lawrence of Arabia* had taken two and a half years to make, *Doctor Zhivago* would take almost as long.

Our studio base became C.E.A. studios on the road out of town to Madrid airport. Between the two there was a very good campsite with all the facilities, including a swimming pool which would come in handy during the summer months. Having decided this was the best spot to offload a film crew, I parked up the caravan and quickly set up a workshop with a team of top class artisans, including Pablo Pérez and Julian Mateos, who had previously worked with us on Lawrence. John Box once again took the helm as Production Designer, with Peter Dukelow tasked with turning a rubbish tip on the outskirts of Madrid into a Moscow street and the Kremlin. I was glad to see that David's 'Dedicated Maniacs' would all be working together once again. Within days of our arrival, enterprising Spaniards set up businesses on the construction lot, salvaging what we threw out and putting up stands and makeshift kiosks, selling anything and everything, from beer and wine to snacks. Before long some smart alec even hitched a line to our power supply. They made themselves at home and before long a bustling mini-metropolis had sprouted out of nowhere. Spain turned out to be a wise choice for a location, despite the obvious differences with Russia's climate and over-optimistic weather forecasts which predicted snowfall over the winter months. This warm, pleasant country converted well to the cold desolation of Russia, with the added bonus that Franco's regime bent over backwards to accommodate us, just as it had previously done with Lawrence. By the time we finished the set it was the height of summer and yet it was my job to cover Madrid in freezing snow. In its place we used tons of crushed white marble dust, which was cheap and readily available in Spain. The very fine stuff was ideal for creating footprints, with the added advantage that it could all be spray washed and used again. To get the sleighs to slide I had little roller skate wheels fitted on the runners, and for falling snow I had some of the best quality hard polystyrene billets milled into shavings, which floated and drifted just like the real thing. It proved so successful that I had thousands of sacks piled sky-high with the stuff. Meanwhile, I placed big extractor blowers to create snow falls from the rooftops. I also made icicles, either from carved polystyrene, or moulded with my falling snowflakes and mixed with white glue to stick on windows. For the more critical close-up shots I covered them with paraffin wax and a light dusting of glitter. It was also far better than salt because it didn't rot the electrical equipment. By the time we were ready to shoot, my gang were all experts at making fake snow.

While we were getting the sets readied, David was still pondering over his choice of cast. He felt Omar Sharif could play Yuri Zhivago, the doctor and poet struggling in a Russia torn apart by the revolution. He was convinced Omar's soft, dark eyes were ideal for the role. But Omar's assets were more than just visual; his gentleness and sensitivity also shone through, although it no doubt helped that he always tried to do things David's way. Another star from *Lawrence of Arabia*, Alec Guinness, was to play the role of Yuri's brother, Yevgraf. Casting Lara – the woman in Yuri's life – proved infinitely trickier, however, and at first it looked as though Sofia Loren would claim the role. In a way, it was an obvious choice as she was married to Carlo Ponti at the time and Zhivago was his production. But my suspicions were aroused when I noticed that Ponti only showed up once before we started filming, never to be seen again. Although David never spoke to me about this, I had a sneaky feeling it was his doing. He liked actors he could handle like putty, but it was clear Sofia Loren was not that type of actress. In the end Julie Christie was offered the role, with Geraldine Chaplin as Yuri's wife. Rod Steiger, Rita Tushingham, Ralph Richardson and Tom Courtney completed a highly professional cast.

We began shooting the very first scene at night with a big set up on the fake Moscow street. The camera was placed in the upstairs room of Gromyko's house, pointing along the whole length of the main street to the Kremlin at the furthest end, with tram cars running along and the big street lamps glowing in the late evening snowfall. We started rolling: the camera picks a crowd accompanied by a band of musicians gathering in the square for a peaceful demonstration...but the mounted police ruthlessly scatter them, and the virgin white snow becomes spattered with bright, red blood. That was the idea at least, but camera operator Nicolas Roeg found lighting the set an almost impossible task. There were delays, and before we knew it we were racing against dawn and David's increasing impatience. He finally snapped and told me to turn on the snow. Nick, however, had turned on the foreground lights at the same time, which effectively wiped out the effect of the new snow, along with most of the set beyond it. David was fuming. "That's it. I'm going to have to let him go," he hissed, "we have lost the entire night's work." As far as he was concerned Nick had made an expensive and unforgivable mistake.

It was a harsh thing to say because Nick had done some wonderful work, but that counted for little now. Somehow, David managed to get Freddie Young – who at the time was filming *Khartoum* – to agree to take over. Without dismissing Nick's contribution I have to say Freddie was in a totally different league. He didn't just light a set; he had a sense of its purpose and knew how to translate David's vision into a powerful image. By contrast, I felt Nick was subconsciously fighting against this by trying to impose his own ideas. The truth, however, was that David scared a lot of people and often had Julie Christie and Omar Sharif in tears. I remember walking into Omar's dressing room one day to find him sobbing inconsolably. I hadn't seen Omar like this before and turned away feeling shocked but not surprised, knowing that David had probably been the cause of Omar's distress. I quickly went to see David to find out what had happened.

"I wonder if Omar's had some bad news from home," I tactfully enquired.

"He's not had any bad news from home at all," David snapped, "he thinks he's a poet because that's the part he is playing but he ain't. He's a cunt and I told him so." I decided not to discuss the matter further but I believe that was round about the time Omar was filming the scene where he was writing poetry by candlelight. Hard though it may seem, and despite the scathing remarks he made about his attempts at poetry, David liked Omar. That, after all, was the reason he gave him the star role in *Doctor Zhivago* (not forgetting his big, brown eyes, of course). Most of us realised that if you wanted to work with David (and Omar already had quite a bit of experience under his belt) getting the 'Lean treatment' came with the territory. As for Julie, by keeping her head down and taking David's occasionally harsh comments on the chin, she proved that she was another consummate professional and, to be fair, David knew it. Ralph Richardson, or 'Ralphie' as David called him, also won his respect, if only because he was one of the 'Old School', although he never expected any special treatment because of it. But it was hard for the rest of the cast. The scene where a woman falls underneath the wheels of a train as she hands over her baby to the occupants almost turned into a real drama. The idea was for her to hand over the baby – in reality a prop doll – to Omar first and then to jump on afterwards, but she slipped between the track and the moving train. It looked worse than it was and she wasn't badly injured, but it was a close call. Many went on to suggest that David showed a callous disregard for the woman, but the truth is we were all too busy with our own problems, anyway (my own concern was for the bloody doll and the thought that it might have broken!).

If anything kept pace with David's direction it was the film's music. Maurice Jarre's sound score, and in particular *Lara's theme*, left everyone in no doubt that this was going to be another huge epic along the lines of *Lawrence of Arabia*. I had the film's famous balalaika made in my prop room – it still exists today although, unfortunately, I no longer have it. Just before we shot the scene in Yuri's bare, cell-like room, I put two tiny pieces of glitter on the strings to enhance Freddie Young's lighting. Shortly afterwards, as *Lara's Theme* swells into a crescendo, Yuri's epic journey truly begins. The scene of Yuri's mother's funeral was shot on a plain in the Sierra Nevada, in the south of Spain. I put together the cemetery in an area close to Madrid and added some Russian headstones and photographs. The open coffin with Yuri's mother inside took a lot of planning and what the viewer sees is not a young model playing dead, but in fact a wax works taken from a mould of Omar's own face.

The film's big scenes often involved the small subtle details, which were hard to plan. A good example of this was the scene shot through a frozen window in which Lara confesses to her student boyfriend, played by Tom Courtney, that she has been raped by Komorovski. They sit opposite one another in profile, with the camera viewing them through the ice tracery on the glass. On the little table between them, there is a solitary candle close to the window. As she speaks the camera creeps ever so slowly towards them. Meanwhile, the candle flame melts the condensation from the window, causing the water to trickle down like tears. Each mark on the floor where the camera dolly was to be positioned had to coincide with the chosen size of the melting hole. This entire scene had to be shot in one continuous take, lasting just over a minute long and without any dialogue. Timing was crucial, and because none of my usual tricks would have worked for this melting scene I was forced to experiment. I got hold of a hairdryer and fitted a long copper tube to the end like a long-barrelled rifle. I then placed boxes of dry ice with slots, through which I could slide false window panes and which I sprayed with water. I practiced a lot to find the right distances from which to direct the blast from the hot air gun on the outside, with the ice inside, so as not to blow the water away.

Without doubt, however, *Doctor Zhivago's* most famous set was the frozen interior of the house in Varykino, or what came to be known as the Ice Palace. While it was John Box's idea, I executed it without any interference from the rest of the crew. Built on the sound stage in Madrid, the entire set – including the furnishings – had to be covered with ice. It took me about two weeks to create the effect and the set behind locked doors and with very few helpers on hand. I used hundreds of rolls of old-fashioned cellophane which, unlike today's wrapping, can be crushed and flattened out to create thousands of creases and wrinkles, each becoming a little sparkling facet of light, like diamonds. In this state, I stapled it everywhere: on the walls, the ceiling and furnishings; sometimes flat, often pushed into ripples or bunched up in places. Once that was done, I boiled a cauldron of white paraffin wax from which I dipped cupfuls to throw at a spot on the cellophane. With my other hand I sprayed cold water pumped from a Hudson spray, which was simply a cylinder with a hose spray. That way I formed the ice into 'icicles' over everything. Soon, I was able to track beads of water and create fantastic shapes over which I scattered salicylic acid powder – otherwise known as crushed, common or garden aspirin – to cover the artificial appearance of the paraffin. Finally, I covered the floor with a thick layer of old-fashioned soap flakes that sparkled in the light. Because it was difficult for the actors to walk on, it was also ideal for reinforcing the illusion that they were trampling over the real stuff.

A footnote to this is that John Box asked me if he could take some credit for the effect on a documentary about the film some years ago. Shortly before doing the interview he phoned me and asked if he could say that he was the one holding the water pistol. I wasn't too bothered at the time, but on the day I dressed that set not even David was on the set, let alone John – I kept the stage door locked. The set's exterior was built in Soria in the north of Spain where it was expected to snow, but didn't. I suspected as much. The tell-tale signs were the flat rooftops we saw on all the houses in the area. It didn't take a genius to realise that countries with more than just the occasional snowfall build houses with pitched roofs.

We waited for days…then weeks, but as the shooting deadline loomed closer we all knew that something urgent had to be done. Yet again, John asked me to fix it. From Barcelona, I brought truck loads of white polystyrene in rolls, about three thousand tons of the stuff. It was fairly rare at the time, although since then polystyrene has found a far more common use, covering thousands of hectares of greenhouses throughout south-eastern Spain. The rolls were spread out far and wide across the Soria countryside and weighted down by truckloads of white marble dust we had salvaged from the earlier scenes. To complete the effect, we lime-washed the few trees that were visible and added a few subtle touches in the foreground. Hey presto, Siberia. Another scene where sheet ice was needed involved the train carrying the deportees to Siberia. The train stops so that the refugees can shovel out the foul straw and bury their dead. As the cattle-trap doors slide open, a flat sheet of ice remains which the prisoners have to break with their shovels. To create this effect we used sheets of paraffin wax in wooden frames.

Some scenes, however, never got beyond the cutting room floor. David initially wanted to include a scene of a marooned train abandoned in deep snow, full of dead passengers frozen like sculptures and half eaten by crows flying in and out of the wrecked wagons. I got it all ready with dummies, a snowdrift and even the crows, which I kept in a big aviary. Alas, the entire scene was removed from the script, something which is not at all unusual.

Another big snow and ice scene was shot with the horsemen who are machined gunned as they charge across the big frozen lake. The truth, as has become apparent by now, is that we shot it in summer and nowhere near a lake. Undeterred, Peter Dukelow graded and rolled the area flat as a pancake. He then created a fake shore line while I dressed the false banks with frost-covered rushes and snow, making full use of white cement topped with marble dust. The 'icing' on the cake, as it were, was the boat that appears trapped in the ice. David had expressly requested that no horses were to be pulled down by stuntmen in the scene where they are mowed down by a machine gun, arguing that he could always tell when horses were pulled down in films. I figured the horses could go down naturally as they do in a steeple chase because they almost always manage to get up and carry on. At certain places I laid steel sheeting and poured boiling soap over it, which I then covered with fine marble dust as previously done on the rest of the lake. David insisted we keep this a secret and the stunt riders were not told. The machine gun fire would be carefully co-ordinated to coincide with the moment the riders were on the slip pads. When we shot the scene it looked even better than we expected. Everybody was taken by surprise as horses and riders skidded and slid…and then got up – except the riders, of course. We did it all in one take and David was totally satisfied.

Not everything was snow and ice. I was particularly pleased with my small contribution to a scene, beautifully shot by Freddie Young in the forest. The idea was to have beams of sunlight piercing the light mist through the forest, which sounded simpler than it was because you can't light sunbeams unless there is something to light, with the added problem that it is difficult to keep light mist constant in exterior shots. Because it required a wide shot, we lit small fires which we fed with wet straw – all at the same low level - around a large perimeter circle, hundreds of yards across. We also hosed the surrounding woodland, especially the tree trunks so that their dark colour contrasted with the rest. This was an example of everyone being methodical and ensuring that every scene had the best possible presentation. On a David Lean film, every frame had to be a work of art. It wouldn't be enough just to photograph the horses riding through a forest – we had to have something much more attractive for the audience to see. David demanded perfection, and for me it was most gratifying to strive to achieve that and to see the end result

– I'd have done it for free, in fact. In much the same way a facial expression can suggest a mood without the use of words, so can a picture. In film production it is the main element in setting a scene.

With the benefit of hindsight, however, I now realise the quest for perfection sometimes became an unhealthy and destructive obsession. The scene in which Zhivago and his wife Tonya watch as a thick cloud of smoke towers above a town was achieved using methods that today would have had environmental activists baying for our blood. Although the scene is only a few seconds long, to achieve the effect we probably burned Spain's entire surplus of disused tyres in one afternoon. While Omar and Geraldine looked on aghast at the conflagration taking place in the distance, I was busy 'dressing' the set by dumping hundreds of old tyres, topped with barrels of tar and old oil, which I then set alight some twelve miles away. I obviously did a thorough job because the black cloud hovered over the area until sunset. I hate to think what effect we had on the surrounding area that day but, mercifully, we never did anything as bad again.

David wasn't keen on doing any battle scenes but felt it was important to suggest the reasons behind the mass desertions in the Russian army, as it was this single event more than any other which tipped the Revolution in Lenin's favour. While the rest of the unit were on a lunch break, I walked up a small slope and built a machine gun emplacement with a dummy Russian soldier slumped 'dead' in the firing position. Emulating the Ice Palace scene, I threw paraffin wax all over it so that it became one piece, like a block of cold marble set against a grey sky. In effect, it was a statue; a gruesome monument to the war dead. Nearby, on flat ground, I packed the marble dust hard and smooth with just the shoulder and the epaulette of the Russian officer's coat barely showing through. Close by a blackened claw-like hand, barely recognisable as human, protruded through the snow. David liked the effect and shot both – it was a stark reminder of what the soldiers were leaving behind. Other times I was called on to produce something far subtler, as in the scene where a sunflower sheds a few petals. "I don't want to hold on to Omar's tears," David remarked and asked me to introduce the scene at a moment's notice. I attached a few petals on the sunflower and tied a fine silk thread which I gently pulled on cue. It was simple but effective. We then flew to Finland for a week to shoot scenes where we needed to include a vast expanse of snow – the only bit of the real stuff in the entire movie – when Yuri mistakenly thinks he sees his family in the distance.

One of David's obsessions in life, besides films and women (and in that order), were Rolls Royces, and halfway through production he treated himself to a new model. He told me he was going to sell the one he drove while filming Lawrence and, keen to get my hands on it, I presented a cheque to his private secretary, Barbara Cole, for the asking price. The cheque was returned to me almost immediately with a note scrawled on the back which said: "I always wanted to give you a Rolls Royce – I think you would look rather good in one." It was signed by David. I was taken aback by his generous gesture and wish I'd kept the note to this day. I sold the Gypsy, thinking it would be great to flash around in a Roller…but then found the large saloon very difficult to park in the narrow streets of central Madrid. Taking advantage of a break in filming I shot off to the Paris Motor Show for two days and bought a little Triumph Spitfire, which was considerably easier to punt along Spain's narrow streets. The Roller was a very special gift, however, so I decided to get the most out of it by putting it to a more practical use. I fitted a discreet towbar under the back bumper so that I could take the caravan back with me to Carboneras when filming ended. I couldn't help thinking that I was probably the only person in the world with a Rolls Royce and a caravan but no house.

When the film came to an end, I was reminded by a Metro Goldwyn Mayer representative that I often did not appear on the credits with a proper job description beyond 'Property Master', a blanket title which did not truly reflect what I did on films, so he asked me what credits I wanted my name to appear with. "There are several due to you," he pointed out, "but you can't have them all – the unions won't allow it."

I shrugged my shoulders. "I'm not interested in credits, just make sure you put some money into my bank account."

Deep in thought, he ignored my comments. "We'll put you down with 'special effects', because we're sure they will get a nomination." They didn't, as it turned out. In fact, nobody noticed the effects, which is as it should be. As far as I'm concerned, if you can tell you're watching a 'special effect' the makers have failed in their job. The whole of Dr Zhivago was a special effect, but nobody saw it as such. That was my reward.

CHAPTER 15

Time on our hands

David came with Barbara Cole to visit me in Carboneras shortly after we finished *Dr Zhivago*. We spent days sitting around by the caravan just chatting, happily whiling away the time without having to worry about shooting schedules or work. It was soon pretty obvious that David had been bitten by the same bug which had attracted me to the area in the first place, and without much fuss he got busy building a house on a piece of land a little further along the beach from me.

I remember one memorable weekend years later, while listening to the first moon landing on my old Zenith radio, I noticed David sitting next to me almost in a trance. He was fascinated by the Apollo XI mission and when he later wrote the film script for *Captain Bligh* he tried to liken ships exploring the unknown world to space travel. He got so excited that he suggested the idea of reproducing the Ice Palace effect in Zhivago on a grander scale, this time involving a ship. I'd never seen him so happy and for a while it looked as though he might be setting up home in Carboneras, but then I got a telegram from Columbia Studios in London, asking me to come for a week or two to do some urgent work on a film that was already being shot. David's heart sank and he pleaded with me to stay. But I was totally unprepared for his next comment. "Don't go. If it's a question of money I have more than I need – you can have some of it." I was taken aback by his generous and somewhat extravagant offer. There was an element of desperation in his voice, and I suddenly realised how important our friendship had become. Naturally I turned his offer down because I could not take anyone's money without working for it. There was an awkward silence and it was now clear that even if I didn't want to go, I was left with little option but to accept the job.

Saying my goodbyes later that day, I got in the Rolls and sped through Spain and France without stopping until I arrived in Nice, where they were doing a film entitled *The Wrecking Crew* with Dean Martin involving silly high speed car chases around Monte Carlo. It was all so forgettable that I ended up working on two films at the same time, although I do remember a scene involving a hovercraft shooting down the main street past open-jawed tourists. There was, in fact, no hovercraft and our only job was to get the crowd to respond by looking suitably stunned – unfortunately, the crowd could not be roused to react effectively.

Irving Allen, who produced *The Long Ships*, unexpectedly showed up and suggested we were wasting precious time. "Have you got a gun?" he asked. I nodded, looking rather perplexed. "Fill it up with blanks," he instructed me. Taking the revolver, Allen then walked up and down the street blasting away while the camera photographed the crowd's reaction. When he emptied the gun he turned to me nonchalantly and said, "Take me back to the airport." It was as simple as that, but that's the way things were done then.

An infinitely more pleasant task required my scouring the beaches to cast background girls for one of the scenes. I had been given strict instructions to find the biggest breasted girls – all topless, of course. I took to the task with my usual sense of rigour (well, someone had to do it). The Americans, not being used to nudity, were a bit nervous about the whole idea, but it really didn't matter because I didn't come away empty handed. I came to the conclusion that the biggest boobs belonged to northern European or Italian women, but not the French (perhaps it was down to their diet and upbringing, but who cares? I wasn't asking). We then moved to the Isle of Wight – my first holiday destination as a young man – to continue filming. I drove up in the Rolls and found I was the first crew member to arrive. Funny to think the last time I had visited the island was as a child enjoying the thrill of my first pay packet. And now here I was, driving around in a Rolls given to me as a present by David Lean. After shooting a few crazy scenes involving hovercraft of various sizes I hurried back home, where I found David still lounging around by the beach. He told me that during my absence he had been thinking about going to India to scout the country with a view to starting a new project. Apparently, he was now thinking of making a film about Mahatma Gandhi

"Barbara will get the house built," he said with a wave of the hand. Soon afterwards he packed his bags and went, never to return to Carboneras. My last memory of him in Spain was watching him drive his red Rolls into the hills, his hand pressing the claxon long after the car had disappeared from view. Years later, he told me the entire Gandhi project had been shelved because he feared too much interference from the Indian Government, who wanted to depict Gandhi as some sort of deity. This was anathema to David, and he was not too impressed with Richard Attenborough's subsequent epic, believing the man had been portrayed with no real flaws. The trip was not a complete waste of time, however. He told me he had met a charming young girl in one of the hotels he had checked into. It turned out that she was the daughter of a family who part-owned the hotel chain. Her name was Sandy and she was destined to become Mrs David Lean. His love affair with India would also outlast the initial disappointment of not filming *Ghandi* and he would return some twenty years later to make *A Passage To India*.

Lord Jim, 1965 (UK) Columbia. 154 minutes. Producer, Writer and Director: Richard Brooks. Photography: Freddie Young. Editor: Alan Osbiston. Special Effects Cliff Richardson.
Cast: Peter O'Toole, James Mason, Curt Jurgens, Eli Wallach, Jack Hawkins, Paul Lukas, Akim Tamiroff, Dalia Lavi.

When I met Director and Writer Richard Brooks at his London office, his first words to me were: "I've heard about you." For a moment I thought he had found out about my exploits with the natives in Yugoslavia, but on seeing my expression he tried to reassure me. "I want you on my picture," he declared. Brooks was an energetic, straight talking American – like most of his compatriots I'd met. Being an ex-Marine, he was also quite tough. But before I began talking about contracts someone pointed out there might be a problem hiring me as the picture was being made at Shepperton Studios, and that would mean dealing with the dreaded unions. It seemed my reputation preceded me, but I had an unlikely ally. Brooks dramatically threw a copy of his script at the person who had raised the objection. "Don't you tell me what I can't have," he snapped. "Change the studio!" I toyed with the idea of quitting for the sake of the production; it would have been the decent thing to do, especially as so many people's jobs were hanging in the balance. The truth, though, was that I was quite skint and wanted the job, so when Brooks jabbed his finger at me, saying: "you're on my picture!" I didn't have the heart to turn him down. It was good to know that a few other friends were also on the film, including

Photographer Freddie Young and Assistant Art Director Geoffrey Drake.

Brooks handed me his script under strict instructions that no one else read it. He hadn't wasted any time, either, as he had all his locations already worked out in Hong Kong and Cambodia. It was great to see that my old friend Peter O'Toole had been cast as Lord Jim, but when I met him he seemed strangely subdued. Perhaps he was unhappy with Brooks' treatment of Joseph Conrad's book. Jim's character was a difficult role to play, in typical Conrad style, but I never thought it would pose a problem for an actor of O'Toole's skill. Clearly, the problem lay with a script that just didn't ignite Conrad's fine narrative. Despite this, I liked Richard Brooks who, it has to be said, could be an intimidating man to work for (if you weren't me, that is). On one occasion, he reduced one of the stand-by prop men to tears after a trifling incident.

To take the heat out of the situation I shouted back at Brooks, "Don't shout at the prop man, you've made him cry! Shout at me, you'll make me laugh!" It had the desired effect. Looking like a sulky schoolboy, Brooks called the prop man over and offered a limp apology.

Nathan Road through the centre of Kowloon, as Hong Kong's main thoroughfare, was inevitably a hot spot for tourists with shops, pubs and clubs. Young girls, all strutting around in tight silk dresses with the slit up the side that seemed to reach all the way up to their necklines, were everywhere. It was while enjoying the local nightlife that I stumbled upon none other than Sam Spiegel walking towards me in the company of Run Run Shaw, one of Hong Kong's richest men. I ducked into the doorway and watched them as they passed by, closely followed by an enormous grey Rolls Royce creeping along the gutter. Sam was a well-known womaniser and it's safe to say that although he may not have invented the casting couch he certainly made good use of it. It was, nonetheless, a surprise to see him talent spotting. I stepped further back into the doorway and watched fascinated for a few minutes before moving off.

Despite the unexpected entertainment, Hong Kong was not on my list of favourite places. The noise was quite maddening at times, but I did frequent Aberdeen Harbour, which was famous for the colony of junks that were used as permanent homes by thousands of people. It was a fascinating self-contained floating town, detached from the rest of the city and full of sampans acting as taxi cabs, with old ladies cooking in the back of them when they weren't rowing passengers to and fro. I was put off from going back when I later found out that every junk had a huge barrel at the stern in which they kept a small chow dog. They would chuck all the old waste food for a few weeks until the dog was big enough to be eaten. Gruesome discovery aside, I did eat at one of the famous huge floating restaurants in the harbour, which were all decorated with garishly coloured lights. But that only lasted for so long. One evening, I went to one of the bars in the restaurant, and there, behind the glaring lights, I discovered another 'culinary delicacy': rows of tiny turtles placed on small glasses, with their legs dangling grotesquely over the edge, presumably to look more appetising for diners prior to being boiled alive. I never went back to the bloody place.

Our next stop, however, was not much of an improvement. Cambodia, a former French colony, was already showing signs of a steep decline even before the ruthless Khmer Rouge took power and wiped out more than one million people barely a decade later. Brooks brought his wife Jean Simmons with him; the little girl I'd picked out in London during the filming of *Mr Emmanuel* all those years back. Maybe it was her presence that made him a little bit edgier than normal but he began shouting that the British crew "were no bloody good".

I decided to give him some advice. "You *would* rely on a film studio to get the crew to go on location. You should get freelancers, who are much better and independent of studio meddling." I never wasted an opportunity to have a go at that lot, and what was even more amusing was that Jean backed me up. Now that I'd got the ball rolling and got his full attention I pressed home my advantage to make a point. "You've also got a problem with production, you know."

"Whatddaya mean?" Brooks cried, looking even more flustered.

"Well, things weren't going well in Hong Kong – the costs looked all wrong – so I decided to hire a private detective to check out what we were spending our money on in our department."

"You did what?"

"Transport charges, for instance, were seventeen per cent more expensive," I leaned towards him, looked into his eyes and delivered the knock-out blow. "Someone's been fiddling you."

Brooks went red. "Names! I want names!" he fumed.

"I don't think I could do that," I calmly replied, teasing him just a little bit more before revealing the name of someone at the production department. By the time we got to Phnom Penh where we were due to film at the Angkor Wat Temple, he'd been replaced and the buyer sacked. At least we could focus on the job at hand without getting sidetracked by crew members who were on the fiddle. The temple itself was like something straight out of one of my childhood comics. Hidden in the jungle, it was covered by huge trees with roots as thick as water pipes, burrowing through the ruins for what seemed like miles. I was so fascinated by the temple that I took every possible opportunity to wander about on my own. In the evenings the place took on an even eerier presence. I watched as thousands of bats flew out of the temple when disturbed. The place had a unique charm and photographer Freddie Young chose round about this time to get married. Dear old Freddie had met a girl at the cutting room department called Joan who would stay with him until he died at the ripe old age of 96. When we finished shooting we went straight to Shepperton Studios, and to my surprise I was made to feel welcome. How times had changed.

CHAPTER 16

The day Armageddon showed its face

Life may have been quiet and peaceful in Carboneras (it was, after all, one of the reasons I moved there) but one sunny morning on 17th January 1966 I became a bit player in a tragic incident that could have resulted in the deaths of millions of people – and I wasn't even making a film. Unusually for me, I was outside my caravan painting a water colour that day when I suddenly sensed something in the skies above. Although I heard nothing I looked up and thought I saw a very fast and high flying B-52 bomber emerge from a rapidly expanding ball of white smoke. I guessed there had been some sort of mid-air explosion. On the table beside me I had a half-frame Pentax and before the plane disappeared from view I took a single picture with it. I then grabbed a pair of binoculars and scanned the clear blue skies for a better view. I could see a number of parachutes fall to earth, which I assumed were the crew, and also noticed a number of bigger, orange parachutes that seemed to be attached to much larger objects. I watched the whole fireball spread wide and form into a perfect smoke ring across the sky. It grew for hours and was still faintly visible late in the afternoon.

By now it was clear something terrible had happened. Bombers were a common sight above the skies of Almería at the time and we usually had two B-52s flying sorties every day. But the truth was even worse than I imagined. A KC-135 refuelling tanker from the US Air Force base in Morón some thirty-five miles from Seville had indeed exploded whilst trying to refuel a giant B-52 in mid-air. The problem, though, was that the bomber happened to be carrying four thermonuclear bombs at the time. The tanker's four-man crew were all killed along with three men from the B-52, but four of the bomber's crew bailed out in time and parachuted safely down to earth. This, in part, explained what I had just witnessed, but the bigger orange parachutes I saw were in fact attached to four Mk28 thermonuclear devices. Three landed close to the village of Palomares, some forty kilometres from where I was standing, while the fourth device fell into the sea, perched precariously on a ledge above a deep trench. Although the explosives on two of the bombs

195

that fell to earth detonated, their thermonuclear payloads had thankfully not been primed to go off. However, nuclear experts soon discovered that radioactive material had leaked into the surrounding countryside. A truck driver friend of mine said he had seen one of the bombs in a field of tomatoes and admitted kicking it out of curiosity. I wondered how long it would take for someone with more enterprising ideas to load one on the back of a truck and sell it off as scrap metal before the military got to it first. Fortunately, a division-sized force of US personnel swooped down on our tranquil corner of Spain and set up camp to clear the mess. I was told it would take months to analyse and remove hundreds of tons of radioactive soil over an area four fifths of a square mile.

Meanwhile, marine experts were frantically searching for the fourth bomb. The Americans sent no fewer than thirty-eight navy ships to the area, including aircraft carriers with helicopters flying everywhere and supplying the onshore camps. In all, there were four thousand personnel, and watching it all were a number of Russian trawlers. Already well known to the fishermen was the existence of a huge underwater trench not far from the shore, and this area of the Mediterranean Sea soon became the best chartered and explored in Europe. But despite their best efforts the military drew a blank. Then about a month later, a fisherman called Francisco Simo Orts told the authorities he had seen two parachutes fall into the sea on the day of the accident about eight kilometres off shore. The first was small and had splashed down some forty metres from his boat. The second, described by Orts as "a big thing, like a stout man", fell one hundred and thirty metres away. The Navy decided that the smaller parachute was the deployment bag for the missing bomb and the larger one, about twenty metres long, was the 'chute for the missing bomb. A team of oceanographers brought in robot submarines and narrowed the search down to a thirty-square kilometre area.

During all the hoopla Almería was crawling with journalists. I was at a bar talking to a US Army officer and happened to mention that I'd taken a picture. An eavesdropping journalist from Associated Press asked to meet me in Madrid with the picture, promising to pay me for it if the quality was good enough. Up to that point I hadn't thought about it much (the film had been left untouched in the camera for more than a month) but we shook on the deal and arranged to meet at the Palace Hotel in Madrid. As I was leaving the bar, a woman I hadn't even noticed before approached me and offered to buy the negative. I turned her down, telling her she was too late. It didn't occur to me that she already knew where I was going to meet the chap from AP.

The next day, as I set off in my Rolls to Madrid, I noticed that a car was tailing me. The roads were rather primitive in those days but I stepped on the gas, thinking I would be able to shake them off, but whoever was driving knew what they were doing and the car stuck behind me all the way to the capital. When I got to Madrid I rushed into the Palace Hotel and noticed the woman I'd met the day before following me in. With my appointment only minutes away, I knew I had to sort something out quickly. I turned and asked why she was being so persistent. She said she was working for the French magazine *Paris-Match*. I congratulated her on her driving and she replied that her companion was an ex-racing driver. When the AP man did not show up on time I felt the woman's determination warranted some sort of reward and decided to give her the undeveloped film. "It's for you," I said. She insisted on paying for it, nonetheless, and gave me a piece of paper with an IOU for 2,000 Francs. Sure enough, the cheque reached me shortly afterwards on the tail of a double, centre-page spread in the magazine with the headline 'Picture of the Year'.

As for the true protagonist – the bomb – it was eventually found, two and a half months later by a US recovery vessel eight hundred metres below the surface, deep inside a canyon. The most intriguing – and worrying – aspect is that the gorge formed part of a deep gash in the sea floor called the Carboneras Fault, where the African and European plates come together. It splits the earth's crust inland a few kilometres from Carboneras and carves a path all the way to Lisbon in Portugal. Retrieving the bomb from such a depth would not be a job for the faint hearted. Step forward professional navy diver Carl Brashear. With a name like that you somehow knew he'd get the job done, and after weeks of trying to recover the bomb it was brought to the surface on March 26.

But the operation didn't run according to plan. A pipe holding a mooring line broke loose and struck Brashear's leg, almost searing it off (it eventually had to be amputated and Brashear became the subject of a Hollywood film starring Robert de Niro and Cuba Gooding Jr many years later although, alas, I was not involved). The Navy searched again and finally raised the device to the surface on

April 7. Not surprisingly, it was found to be damaged by its second impact. It begged the question what would have happened if any of the bombs had gone off. A thermonuclear weapon of this type had a 1.5 megaton warhead, which was about eight hundred times more powerful than the bomb that destroyed Nagasaki in 1945, and if one of the bombs had exploded on land there would have been a catastrophic chain reaction, triggering two of the bombs and wiping out most of Western Europe and Northern Africa in the process. And had the fourth one detonated beneath the sea the resulting tsunami would have reached 2,000 kilometres an hour and changed the shape of the planet. It's not a good place to have a nuclear explosion two hundred metres down, unless of course you want to make the Mediterranean Sea bigger. As a footnote, the radioactive soil that was removed was eventually taken to the Savannah River nuclear waste disposal site in Southern Carolina, where I suspect it remains to this day. More than forty four years later, the US and Spanish governments are still trying to clear the area of the contaminated soil that wasn't removed at the time, but that's another story.

CHAPTER 17

How to blow up a Beatle

How I Won the War – 1967. 109 minutes UK. Petersham Pictures.
Producer: Richard Lester. Director: Richard Lester. Writer: Charles Wood (based on the novel by Patrick Ryan). Photographer: David Watkin. Editor: John Victor Smith. Special Effects: Eddie Fowlie.
Cast: Michael Crawford, John Lennon, Roy Kinnear, Lee Montague, Jack MacGowran, Michael Hordern, Jack Hedley.

How I Won the War was a product of the late sixties. Not only was it an anti-war film but it had Beatle John Lennon in the cast; perhaps the most high-profile celebrity on the planet at the time. Pity the same couldn't be said for the film, which went down like a lead balloon on its release. At least we filmed half the movie barely a few kilometres from my home, which was very convenient (in a way, it was as close as I would ever get to doing a nine-to-five job!).

We started filming in Hamburg close to where the NATO forces were based. Richard Lester revelled in the idea of shooting scenes with tanks rolling over buildings and smashing up cottages, and we even had a squadron of Churchill tanks helping out. In order to get hold of the tanks we kept quiet about our real intentions and the guys who loaned them to us didn't have a clue what we were doing and perhaps thought we were making some sort of heroic war epic. I hate to think what the locals thought about it all, seeing as their city had been flattened during World War Two less than twenty-five years earlier.

In one scene we had the tanks thundering across a bridge with an ecstatic Michael Crawford standing in front of the lead tank after having bought the structure from the Germans (don't ask why, but that more or less summed up the surreal nature of the film). In front of them, a German officer, who had just received a fat cheque from Crawford, innocently waves them on, only to get flattened like a pancake by the first tank. The subsequent mangled mess, which was my job to create, included an arm still holding the cheque. That was the high point in Germany. The crew then flew over to Almería to shoot the rest of the film, including all the desert scenes, while I drove over in my Rolls.

"I'll see you there on Monday morning," was my comment to Richard on the Saturday. It was one hell of a non-stop drive. The confused plot rumbled on, this time with the ramshackle gang landing behind the enemy lines in North Africa. We borrowed a landing craft from the American Sixth Fleet without them knowing what it was going to be used for (we were getting rather good at this by now). To convince them to lend us the vessels we made up all sorts of nice sketches to give the impression we were making a decent war film in which the heroes came up smelling of roses. Behind the trucks in the landing craft was a humongous Roller that Crawford's men had been ordered to transport behind enemy lines in order to prepare a cricket pitch, as one did in wartime.

Among my tasks was staging the shooting down of an aeroplane, which I did by using a catapult close to the edge of a hill, and blowing up a jeep with Michael Crawford in it. Here, the scene called for a bit of staged blood and guts, as Crawford's driver has his legs blown off. I simply got hold of some sheep's legs to substitute the real legs, folded the meat back off the bone and buried them in the sand. Most of the endless gags in the film weren't even in the script, but this was how Richard liked to work. That wasn't a problem, but when I discovered that John 'I'm-going-for-a-gin' Stoll had been hired as Art Director I knew the film would hit the buffers. True to the chaotic and somewhat improvised nature of the film I dressed the set for the Battle of the Alamein, which required the inclusion of a number of blown up tanks, only to be told by Richard that we'd got the location wrong.

"Where are the gliders?" he asked nonplussed.

"No one's told me anything about gliders," I replied.

"I told John I wanted wrecked gliders all along the hill top! Where is he?"

At that precise moment John was getting blotto at a bar near the airport, and it was only seven in the morning. I drove over and found him with his head in a puddle of wine with some bits of onion strewn around him.

"Come on John, I think Richard wants to see you."

He groaned as I dragged him back to the set to face the music and a very angry looking Director. "Where are the gliders, John?" Richard demanded to know.

Bleary eyed, John straightened up momentarily and blurted out, "They proved to be a lot of trouble, so I didn't bother." Richard went a deep shade of purple, but there was little he could do about it this late in the day.

John Lennon proved to be far less problematic than Stoll. His character is killed off in a particularly gruesome way by being blown up in the sand dunes of Almería. John was very uncomfortable with acting, despite having appeared in *A Hard Day's Night* and *Help!* with The Beatles some years earlier. Clearly, he hadn't grown in confidence as a result of the experience.

"I'm not an actor, Eddie, what do I do?" he asked nervously.

"I'll tell you exactly what you've got to do, John. Just follow my instructions." I pointed into the distance. "See that tall tuft of grass? Just walk straight to it and ignore this thin strand of wire I'm attaching to the back of your ankle." As the cameras were about to roll he grabbed his rifle and took a good long walk to the agreed point. When he got to the tuft of grass I pressed a button and my bomb blew up underneath him. But that was only the first part. I had attached the wire to an aluminium plate on his chest, and stuck to that was a condom designed to burst its contents of fake blood from his belly when I triggered a tiny explosive charge. He looked shocked as he fell to the ground, but the scene wasn't yet over. He then had to hold his guts in as the camera zoomed in on the wound and the blood pumped out from between his fingers. To this day I still can't figure out if he did a splendid job of acting or whether he was in a genuine state of shock. In a way I felt sorry for Lennon. He couldn't even sit in a chair between takes without hordes of photographers, armed with lenses three-feet long, mercilessly snapping away at him. I saw him continually lying down on the ground and putting his face in the crook of his arm in a vain attempt to hide from the paparazzi.

It wasn't always like that, of course. Ringo Starr came out with his wife to visit John, and to while away the time I invited both of them to my house in Carboneras. John arrived in a thumping great black Rolls-Royce. In fact, everything was painted black – his favourite colour – including the tinted windows and the chrome. They were looking for thrills and the best I could offer them was to lend them my rubber boat – a Zodiac – and to let them take it out to sea. They must have had a good time because I didn't see them again for the rest of the day. There was still no sign of them as dusk came, and I was about to call the Civil Guard when they showed up looking sheepish. God knows what they had been up to, but the dinghy was in such a bad state that it looked as though it had been rolled down a hill.

One of the more interesting special effects to create (and one most film makers today seem incapable of achieving satisfactorily) is blowing up a vehicle. The scene in question had Michael Crawford lighting up a trail of petrol with a match to blow a truck to bits. The fact is petrol doesn't light up *that* easily on sand and you can't put a match to it even if you try. The way I did it was to lay down a couple of hundred yards of copper piping with holes and then to pump gas along it – it was as simple as that. Nowadays, special effects experts have it easy as it's all done on the computer after much planning. The problem with that is that it's over the top; a motor car doesn't blow up like a petrol refinery and it certainly doesn't summersault through the air when it rams another vehicle. Thanks to Richard's desire to improvise as often as possible I was forced to come up with things like this on the spur of the moment, all the time. At times it seemed as though he was trying to catch me out and, inevitably, this led to some friction. We teased each other and I began calling him 'Dick', but after a while he hinted that he preferred being called 'Richard' instead. It was all good natured fun, however. The fact is I always gave the real 'dicks' in the business a wide berth, and Richard and I would go on to work together on quite a few more films.

CHAPTER 18

Give me a David Lean set up!

The Charge of the Light Brigade. Great Britain. 1968. De Luxe Panavision. United Artists. Producer: Neil Hartley. Director: Tony Richardson. Writer: Charles Wood. Photographer: David Watkin, Peter Suschitsky. Music: John Addison.
Cast: Trevor Howard, John Gielgud, David Hemmings, Vanessa Redgrave, Jill Bennett, Harry Andrews, Peter Bowles.

Throughout my career in films I came across many oddballs whose eccentric requests made me smile on occasion, but one particular Director went beyond the call of duty, especially when it came to treating animals. Step forward Michael Winner.

It happened while we were intending to make *William the Conqueror*, a film that Winner was to direct but which never got beyond the planning stage, and no wonder.

I was hired as Property Master, and as Winner wanted to shoot in Spain we met in Madrid to discuss the props that would be required for the film. It became clear that he wanted only the genuine items, including the silver embellishments for the shields. I pointed out that the budget wouldn't run to the real stuff, but he was pretty insistent. I let the matter drop, trusting that he would forget about it once I showed him a bill for real silver. We then went on a reconnaissance trip to Urbasa in Pamplona in the north of Spain to look for locations. There were fine ancient oaks spread across a lush green countryside that could quite easily have passed for southern England in the 11th Century. All seemed to be going well until we walked to the edge of a precipice. With a sweep of his arm, Winner spoke. "The men will come out of the trees in a surprise attack and drive the horsemen over the precipice," he said, pointing downwards. I kept silent and that evening back in our hotel we met up to discuss the ideas I had about the cliff-top fall.

"I'll use rubber dummies for both men and horses," I suggested.

"Rubber horses? What rubber horses?" he asked perplexed.

"I can get waterbed manufacturers to manufacture life-like horses."

Winner went red like a plum tomato. "What are you talking about? I want real horses falling over that cliff!" he scoffed.

Staring blankly at him, I came to a quick conclusion. "You know you're never going to get the film made, Michael." I tried to reason with him once more by proposing we use stuffed horses for the long shots.

"Who wants stuffed horses!" he said, ridiculing my idea as though I had suggested we use flying pigs instead. "They've got to be real," he repeated petulantly. I looked for a misplaced sense of humour (which has been known to exist among directors) but couldn't find one.

With a sigh I turned to Michael and looked straight into his eyes. "Well Michael, count me out of this one." We left it at that and not long afterwards I heard the project had been shelved even before the casting stage. A few years later I found myself sitting next to Winner on a plane and during our conversation I brought the subject up by way of a question. "Why are you always so shitty to everybody?"

To his credit he was amused and replied, "It works, doesn't it?"

Director Tony Richardson, who leaned very much towards the theatre, was a completely different kettle of fish. For a start he was charming and witty; two qualities which were notably absent in Winner. I felt, however, that Tony had a lot to learn about movie-making and the shame was he did a lot of it while directing *The Charge of the Light Brigade*, despite having a great cast at his disposal. We met at his Kensington home for a strategy session before going on location to Turkey and I soon got a sample of his wry humour. He was surrounded by a loyal crowd made up of his wardrobe department and other assorted theatre cronies, who were keen to show how much they admired him.

He leaned across the table, as if savouring the audience's attention. "I want camels in this. David Lean had camels and I want camels." There were a few giggles in the room while I sat stony faced, pretending to make notes on my pad. Noting that I was seemingly unimpressed he pressed on, "And I want elephants too!" There was more dutiful snickering while I scribbled further, refusing to bite.

As the evening wore on it became clear he also wanted me to build a huge British army camp before the battle, with rows of immaculate white army tents "that would dazzle in the sunlight". I reassured him that his tent town would be on schedule, and on budget. "It'll be just like you described it in your script – maybe better – although I doubt you'll get any elephants," I couldn't help adding. The room fell silent.

As soon as we got to Turkey I went straight to the Red Cross, the Red Crescent and the Turkish authorities, knowing that, as an earthquake zone, they would have thousands of army tents in store. They were happy to lend them to me in exchange for a generous contribution to earthquake relief. After days of back-breaking work I stood on a hillside to view our pristine tent town, which lay sprawling over a vast plain, ready to fool the most fastidious of army historians. In the distance I spotted a Stork as it began nesting on a small tower on the approach to the valley. I took a big breath and closed my eyes, taking stock of all the past days' hard work. Just then I felt an enormous bang that threw me to the ground. Half dazed, I staggered to my feet and dusted myself off. Looking to see what had happened I turned and saw a patch of scorched earth a few metres from where I had been standing. I immediately thought it was Tony playing some sort of practical joke but then realised it had been a lightning strike. Some directors have friends in high places, I mused. But I hadn't forgotten about Tony's camels. I took a Polaroid of them snoozing away and sent them to Tony with a note saying: "You are now the proud owner of these two camels. Elephants are proving rather more difficult to obtain, although I'm currently in negotiations to have two flown in from Ceylon." I knew that would put the wind up him and an urgent telegram rushed back saying: "Forget the elephants!"

At least we agreed that the British Army's pristine red tunics would have to look dirty and faded if they were to fool an audience into believing they had been worn on a long military campaign. I took hundreds of costumes, and while testing one I realised they hadn't been pre-shrunk. I didn't dare alter them too much, otherwise cinema audiences would have been presented with a Charge of the Dwarf Brigade, but I wore out the elbows, cuffs and greased them all round the button holes. When the wardrobe mistress saw them she practically fainted. It was all too much for the woman, who abandoned the picture in disgust. It was not the sort of effect I usually had on women, but there you are. Perhaps she thought we were going to do an opera or something similar and didn't understand the importance of making the props appear as genuine as possible on film. All in all I don't think I was too popular with the crew, but I did get on very well with the cameraman and, believe it or not, Tony – and that was all that really mattered. Despite our good working relationship, Tony never got over the fact that I had worked with David Lean and he never let me forget it, either.

"Go and get me a David Lean set up!" he demanded, which I understood to mean a large panoramic view. I happily obliged.

"Right. You'll need a 35mm lens to shoot an entire army going along the top of a plateau in silhouette," I said teasing him.

"We haven't got a 35," he whined (I knew that because they were using funny old lenses to give a dated feel, which in itself was a rather good idea). Still, he calmed down a bit after that. The Light Brigade may have come a cropper on that fateful charge in 1854 but we shot the scene over a number of days without any major mishaps, pity the same could not be said about the retreat. "After lunch I would like to rehearse the retreat," Tony announced, to which I replied, "As far as I'm concerned, you can shoot it now." What he didn't know is that I had lorries waiting over the hill loaded with stuffed horses and dead animals we'd got from a local slaughter house.

But Tony had other ideas. "Can't I have some of these horses run along...and then blow up?" I quietly replied 'no', in a scene painfully reminiscent of my previous encounter with Michael Winner, but Tony also proved to be a persistent bugger. "Couldn't you get them to eat some dynamite?" I chose to ignore him, but later on I thought of teaching him a lesson and hatched a little plan.

During a lull in shooting I asked him to have a look at the carcass of a horse which had succumbed under the harsh conditions. I got an axe and chopped its head off for effect and pulled it away just a little. "Here's a wounded horse for your close up," I said. He went pale and almost threw up – it was quite obvious he had never seen a dead animal before.

After a feeble instruction to film the remains with the second unit – which I ignored – Tony finally dropped the matter of shooting dead or wounded horses. I could see that he was still desperate for a little cinema vérité, so for the shots of the retreat I attached slabs of raw meat to healthy horses and sprayed fake blood everywhere. The effect was suitably gruesome for cinema audiences with the obvious advantage that none of the horses suffered. It was important that the battle scene look chaotic and not staged in any way, although nothing was done randomly. I had truck-loads of our props thrown from the trucks, leaving mounds of dead horses and soldiers positioned where they fell and increasing their number as we approached the Russian cannon emplacements.

The final detail was to get a crew member driven in a jeep to spray fake blood from bottles and to throw a few swords around. When Tony came to inspect the work he couldn't resist having a dig: "An American prop man would have gotten me real arms and legs from the mortuary." It was a petty remark which irritated me but I chose not to show it.

"Better get one then, because I don't do that. Be satisfied that I have got you all these torsos without arms and legs."

The entire project was becoming an endless slog, what with Tony's tiresome sarcasm and Turkey's unfavourable rainy climate. "Why are we here in this bloody wet valley?" I wailed in exasperation. "We could have done the whole thing in Spain and got better horses as well!" But Richardson was having none of it, and I later learned it was because his then wife, Vanessa Redgrave, was firmly opposed to the idea of filming in a country ruled by a fascist dictator.

Tony's obsession with using as few extras as possible was a constant headache and I needed to come up with impromptu solutions. At one point it got so bad that I had to manufacture the Russian Army out of plywood. We needed lines of infantrymen massed behind the Russian cannons; the problem was that we only had about enough to guard Buckingham Palace on a quiet day. My solution was to nail five plywood soldiers to a batten, with each batten carried by live extras dressed as soldiers. That way Tony had seven Russians for the price of two, plus the cost of the wood and my time – and all without a fascist dictator in sight.

I stood on the same hill where, months earlier, I had almost been killed by a lighting strike and gazed at the small bell tower where the stork had been nesting. In the time it had taken us to make the film its chicks had all grown and flown away. We then went to Istanbul and the Black Sea to film the scenes of the British Army landing in Balaclava. It was a relief to leave Ankara, which was just about the filthiest and most disgusting place I had ever been to.

The city was fuelled by black coal which blackened everything in sight, and when mixed with the harsh winter the rains covered the entire metropolis under a mushy layer of dirt. By contrast, Istanbul seemed a world away. I booked a large room at a luxurious hotel, thinking the worst was over. But I'd hardly been there a minute when a massive earthquake shook the entire building while I was having a shave. I managed to finish the job before rushing downstairs in a lift (a silly thing to do in hindsight) and when I got to the lobby I was met by seething mass of panicking tourists, many of whom had been caught while taking a shower and were running around in circles with towels wrapped round their heads. Some elderly American women, clearly unhappy that the hotel receptionists could not control an Act of God or provide a satisfactory reason for the phenomenon, stampeded into the street in various states of undress looking like ghouls out of a horror movie. It was all too much to bear. I needed to get away and went down the road to a ramshackle shed to get a stiff drink, thinking that if this fell down at least I wouldn't be hit by a mass of falling masonry or mowed down by a fat American.

We shot off to London for the final scenes, including the ceremonial departure parade of the Light Brigade at Aldershot. The Producer arranged it with the military establishment to lend us their swords. However, it was only at the last minute that the Army discovered that most of its supply was packed in grease and decided it would be too much trouble to unpack and clean the whole lot. We were now facing a parade of sword-less soldiers because my Wilkinson swords were still in Turkey. Tony was understandably pulling his hair out. I thought about the problem and decided to use one of my more useful contacts. I borrowed one sword and went to see a friend, Harry Pottle, who had been the Chief of the foundry at the old Denham studios and who now had his own factory. Confident he could make anything, given sufficient notice, I took Pottle at his word and told him he had forty-eight hours to manufacture around three hundred bright and shiny aluminium swords. He didn't even blink. The factory worked round the clock and on the morning we had set aside for the shoot, with our cavalry mounted in full uniform sans swords, I arrived in a truck in the nick of time with the sabres. My prop men ran up and down the parade ground, handing out swords. Afterwards, nobody made any jokes about not being able to cut the butter with them. They wouldn't have dared; the swords looked great and glinted in the sun just like the real thing. That more or less wrapped the whole thing up, but it didn't leave a pleasant taste in the mouth. I resolved there and then that I would stay away from making war movies in the future. Curiously, just as I arrived at this decision I got a call to go to Pinewood Studios to meet Harry Saltzman, the producer of the James Bond films. It turned out he wanted me to work on – wait for it – *The Battle of Britain*. He had all the accoutrements of a producer, including a big office with a big desk, and even bigger promises. But I wasn't impressed and flatly turned the offer down, saying I was busy working on Tony's film.

"Well, quit!" he insisted.

"I can't do that."

"Well, as soon as you've finished you'll work for me."

"When it's finished I've promised to do something for David Lean." There was no David Lean picture, of course, but Saltzman was beginning to get up my nose.

"That picture will never happen," he snorted. I knew that, but he didn't.

"Sorry. I'm not going to do it."

"Are you saying no to me?"

"Yes, I suppose I am."

Years later I bumped into Saltzman at Madrid airport. He came off the airplane with Brigitte Bardot, who was about to make *Shalako* with Sean Connery in Almería, of all places. He spotted me, which was quite unbelievable in itself, and sauntered across.

"You are the man who said no to me," he said, jabbing his finger at me, and without waiting for a reply he turned on his heels and joined Brigitte. The moral of the story is: if you want to be remembered by a big-shot say 'no', because he is always surrounded by 'yes-men'. In any case *The Battle of Britain* seemed a bit of a bore and wasn't much of a film for a Property Master – I had lived through the real thing, after all.

CHAPTER 19

Tell it to me straight, Eddie

Ryan's Daughter. 1970. **Great Britain. Metrocolour/Panavision 70. MGM.**
Director: David Lean. Writer: Robert Bolt. Photography: Freddie Young. Music: Maurice Jarre. Producer: Anthony Havelock Allen, Stephen Grimes.
Cast: Sarah Miles, Robert Mitchum, Christopher Jones, John Mills, Trevor Howard, Leo McKern.

After working on what was probably one of the worst westerns of all time, *The Desperadoes*, I joined the crew of another western, *100 Rifles*, with the stunning Raquel Welch...until I fell out with the American Production Manager who tried to interfere with my department (hadn't he heard by now what happened to anyone who did that?). The truth is I don't like westerns. They're miserable bloody things because there's nothing in them; only horses and six-shooters. I left the set feeling relieved rather than angry and drove back to Carboneras, wondering what to do next. But it wasn't long before David came to the rescue once again. I got an interesting telegram from him in Rome that simply said: "Don't start anything, Eddie. Robert Bolt and I are writing a little gem." About a week later he phoned me, hardly able to contain his excitement. "Can you come immediately? It's no longer a gem; it's going to be something bigger." His enthusiasm was infectious. For the first time in ages I was really looking forward to a project and agreed to fly over to meet both him and Robert. They told me it was going to be a love story set in the west coast of Ireland at the time of the 1916 Irish uprising. I was given a bunch of lira notes the size of bed-sheets and told to get the rest of the money I needed from backers Metro-Goldwyn-Mayer before going on to Ireland to look for locations. I thought 'fuck that, I'll go to Spain first'. The fact was that it was more reliable to shoot in Spain as the country had good technicians, so when I arrived back in Almería I set off in the Rolls in the wrong direction, checking the coasts of Asturias and Galicia in the north because they were both green. I soon realised however that they were too green and the skies too blue; it was not the right background colour at all, it had to be grey, because *Ryan's Daughter* was going to be a bleak story. I spent a couple of nights at the Royal Gardens Hotel next to Kensington High Street studying maps and drew a ring around a place called Dingle, which had the most rugged coastline. I decided to go up the Welsh coast first and cross over to Ireland by ferry from Anglesey, just to cover my arse – it wouldn't look good if someone were to ask me if I had bothered to check Wales out. I then drove to the west coast of Ireland and came across some spectacular views but was worried about how remote it all was. Then, just as I was driving down from the mountains to the small fishing town of Dingle, I noticed that a new hotel was nearing completion. I took it as an omen. 'They're building this for me,' I thought. I may have even been the very first guest at the, as yet, unfinished Skellig Hotel.

I spent weeks looking for locations, going up and down the coast into Donegal and Cork, not once but many times, with the aim of getting to know every nook and cranny. Very early on I realised there was no point following local signposts as many had been twisted in their sockets. What took me a bit longer to realise was that you couldn't be guided by the locals either, as they also seemed a bit loose. Arriving at a junction feeling completely lost, I spotted a farmer and asked him how far we were from a certain village. He scratched his head and gave me elaborate instructions on how to reach it, adding that it was some 20 kilometres away.

"That far!" I said in surprise.

"Well, it's only a quarter that if you go in the opposite direction," he added helpfully. He may have been a sandwich short of a picnic but everything else felt right about Dingle.

It wasn't just the locations but the atmosphere that made it especial. When you are looking for film locations you have to feel that the ambience is right. And if 'dark' was the mood I was looking for I found it here, in all its primeval intensity: the misery of the west coast of Ireland, with the haze drawing strange patterns on rocks or hanging over ancient tumble-down cemeteries, and the breathtaking sight of cumulus clouds towering like enormous castles over the Atlantic Ocean. I also found suitable storm cliffs quite close in the Bridges of Ross, south of Kilkenny. This is where the weapons would be brought ashore by the IRA in storm conditions.

By the time I found all the   locations and had them in Kodachrome it was autumn. I asked David to check them out, which he wasn't keen on doing because he was still writing the script with Robert, but I insisted. "Well, if you don't come now we won't be ready for next year because there isn't a suitably moody village around and we'll have to build it." I could see he still wasn't keen, so I dangled a carrot. "I've got a nice suite for you in the Great Southern Hotel in Galway and in the private sitting room there is an open peat fire." It worked.

A week later David turned up with Robert Bolt, his wife, Sarah Miles, who was also the film's leading lady, and his new love, Sandy, the charming girl he had discovered in India. I set up a slide-projector in the room and showed them some of the thousands of pictures I had taken. I clicked one after the other without making a comment, hoping to whet David's appetite. "Go back," he said excitedly. "Where's that?" At the end of the display all the locations David chose had been taken around Dingle; this is where we were going to build our very own Irish village and shoot *Ryan's Daughter*.

But we still needed an important location as the script called for a scene with woodlands. I'd heard from the locals about a mysterious Englishwoman who owned a beautiful plot of land with a small forest. It sounded perfect, and when I was told that she had barred entry to all-comers I was even more determined to meet her. I drove over to the house, past a wonderland of trees and a carpet of bluebells, and parked the Rolls right across the front door. As I went to ring the bell I was met by a fox, casually walking past with a huge salmon in its mouth. I was still getting over the sight when the heavy front door swung open and I was greeted by an imposing woman – the sort that wouldn't look out of place in a St Trinian's film. I introduced myself with all the charm I could muster, telling her I was from Metro Goldwyn Mayer and that I would like to film some scenes of her beautiful woodlands. "I see. I'm Mrs Grosvenor," she replied dryly, clearly not wholly convinced by my introduction. She said she had inherited the house along with the whole of Killarney – including the lakes – from a Lord Castleross.

Almost as an afterthought I was ushered into her palatial home and she offered me a drink. She meant tea, of course, but I had other ideas. "Have you got anything a little stronger, like a Scotch?" It broke the ice.

"What a good idea! I think I'll join you." she replied with a playful smile. In half an hour, over a Scotch, she agreed for us to film in the grounds outside the house, thereby confirming my view that whisky is an excellent tool to negotiate with.

One day in Dublin, while enjoying lunch at The Shelbourn, I got a pleasant surprise from an old friend of mine. I received a heavy tap on my shoulder and on turning round, ready to reprimand the clown, I saw Peter O'Toole beaming at me. "Tell David I want the part of the idiot in that script he's writing!" How he got to know about it I'll never know, since the script was not yet finished and no one but ourselves had seen it. I'd also heard he and David had both fallen out, but Peter was undeterred and he instructed me to tell David not to speak to his agent but to him directly. "I'll do it for nothing!" he ended.

David would have been happy to comply but he had already made up his mind and given the role to another old friend, John Mills. It was clearly an Oscar-winning role and Peter had sensed it, but it was not to be. David offered the part of Father Collins to another old pal instead, Alec Guinness, but he wasn't too keen, arguing that the portrayal in the script was not realistic, so he was dropped and Trevor Howard got the role instead. But if Mills and Howard were good choices, *Ryan's Daughter* will unfortunately be remembered for the awful decisions to cast the hopeless Christopher Jones in the role of the British officer Randolph Dorian, and Robert Mitchum who was also totally miscast, and a nasty bugger to boot. Jones had been chosen on John Box's recommendation, to David's eternal regret.

Things got so bad in one scene that David asked me to show Jones how to play someone suffering from shell-shock. I wasn't exactly known for my acting abilities beyond the occasional stand-in as a woman, but whereas Jones could only think of trembling feebly by the bar, I decided the scene called for a more theatrical performance. I'm not sure if it's what a shell-shocked soldier would have done, but I thought of cowering behind the fire-grate and half-way up the chimney. David agreed and Jones was instructed to re-enact my improvised performance before the cameras. To his eternal embarrassment, Jones's speaking abilities were also questioned and he was eventually dubbed by another actor.

If this was bad, Robert Mitchum proved to be an even worse casting choice, despite being a huge film star. He was not only totally unconvincing in the role of sexually repressed school teacher but proved to be a behind-the-scenes trouble maker from start to finish. Sometimes he'd lock himself up in the caravan, refusing to come out for a scene. On other occasions he'd vanish, mostly to spend time with four or five young women he had especially flown over to take part in one of the many private parties he often threw, although that wasn't enough to keep him satisfied and he ended up having an affair with Sarah Miles. He wasn't popular with the locals, either, and at a party he and Sarah organised, a gate-crasher punched him square in the eye following an argument. Shooting had to be postponed and he was urgently flown to London for treatment. Fortunately – or unfortunately, depending on one's view – he was well enough to resume shooting shortly afterwards. But there would be more trouble from him throughout. While we were quietly on the set with the crew standing around and the camera at the ready Mitchum noticed the Producer, Tony Havelock, arrive. "I smell shit!" he shouted for no reason. David pretended not to hear, but I could tell he was furious. I was not surprised by his outburst. I realised Mitchum had a habit of zeroing on someone, myself included, if the mood took him. Days later, during a heavily overcast, grey morning when no shooting was possible, I suggested to David to do a dull weather scene which required Mitchum to stand at the edge of the sea in his nightshirt. David was up for it but not Mitchum, who was put out by the fact he would have to stand around in the cold. After much cajoling, he grudgingly agreed to step forward by the sea's edge while I stood below him, making a few adjustments to the dynamite box props. Suddenly, he lifted his nightshirt and decided to go for a piss there and then. I stepped smartly aside and he missed, but he made his point – I made sure I'd make mine towards the end of filming.

Despite appearances, *Ryan's Daughter* wasn't all bickering behind the scenes, and thanks to David's masterful direction the film was a visual success. In the opening scene when Rosie Ryan's parasol gets blown away, David wanted it to drift past a cemetery, fall over a cliff and into the water below, "like a parachute". Of course, an umbrella wobbles and rises with the wind, and seems to prefer falling upside down if blown. To solve this, I built an enormous fishing rod with the longest bamboo pole I could find. Then we constructed an overhead winch mounted on top of a trolley, which was mounted on rails and designed to hang over the cliff. That way I could stand up and work the contraption with a nylon thread and swing it round over the sea like a puppet. Hidden from view we had a man at the bottom whose job it was to pull the umbrella down using another thread to control the updraft. It worked first time. The really difficult part was when it came to filming the love scene in the woods between Miles and Jones. As there were no deciduous trees north of the equator, David toyed with the idea of moving the entire film crew to somewhere like New Zealand. I had different ideas and told him we could build the set here, but he dismissed it out of hand. "Don't be silly Eddie, you can't match summer." I said no more and got down to work, determined to prove my point.

A while later I went to another village not far away and rented a little dance hall I'd found just outside Dingle. I felted the floor over, put some soil and turf, and sowed grass and watercress seed; anything, in fact, that grew quickly. I dug up some plants from the forest and sent them across to the other side of Ireland. I put them into cold storage for a couple of weeks and then brought them back into a hothouse. I even got birds and butterflies which I shipped over from a butterfly farm in Romney Marshes in England to add to the atmosphere. Finally, I built the woodlands and the bits on which Jones and Miles, to put it bluntly, were going to screw. The idea was to have a number of grass-covered panels slide in and out to allow a camera to get close enough to the couple at ground level. I didn't tell anyone about what I was doing until the time came to show David.

One night after we finished shooting I asked him if we could go home in his Rolls. Taking a detour, we arrived at the dance hall and entered. When I pulled back the net curtain he was stunned. The fact I had gone ahead and done it behind his back probably gave him as much cause to smile. Here was a relatively cheap solution and one that would save everyone a lot of time. By now, I think David expected me to pull a rabbit out of the hat like this every so often. We didn't have to discuss it, either. It was part of that bond we shared. The scene itself had David in a fix, however. Pulling me to one side during a break, he admitted he was unsure how to shoot it.

"I don't want to do what they always do nowadays, which is just to show them fucking. But I don't want them to accuse me of not being modern, either."

I noticed that Miles, who had just got off her horse, had a red scarf round her neck. "Let him just reach out and pull the scarf in a seductive way," I suggested. "We can watch it slither into the mouth

215

of the fern and they can then begin to clinch. In the climax we can film the dandelion seeds scattering by the wind and drifting away."

David liked the idea and was now feeding off it. "I'll have them fall onto dark water, and you can make me a little pool so that the seeds drift away under a little rock. Then we'll cut to a scene showing agitated leaves backlit by the sun." Today, there is probably no director on earth who would film a love scene like this, but subtlety and good taste are in short supply these days.

Whatever the scene's alleged shortcomings, the real problem was the lack of chemistry between the two lovers. The fact was Cristopher Jones didn't get on with Sarah and was very uncomfortable shooting the scene with her, especially when he had to lean down and kiss her tit. The fellah just couldn't hack it and David got very angry. In the end, it took some pretty practical advice on David's part to get Jones to perform. "Look, it's like this," he said exasperated, leaning down and biting her bosom. Sarah loved it, and I too got into the spirit of the occasion. "Sarah, your nipples are going down, you know, they've got to stay up all the time. I've put this little plastic cup with ice behind this little tuft of grass. Just before we start rolling touch your nipples with it." She did as she was told, but then Sarah was a bit of an eccentric.

Yet, of all the locations and effects in the film, the one that really stood out was the force of the storms – all real and courtesy of the Hand of God. I knew the script called for at least one splendid storm sequence and I felt that this was the ideal place to shoot the scene. However, we both realised that filming under tempestuous conditions would be dangerous. Our solution was to drill into the rock during calm days and cement in ring bolts, through which we threaded chains to hold down our equipment, the cameramen, and a priceless Film Director. Lashed by the winds, the rain and the sea, we shot many of the scenes wearing wetsuits, barely able to stand up, but we soon became adept at shooting in a force eight, then a force ten and finally in a force eleven gale. At the height of the tempest we had rain pouring down the cliff, creating huge waterfalls that somersaulted backwards. It took my breath away and I wondered if the chains would hold. They did, but we still had seven unfinished beach sequences to do. David was desperate and wondered when we would be able to finish the film.

"We can't wait until next summer," he said.

"We'll have to find some other beaches." I replied. "I've seen pictures of beaches down in South Africa."

David suddenly perked up. "When are you going to South Africa?"

"Whenever you like."

"Well, now!" I started getting out of the wetsuit inside his caravan. "Not now, I meant tomorrow. Do you want anybody from the art department with you?"

"No thanks, nobody from the bloody art department, just someone from the money department." I flew down that very next morning with the production manager, a little man called Doug Twiddy, who was a one-eyed, ex-commando and a good friend. We arrived in Cape Town within hours. I skipped the hotel and walked across from the check-in desk to hire a light aircraft. We flew all round the coast and the following morning we took a helicopter to land in those places I'd seen on both sides of Table Mountain the previous day. I took all the pictures and scooped a handful of beach sand into a plastic bag. I then flew back to Ireland through London – all in three days and getting only one night's sleep.

When I got back to the hotel I spotted David, sitting in a corner working late. He looked up, frowning. "I thought you were going to South Africa," he said a little sharply.

"Done that," I replied smugly.

"Don't be silly, Eddie."

Without uttering a word, I emptied the plastic bag containing the sand I had collected in South Africa on the table. "This is for Freddie. Let me know if it matches the colour from the beaches here. If it does we can pack up here and get down to South Africa to finish the film."

All the while I had been crossing my fingers and touching the table. There was a pause and when he finally spoke it touched my heart. "You know Eddie, you're the only one who tells it to me straight. Everyone else says it might be OK, so that I'm the one who falls in the shit if it isn't." We flew to South Africa to film the scene – and I challenge anyone to spot the difference in the film. By now I knew David's requirements at least as well, if not better, than him. Many times at a new location, when he was wandering around looking for shooting angles, I would casually walk to where I felt the best spot was and stand in silence, pretending I was admiring the view. After a while he would wend his way to where I was and I would discreetly move off. Not a word was said, but the truth is we had an almost telepathic understanding after having worked together for so long. David was delighted with the beaches I'd found and he was particularly taken with the rusting ribs of an old steamship protruding from one stretch of sand. "This is where the English officer has to die," he decided. After shooting was completed David asked me to hang around while he cut the film, and while I was sitting around with nothing to do I met a very charming girl who worked at the Skellig Hotel. Before long we started going out, often in the company of David and Sandy for dinner, and when David finished editing and it was time for me to return to Spain I invited Kathleen to join me. She's been with me ever since.

Before wrapping up, I had a little unfinished business with Mitchum. In the final scene where his character is punched in the face as he attempts to rescue Rosie from a baying mob, David kindly offered me the role of the chap who delivers the knock-out blow. Mitchum smelled a rat and thought this was David's way of helping me get even, but the fact was I barely laid a glove on 'Big Mitch'. The film received a knock-out blow of a different kind, however, at the hands of the critics.

David and Sandy went to LA full of confidence – as we all were – to present the film, but Pauline Kael, *The New Yorker's* notoriously crass film critic, was quite scathing. She wrote that it was "gush made respectable by millions of dollars tastefully wasted". She was right about it costing millions, but so did most MGM productions made in the US. She also failed to mention that in those days taste was very often only found in the mouth. MGM's answer to the critics was to promote the film relentlessly, and they even got me to help. For three weeks I raced around the US, appearing on talk-shows, at college campuses and giving more than seventy reviews. I remember talking virtually non-stop and became heartily sick of listening to myself.

But the one exchange which remains with me to this day is not about the movie itself. While waiting to be interviewed outside a New York TV studio I asked a passer by for the time. Looking at me disgustedly he shouted, "Goddamit! There are millions of people in this city and you ask me the time? Why me?" I'm glad I didn't ask him for an opinion on *Ryan's Daughter*. Clearly, things weren't going well. David was convinced the film was good technically, but he secretly agreed with me that it could have been cast better. What finally did it were the disastrous reviews, which left him with such a bitter taste in the mouth that he retreated from the public eye. Worse still, he didn't make another film in fourteen years; years lost not just for him but for the film industry as a whole. The lasting irony, however, is that *Ryan's Duaghter* has since become many people's favourite – particularly with women, who feel it has a particular relevance to them.

CHAPTER 20

One swordfight after another

The Three Musketeers and **The Four Musketeers**, 1973. 105/116 minutes. Fox. Producer: Michael Alexander, Ilya Salkind. Director: Richard Lester. Writer: George MacDonald Fraser (based on the novel by Alexander Dumas). Special Effects: Eddie Fowlie.
Cast: Michael York, Oliver Reed, Raquel Welch, Richard Chamberlain, Frank Finlay, Charlton Heston, Faye Dunaway, Christopher Lee, Geraldine Chaplin, Jean Pierre Cassel, Simon Ward.

All that hard work trying to turn sunny Spain into snow covered Siberia during *Doctor Zhivago* years earlier placed me in good stead for getting another job. I got a call from Sam Spiegel asking me to work on the epic *Nicholas and Alexandra* because I was regarded as a bit of an expert creating 'phoney-baloney' snow; a qualification not recognised by the film industry to this day, I believe, but who cares? I was hired as the film's special effects expert, and the good news is that we would be filming in Madrid with film technicians who knew what they were doing. I hadn't been on the set long when I got a big fat cheque from MGM in appreciation for all the work I'd done promoting *Ryan's Daughter* across the States. The money was gratefully received and while I was away I had a small hotel built in Carboneras on a plot of land I'd bought by the beach. Kathleen helped me to get it up and running but it wasn't easy, as I was running out of cash. Help came in the nick of time in the shape of my old friend Don Chaffey, who arrived in Almería to direct a low-budget film called *Charley One-Eye* with Richard Roundtree. The other unlikely star was a one-eyed chicken, although to this day I don't really know what it was about. I wasn't complaining, though, as we were filming about an hour's drive away in the Tabernas desert, where all the other cowboy films of the period were being made at the time. An offer for a new job in Hungary to work with Richard Lester on *The Three Musketeers* gave me something more positive to think about. I flew with Kathleen to Budapest in search of locations but was disappointed with what I found. The Hungarians wanted to get involved in financing the project and I knew from bitter experience what communists were like when they meddled in film making.

It was nowhere near as bad as Yugoslavia, but when Lester came out I was quite blunt and told him I didn't think this is where we should be making the movie. "It's no good. I can't find good enough locations."

Lester looked horrified. "Well don't tell the Salkinds, or they won't make the film."

"Yeah but I can't tell them a lie, because in the end I'll be wearing it."

"Don't tell them," he pleaded, "there's no need to; let's just get the movie started."

I stood my ground. "No, I'm not going to do that, I've got to tell them."

I did, but didn't want to leave without at least trying to come up with an alternative. I bumped into Alex Salkind at the studio in Budapest and tried to reassure him. "Give me a week in Spain and I'll have all the locations for this movie...but don't tell the Hungarians you're leaving." The reason for all the subterfuge was simple: we were going to renege on the deal. Within five days I had enough locations ready to persuade the Salkinds to change their minds. The fact is it was always easier to film in Spain because the authorities never put up any objections and bent over backwards to have films shot in their country. But there was an added incentive for film makers: officials were also easy to bribe.

Once in Spain it took us a week to find all the locations and the vast array of technicians with whom I had worked on other film projects. The producers gave the okay and the film was on again. I realised that this was going to be a very different sort of film from the ones Richard had got me used to working on. There were the usual stream of gags and last minute requests from Richard, but the locations were far more beautiful and interesting. We shot at the Royal Palace in Madrid, the Summer Palace in Aranjuez, the Palace Gardens in Segovia, the streets of Toledo and the famous monastery in El Escorial. Our musketeers – Oliver Reed, Michael York, Richard Chamberlain and Frank Finlay – were superb and with Roy Kinnear as the stooge the laughs were guaranteed. Christopher Lee was also a real heavyweight, this time as the villain, and needed very little direction from Richard. Americans Charlton Heston, Faye Dunaway and Raquel Welch – as Spike Milligan's unlikely wife – completed the star cast. The film also gave me an opportunity to work with swords once again. God knows why they were called musketeers because they were never seen within a mile of a musket. Instead, I was asked to produce hundreds of rapiers: trick ones, telescopic ones, telescopic ones with blood on them, as well as swords to stick, pierce, or slice into something; virtually anything, in fact, as long as it didn't kill or maim anyone. I got stuck into sword production, and in Toledo, (one of the world's most famous sword-making centres) I gained a lot of useful knowledge hanging around the many workshops, where I also met an expert swordsman from the mountains of Montenegro. He had set up his own business in the town and kindly produced the more exotic swords which were required for the film. Toledo also served as a wonderful backdrop and I helped convert the square outside the cathedral into a market place.

All seemed to be running smoothly, but unbeknown either to me or the cast, the producers had hatched a cunning plan to get more bangs for their bucks by making two films, not one. The problem was that the actors had been contracted to make only one film, and when they found out what the producers were planning they went spare and charged Producer Alexander Salkind in lieu of the second, which became *The Four Musketeers*. It's impossible to know what effect, if any, this had on the actors' performances, although I'm convinced the fight scene involving Raquel Welch and Faye Dunaway was not entirely staged. I sensed there was bad blood between the two of them, more so with Faye, who kept herself to herself and always chose to retire to her caravan when her scenes were done. By contrast Raquel, with whom I'd already worked before, was outgoing and far more amiable with the crew. During the fight I noticed that although Raquel was big in the obvious places, she was in fact fine-boned and in truth would have been no match for Faye if the fight had been for real.

In one scene, where Raquel had to hide from Richelieu's men in the market place, Richard thought it would be appropriate for her to do so in a pile of melons. I wonder why. It wasn't just the human characters who appeared over-sexed. Geraldine Chaplin had a pet pug dog by her side that was continually humping people's legs. It became such a nasty little habit that Geraldine threw him out of her caravan after one of his uncontrollable fits of passion. Unable to find relief in the caravan, he turned his attention to a large female dog running around the set. The little pug lost his mind, frantically trying to mount this canine goddess. Feeling sorry for him, one of the grips got an apple box – a sort of stool normally used to give actors more height – to help him rise to the occasion. Once in place, the bitch backed up to it. The pug didn't need telling twice. He quickly mounted and humped the bitch to his and, presumably, her heart's content. It was unquestionably the highlight of his career and was cheered on by many of the crew who voted him an Oscar – something no actor on *The Three Musketeers* managed to achieve. I hate to think what the puppies must have looked like, though.

Joking aside, the actors playing the Musketeers were all hardworking types and I had no problem with any of them except for Oliver Reed, who was a bully by nature and was always demanding and difficult to work with. Richard, with all his usual charm and diplomacy, managed to ride along with it and often turned it into an advantage, but the rest of us learned to be careful with Ollie, more so when he was drinking (which he did for most of the time). We found the best way of dealing with Ollie's often loutish behaviour was to pander to him. There was no better example of this than during a sword fighting scene with Christopher Lee. Perhaps because Lee was very handy with a rapier and was showing Ollie up a bit that he turned to me in the middle of the scene, looking very flustered. "This sword's unbalanced!" he spluttered. I took the offending rapier, gravely nodding my head and promising to "get a better one right away".

Out of sight behind the set, I turned and hurried back again, handing him the exact, same sword. "Try this one Ollie," I said, smiling confidently.

He took it and waved it about like an Olympic fencing expert. "That's better," he announced and got on with the scene.

Fortunately, there were enough challenges on the job not to have to worry too much about temper tantrums. Richard came up with the clever idea of having a huge sword fight on ice between all the four Musketeers and Richelieu's men. As there was no snow around Madrid during the summer months I knew I would have to reprise the work I did on *Doctor Zhivago* by designing another frozen lake. In the event it was shot on a record hot day in a shallow valley. I dug holes filled with water where a swordsman could break through the ice and fall in. These were covered with broken sheets of thick Styrofoam and sprayed with wax. Richard wanted two such holes close to each other so that two men would sink very slowly as they reached across the remaining ice to continue the fight. To regulate the speed at which the men sank, I placed elevators controlled from the camera position. For it to be totally convincing, the frozen lake had to be at least as slippery as an ice rink. At a factory which made wax polish I had them fill drums of the white stuff, which we splashed everywhere and fine sprayed with water. In the event, it turned out to be too slippery. Nobody could walk on it and the crew could hardly photograph the action. The crew all fell about in hysterics, but it was probably one of the funniest sword fight scenes ever.

We staged another sword fight, which was almost as funny, in a big laundry and dining room with great vats of dye, all attended to – naturally – by buxom young girls. We added ropes and lines from which the musketeers could swing, or fall into the vats, while fighting. I used every kind of trick sword in the arsenal for this, and for another scene in the Musketeers' gymnasium I even built sword-fighting machines. I fed off Richard, who kept dreaming up gags on the spur of the moment, often leaving me with no time to prepare. It seemed almost like a game for him, as if he were trying to catch me out, so I had to anticipate his every move.

Once, he started kidding that I should include loads of rats in a scene. I didn't take him seriously at first but when he moaned that there was a rat catcher but no rats for him to catch I blurted, "They got away, Richard, but I'll get you some more." And I did, in a manner of speaking. I couldn't find any rats so I got hold of a bunch of guinea pigs and stuck pieces of string on their backsides to look like tails. "Here's your rats, Richard." Always be ready to improvise, I say.

The film crew moved to an old monastery on top of a high hill on the road to Valencia to shoot a scene in an empty church under a huge disk of coloured light emanating from an enormous, circular stained-glass window. Richard wanted to include a fire inside a huge wooden structure like a multi-storey barn, while a fierce sword fight between Reed and Lee takes place inside the church. The blaze was so fierce that the camera crew shot the scene far away using long lenses. I had the structure rigged to collapse on cue, which was relatively easy except for the fact that I also had to protect the church wall. To solve this, I had it painted with silicone. It worked brilliantly and no damage was done. To celebrate the end of production we had a huge end of film party, which was like a red rag to a bull for someone like Reed. He got wildly drunk and smashed up the venue, frightening the poor locals so much that they called the Civil Guard. They were thoroughly bemused by Ollie's antics, but a few calming words from the producers and Richard seemed to do the trick and we managed to assuage Franco's bovver boys.

The film was, in fact, incomplete and needed one final battle scene. The problem was that there was no set, no location and – more importantly – no more money. Nevertheless, that was the end as far as the crew were concerned. I thought about it and decided the battle scene could be done in my own backyard where we filmed Aqaba in *Lawrence of Arabia*. I scribbled details of the proposed scene and sent it to the producers. We then got the crew together and built fifteen period field guns, and on a low hill put up the base of the fortress with a very tall pole and a flag flying on the top. The rest of the fortress was painted onto a piece of glass, which the camera shot the scene through – a glass shot, as it's called. All I had to do was to ensure that the smoke from my cannons and the dust from the battle didn't rise up from the real action and disappear behind the painted bit on the glass. When we finished the scene and had it all in the can, I got in the car and drove over the hill back home. The phone rang just as I stepped indoors. It was David, inviting us to visit him and Sandy in Rome.

CHAPTER 21

Different tights for different folks

David enjoyed driving almost more than he loved making films, and he loved women virtually as much. The problem was that while he was an expert at the first two he wasn't much good with women. All his relationships eventually turned sour and David, like most people, was partly to blame for that. The fact was he didn't like anyone else taking centre stage and he certainly liked his women to remain in the background. I don't think he was strictly aware of it, but there's no doubt in my mind that he thrived being in control. It's as if he ran his life with the same, often despotic rigour as when directing a film. I suspect his dad was a bit like that. He didn't like David much and once said he wasn't worth educating. Such a cruel remark must have left a big scar, but it didn't prevent David from admiring his late brother, Edward. "You're like a brother to me," he often said to me, and knowing how he felt towards his older sibling I took it as a great compliment. But if David was seeking a lifelong partner, and in spite of all his previous failures, I think he found her in Sandy. It seemed – for a while, at least – that things on this front were looking much brighter for him.

In the succeeding years after the commercial and critical failure of *Ryan's Daughter*, David more or less disappeared from the public eye, but it was during this period that I got to know him much better. Free from the constraints of filming, David dropped his guard and we took the opportunity to socialise together with our respective partners a lot more. Our trip to Rome, where David was living at the time with Sandy, was the first of many such visits and tours. Driving along the Via Veneto past long rows of exclusive properties that were fenced behind high walls (which I suspected were designed to keep people out as well as to hem the owners in), I got the feeling this was not a particularly safe area to live in. There was even a police station built specifically to guard the complex. I stopped to ask directions and just then, in the distance, I saw David step out into the middle of the road to greet us. Later in the house Sandy told me that David had been sitting quietly in the living room, when he suddenly got up and said "Eddie is about to arrive." Once

226

again, David had made a reference to the telepathic link I was convinced we shared.

My doubts about the Via Veneto were confirmed some time later when David and Sandy were burgled in the middle of the night. Although nothing happened to them, the incident convinced David it would be safer to make a more permanent home in London. Soon afterwards he bought two adjoining, bombed out warehouses in Limehouse, in London's Docklands, and set about building a home and riverside garden. In the meantime, he stayed in hotels which he used as a base for his frequent visits abroad. It was a great life.

When we were in London David often invited us to dine at The Savoy Hotel Riverside Restaurant, where he booked his favourite table by a window, overlooking the river and his beloved great London trees. He seemed so happy that on one occasion, while having dinner, he suddenly stood up and started dancing along to the orchestra like a young man. He seemed to be putting the critical and commercial failure of *Ryan's Daughter* well behind him and it was heartening to see. They may have killed his love for making films, I concluded, but for now at least he seemed to be over the disappointment and was taking it in his stride.

I, on the other hand, was still very much active and before leaving London I got a message to go to Paris to meet Roman Polanski, who was planning to make a film about pirates. When I met him in his apartment he wasted no time in asking me details on how best to film galleons. But I was turned off from doing the project when I found out he was going to be working with a French crew. All he wanted was the benefit of my experience of filming at sea, and although I didn't have a problem with that and was willing to pass on a lot of my hard-earned knowledge, I wasn't keen on getting involved beyond that. The doubts I had about the professionalism of our Gallic friends were more than justified when I later learned that a French designer had built a great cumbersome raft with a mock-up of a Galleon fixed on top that could barely move. *Pirates* was eventually made in North Africa but it was bloody awful. One of the most important considerations when filming a boat is that it should be manoeuvrable; you must be able to move it around because all the ropes make shadows that shift with the sun. This is why I always fitted four anchors to a ship to help reposition it as and when required.

Kathleen and I spent a few days in Paris at Alexander Salkind's invitation. We stayed in an hotel and spent hours talking movies with him, his son Ilyia and his wife, Bertha. During our conversations the idea of filming *Superman* was broached by an excited Ilya, who tried to hire me for the project and kept dropping heavy hints such as "How would you like to do that?" and "Think of all the special effects you could do!". I had a feeling that my work on *The Three Musketeers* had pleased them, so I played along and suggested making the film in Spain. While he thought about it, I was hired to do the props and the special effects for another film about a hero in tights – albeit one with substantially fewer powers.

On returning to Spain I quickly got down to work on *Robin and Marian*, another great movie project of Richard Lester's. His old friend from The Beatles' days, Denis O'Dell, was the producer, with Sean Connery cast as Robin and Audrey Hepburn as Marian. This version of the thief who stole from the rich to give to the poor was, if not the most exciting, certainly the most moving and humane attempt at retelling the popular story. Connery was an older, war-weary Robin returning from the Crusades and hoping to relive the good old times as though nothing had changed in the intervening years. His efforts to re-unite all his merry men backfire for the most part, but his failed attempt to woo Maid Marian, who has now become a nun in a secluded monastery, provides the pathos to the story. At least that was the plot, but it was far more interesting behind the scenes. I suspect Sean – being a true Scot – wore pretty much nothing below his leather-like kilt, which was also an odd-looking piece of costume. Evidently not everyone agreed on the set. In the scenes where he was required to climb up the branches of trees I noticed how female crew members would often pass below and glance upwards, perhaps hoping to get a big surprise. As for Audrey, she had a real youthful sense of fun. On one occasion I was asked to bring her to the set, as the Assistant Director had "lost her". What they didn't know is that I had hidden her – at her request – and that she would not appear until she was ready to be found. To help her disappearing act she stayed in an old stone cottage in the forest where I kept my props. I peered round the door and shouted out, "Come on kid, you're on!"

She jumped to her feet and put her arms around me, squealing in delight, "Nobody has called me 'kid' in years!"

It looked as though it would turn out to be yet another great game like the ones I used to play at Hampton Court and Bushy Park as a child, where I acted the role of Robin Hood and cast the parts of the other kids, except that we didn't have a Maid Marian. As we started preparing the set in Pamplona, I couldn't help but wonder why Hemingway had been so attracted to it, save for the fact that he was obviously drawn to the unpleasant and thoroughly cruel activity of the Bull Run. Although we stayed at a good hotel it was impossible to sleep at night without having to endure the raucous singing of groups of drunken men in the streets below. It was all too much for this film specialist, and as soon as we found our main location, Kathleen and I moved to a countryside hotel not far away for a bit of peace and quiet.

While rapiers were needed for the musketeer films, bows and arrows (English longbows, to be precise) were the order of the day for this movie. Like the swords, I trained arrows to perform all manner of tricks, from flying down an invisible tight wire, to sticking to tree trunks – or people – and flying high over the parapets of castles. The phrase 'I-shot-an arrow-into-the-air-it-fell-to-earth-I-know-not-where' did not apply to me or my compressed air, arrow-firing machine.

The main set was Robin's forest hideaway made in a hollow of a depression, constructed by me with tree branches and totally camouflaged from the outside. It was so roomy and comfortable that we decided to film inside it. You could say I'd had a lot of experience with this type of set, having built many as a boy on the sides of the River Thames near Petersham. Little did I know back then that I was doing an apprenticeship. *Robin and Marian* was without doubt one of the most enjoyable films I ever worked on, thanks in no small measure to Richard Lester and cameraman David Watkin. Richard was always ready with a prank while David was totally laid back and a barrel of laughs. Besides being a top man at his job, David's confidence in everything he did was quite inspiring. Having lit the set, it was normal to see him sitting in his director's chair with a newspaper over his face, sleeping soundly whilst confusion and mayhem reigned all around him. Electricians throughout the business fondly nicknamed him 'Wendy' – a moniker which stuck and was later given to a battery of encased lights he invented to floodlight from a great height.

By far the cleverest of the lot, though, was Ronnie Barker. He may have been a comedian, but he was super-sharp. If he noticed anything remotely odd, he would instantly apply a wickedly funny line to describe or lampoon it. One evening alone in his hotel, he recorded a monologue about the crew to while away the time. He gave a copy to some of us – I still have mine. Here's the transcript of it:

This is the story of bold Robin Hood and his band of obscene merry men.

You've not heard it before and I fear, what is more, you're not likely to hear it again.

It's the story of robbers who live in the woods with the catering vans and the rabbits.

It's the story of farmers in big green pyjamas and nuns with extraordinary habits.

Now Robin came home from the wars with his friend – the one friend he counted upon.

A guy big and mean, known as Tiny Latrine, whom Robin renamed Little John.

Now, the man that our heroes had come home to kill was the bold Sheriff Shaw of Nebraska, who was living in sin in a room full of gin in a clip-joint they called the Alaska.

The man was a coward. He walked round the town in chain mail – the thicker, the better. He was nervous as heck, so when he had sex he would always put on a chain letter.

Now young Robin had failed – ever since he was twelve – to seduce a young virgin named Marian. You could touch her crotch but not very much 'cause her mother was strict Presbyterian.

One day, she strolled past the butchers' in town, saw Robin and shouted 'What ho!'

She hoped he'd turn round 'cause she owed him a pound 'cause he'd given her one years ago.

But he just walked ahead, past a shop that sold bread and he waved to old Stanley, the baker. He waggled a finger at the street corner singer and two at the town undertaker.

So she ran down the street and was cheered by the crowd 'cause her tits were such wonderful wobblers.

So pleased it was he, she sank to one knee and kissed him just down by the cobblers.

So next morn in the wood, there she lay with young Hood, she was driving him out of his wits. And the Sheriff, she spied, 'Buenas Knockers!' he cried, which is Spanish for beautiful tits.

'Take no notice,' said Marian, 'bold Sheriff Shaw is renowned for these kinds of offences.' But Robin moved quick and grabbing a brick gave him one in his weekly expenses.

Then Sir Ranulph rode up with a hat like a stove, but Burmans had dropped a big clanger. It stayed on OK but it faced the wrong way, which forced him to look back in anger.

Then into the picture stepped Denis O'Dell, who had come up to see the fiesta.

Though he'd set out alone he was tailed unbeknown by two dicks, known as Shepherd and Lester.

Then the shooting broke out. It was such a good fight that nobody wanted to spoil it.

Will Scarlett had fun, shot a horse and a nun, while Tuck shot his bolt in the toilet.

All the peasants joined in with bold Robin's gay band – they turned in their tens and in twenties. The men in the farms were all up in arms and old Jack was up his apprentice!

All the soldiers refused to go into the wood, so they brought up the women to rally 'em.

Old Friar Tuck said 'I'll try a fuck!' and Will Scarlett said 'I'll try a valium'.

Now bold Sheriff's army was big, fit and fast. They arrived in a lorry each day.

But poor Robin's was small and no use at all, so he just couldn't get it away.

So his brave little band were all slaughtered that day, split asunder from top and to bottom.

They crouched behind trees with their hands on their knees – yes, the catering had finally got 'em!

Now Nottingham Forest is once more serene, not a hint of that previous menace.

But it shows it don't pay to stand in the way of Dusty two dicks and a Denis!

After the film was in the can we drove to London to see David and Sandy's progress with the new house. From there, we went back to Budapest at the request of Alexander Salkind to recce and cost for a film script written by his charming Mexican wife Bertha. It was a strange and unusual story about a community of characters who lived in the drains below Paris. She hoped to get Peter O'Toole to play the leader of these people, and among the plot's many twists and turns there was to be a flood that would sweep the domain away. After looking at many caves and tunnels, as well as some wine vaults, I decided that although costly in financial terms and special effects, the film could be done. We submitted the project to Alex, who had the infinitely harder task of finding the finance to make it. As it turned out, he was unable to find the cash and the project was shelved. But before I had time to digest the fact, a copy of *The Prince and the Pauper* was dropped on my desk with a message asking me to find locations as a script was being prepared for a film adaptation of Mark Twain's work. Budapest was ideal for many reasons, including its wonderful architecture…and the fact that I was already there. However, the country was quite run down, thanks to the Communists and the telltale signs of shrapnel on buildings; the aftermath of the violent struggle to throw the Russians out during the 1956 rising.

We ended up in a nice little medieval border town called Sopron near Vienna, where we dropped off script writer George MacDonald Fraser. He crossed the border to catch a plane and promised to be back with a completed screenplay within three weeks, which he did. Having previously seen Vienna's sewerage system, I knew that they were remarkably commodious, with clean lit sidewalks and barges. It was also where some of the scenes were filmed for *The Third Man*. I did note, however, that the Danube was anything but 'blue'. Looking down from the famous Széchenyi Chain Bridge, the river was in fact grey and filthy, with all kinds of stuff floating by, including hundreds of used condoms. Walking back home after a drink on our first day we passed a college of music and heard a rendition of *Happy Days are Here Again* blaring out from one of the open windows. Ever since that day in the middle of the desert when I heard Colonel Bogey's March blasting through the radio as we were about to start filming *Lawrence of Arabia*, I always looked for a sign – an omen – before embarking on a new project; it wasn't something I openly spoke about with the rest of the crew and it certainly wasn't a precondition for working on a film, but it nonetheless gave me a small ripple of excitement to sense it.

There was also no question that Hungary was an infinitely happier place than, say, Yugoslavia. After shooting finished I was asked once again by the Salkinds if I wanted to do *Superman*. They suggested I check the Samuel Bronston Studios in Madrid, which had been the home of many big Hollywood productions in the past. Bronston, however, owed the banks a lot of money and fled town before the studios were embargoed. When I got there I found them in a very sorry state but felt they could be made to work. After initial enquiries the bank seemed very co-operative, but the socialist mayor of Madrid (showing a calamitous lack of vision) put a spanner in the works and had the studios pulled down. In their place, some ghastly workers' apartments were erected instead. That put a lid on it for good and was the main reason why *Superman* went to Pinewood in England. Undeterred, the Salkinds still wanted me to work on the film and asked me to fly to England, but I declined for a number of reasons; the main one being that I didn't want to work on a British studio-based film.

A straight jacket

Back in England, we got another invitation to join David and Sandy in London. While having dinner with David at the Barclay Hotel, the head waiter came up and pointed at a man in a chauffeur's uniform standing in the lobby who had instructions to deliver something to me. Feeling somewhat embarrassed by all the fuss with David looking on I was then handed a package containing a script for the film *Full Metal Jacket*. In an envelope was a note signed by Stanley Kubrick, asking me to read the script that same night and to be his guest for lunch at his home the very next day. Later in my room I went over the script in more detail, but it quickly became clear to me that this was not a film I wanted to get involved with at all. Scenes of soldiers standing all round a recruit and pissing on him were not my kind of stuff, so I forgot about the whole thing...until the next day, when I got a phone call from Kubrick himself. "Now that you've read my script you'll want to do the movie," he said, taking it for granted that I would naturally want to work for him.

I hated to burst his bubble, but I had been manoeuvred into an awkward situation. "I'm not too sure about that, Stanley," I replied between gritted teeth.

"Well, come and have lunch and we'll talk about it, anyway," he insisted.

Everyone knew Kubrick was a perfectionist but he also had a bad reputation for treating film crews with disdain. Working with a prickly director was nothing new, but I drew the line at treating the people who worked under you like muck. I also heard that Ken Adam had ended up in the nut-house for a while after working for him on a film, and that was the sort of extra baggage I was not prepared to take on with the job. I drove all the way up to north London to his home near Borehamwood film studios, where he owned a large plot of land that included a village, no less. When I arrived he greeted me with open arms and ushered me into his office. The first thing he did was to offer me lunch, consisting of a stale-looking sandwich which he unceremoniously thrust into my hands. As I gazed at it intently he sounded off with all the bluster of a typical Hollywood film director: everything was bigger, louder, noisier and more expensive. "I've fired the art director and I want you to go to the site of the old Beckton gas works and turn it into a Vietnam battleground right away!" He obviously hadn't been listening to a word I'd said the day before.

"I'm not going to do it, Stanley," I said, interrupting him in full flow. You could have heard a pin drop.

"What do you mean you're not going to do it?"

"Well, it's like this Stanley," I said, trying to be as tactful as possible. "You make great movies, but you have a certain reputation with your crews and I've decided not to get involved in it." I can't recall much after that, although I do remember not finishing my sandwich.

I never saw him again and although the film eventually got made and became quite a success without me, I didn't regret not taking the job on. I decided a long time ago that I would pick and choose the films I wanted to work on, and there was nothing about Kubrick or his film that inspired me enough to make me want to change my mind. Fortunately, I didn't have time to ponder over my decision. David and Sandy were going on a trip around the USA in his Roller, which they arranged to ship across on the QE2. As they were about to board I gave David a book I'd read about Captain Bligh written by John Howe, which had been Book of the Year. I had written a short treatment on it and suggested he might read it. "Chuck it over the side if it's no good," I added, and thought no more about it. We drove back to Spain, but not for long as I was about to fly to Athens to film *The Greek Tycoon* with Anthony Quinn and Jacqueline Bisset.

The Greek Tycoon, 1978. 107 minutes. Universal Pictures.
Producer: Allen Klein, Ely Landau. Director: J. Lee Thompson. Writer: Morton S Fine.
Cast: Anthony Quinn, Jacqueline Bisset, Raf Vallone, James Franciscus.

Anthony Quinn was a Greek tycoon who was having an affair with the wife of an American president who happened to look remarkably like Jacqueline Kennedy. Quinn's character may have been called Theo Tomasis, but it didn't take a genius to figure out that the film was really about the shipping magnate Aristotle Onassis. We were making a film about a filthy rich couple alright, but the producers told me they were short of cash and could not afford the expensive props that were needed. As always it was left to me to sort things out.

When I arrived in Athens I wasted no time in rubbing shoulders with many of the city's richest men with a view to getting all the props I'd need at bargain basement prices, or even better, for nothing. Visiting many luxury yachts – most of which seemed to spend their time moored in the harbour – it was clear that they were being used more as status symbols than fully working vessels. It didn't come as a surprise then that the idle rich were keen as mustard about having their expensive but inactive playthings paraded on film. We were soon knee-deep in yachts, Rolls-Royces, Ferraris and helicopters, most of which were loaned to me free of charge. For the scene of the wedding party there had to be a crowd of yachts sailing around the harbour celebrating the event. One was a magnificent sailing ship I had previously spotted aboard a helicopter while scouting for boats. As I flew over it, it appeared to be crewed by a bunch of completely naked young women. Convinced the unusual crew had brilliantly captured the mood of the film, I asked the owner if he was interested in having his boat appear in the movie. Needless to say, the young American jumped at the chance. It was much later that he revealed that the boat was not only not his but that he wasn't a millionaire. It turned out he had got

235

into the habit of spending the large salary he earned on the rental of the craft for himself and his numerous lady friends for a set period each year. When he told me that his real job was inspecting the sewers of New York I nearly fell off my chair, particularly as he worked for only six months of the year! If true, he certainly made the best of a bad job.

We dashed to Crete to shoot some additional scenes before returning to Athens for some night shots on Tomasis's yacht. But shortly afterwards, in the early hours of the morning, the production manager Eric Rattray came on board and told me to get in touch with David Lean at Warner Studios in Los Angeles. It seems he had desperately been trying to contact me.

When I phoned him, he sounded quite worked up. "Where are you? We've been looking all over the world for you!" I told him what I was doing, but he wasn't listening. "Get over here right away," he insisted. "Come over to the Bel-Air Hotel. We're going to do your thing."

At first, I wasn't sure what he was talking about and then the penny dropped. I couldn't believe it, but it seems David had read my treatment on Howe's book about Bligh, after all. I rushed back, but knew *The Greek Tycoon* was now history as far as I was concerned. I wondered how I would go about telling the Production Manager that I was no longer going to be working on the film. "Look," I said, "we've only got two weeks to go and all the rest of it is on the bloody boat, so you don't really need me anymore." To my relief, they were very good about it and released me without any fuss. If only all productions managers were like this.

CHAPTER 22

Living the life

When we touched down at Los Angeles airport I wasn't expecting to get the sort of red carpet treatment normally reserved for movie moguls. I couldn't quite work out why I was being fussed over and why I was being introduced to all the top brass at Warner Brothers'. Then I realised this was all David's doing. He had evidently told everyone in Hollywood that I was the mastermind behind the new version of *The Mutiny on the Bounty* story. I can't pretend it wasn't an enjoyable experience – it was – but the real kick was watching how David had been re-energised by the project. There was no doubt in my mind that it had rekindled his enthusiasm for making films, and I felt doubly pleased thinking that perhaps I'd played some part in this. His enthusiasm was threatening to run away with him, however. During a brief respite from all the hullabaloo he pulled me to one side and confided that he wanted to make not one but two films, and then suggested I be the producer as well. I was mortified by the idea and told him that I was "not that kind of man". I knew my strengths and weaknesses, and wheeling and dealing like some cockney version of Sam Spiegel was not my thing. The project had also whetted the appetite of other big fish and Robert Bolt came out to California, revelling in the five-star treatment like the rest of us, although he was clearly more used to it than me. The decision was then made for us to fly out to Tahiti to look for locations, little realising that it would turn out to be a four-year, all mod-cons holiday.

Our first stop was the Rangiroa Atoll, one the biggest atolls in the world close to Tahiti, which David was determined to see, having flown over it many years before. He was convinced we could use it as a giant tank in which to shoot the entire film, but I quickly put him off the idea as it was totally impractical. Nevertheless, the stopover was exactly what the doctor ordered; we stayed in native huts with all the amenities, cruising around all day long in a Boston Whaler and taking pictures while Robert and David got on with the script. John Box had also come out to work on the film as Art Director and the five of us (David, Sandy, Kathleen, John and me) spent day after day cruising around the huge atoll. John hated it. He quickly got bored with the lack of activity, and when he decided to go back to the UK for Christmas David hit the roof. The truth, however uncomfortable it may have been, was that we hadn't done anything yet. While David and Robert had been working on the screenplay the rest of us twiddled our thumbs in Bora Bora with nothing to do. Personally, I wasn't bothered at all because I was definitely enjoying my time in paradise. I once came ashore aboard a canoe, dressed as Santa Claus, ringing a bell and handing out gifts to old American lady tourists at the hotel. I can't quite remember what made me do this, but living on a small tropical island for long periods does funny things to you. Kathleen and I later flew to Samoa where I met my old friend Aggie Gray. We also went to Tonga and the Cook Islands for a few days and spent a couple of nights with David and Sandy in Aitutaki; a huge blue lagoon where the Bounty mutineers went first in their search for a safe haven.

All this was of no interest to John, who was clearly feeling like a spare part. It was all heading for an unpleasant showdown. John still wouldn't budge and David, looking irate, pressed him further. "Are you with me on this film or not, John?" The answer was not what David wanted to hear from one of his band of 'Dedicated Maniacs'.

"I'll have to ask Doris," he feebly replied, referring to his wife.

David reacted in his predictably explosive way. "In that case, you may as well go…and don't come back!" he shouted.

John left, feeling quite humiliated and knowing that it was virtually impossible to gain David's trust once you lost it. Despite this, as soon as he got back to Hollywood he foolishly started spreading a nasty rumour that David Lean had gone mad and was going to spend fifty million dollars on a film that didn't even have a script. When we got to hear about John's folly, David quickly set about an exercise in damage limitation and went on the attack by publicly announcing what we all already knew; he was going to make not one but two back-to-back films about the aftermath of the mutiny, and for far less money than had been suggested.

While this was going on, I rented an apartment in the harbour, right in the middle of Papeete. It became our home for the next three years and we used it as a base from which to fly to the other islands in search of locations. There was only one downside. Because of immigration rules I was advised – nay, forced – to take French citizenship. Seeing as we were having so much fun I concluded that it was a small price to pay for living in such splendour. To show we meant business we started building *The Bounty* in New Zealand at a cost of some six million dollars, using the original drawings of the ship which were kept in Greenwich but with far more sophisticated interiors. I flew back to England to do more research on the film and while at the National Maritime Museum in Greenwich, I came across Captain James Cook's log book. In it, he recounted an incident that almost cost him his ship while negotiating Tahiti's dangerous coral reefs. It seems Cook was forced to cut one of the anchors adrift when his men were unable to prise their ship free. Since then, historians and other experts had been baffled as to the anchor's exact whereabouts. Most were convinced it lay some way out of a natural lagoon called Cook's Anchorage, on the far side of the island, but they had drawn a blank. With time on my hands I thought I'd have a go at finding the damned thing, convinced that the mystery needed to be approached from an entirely different angle.

While filming *Ryan's Daughter* almost a decade earlier I spent hours observing the storms and the behaviour of the waves. Any ship sailing through a group of small islands would be at the mercy of these. Back in Tahiti, I sat down to observe a pass through a reef where there were strong currents. I reckoned that this was the spot where Cook's ship had been sailing through when he lost his anchor. While pondering over how I'd get hold of the necessary diving gear to explore the area, I chanced on a French–Tahitian called Charlie Lehartel who happened to be a wonderful skin-diver. It didn't take much to convince him to dive in the area where I'd roughly calculated Cook's anchor could lay buried.

After a few fairly deep dives, and just as we were about to call it a day, he rose to the surface with a big smile on his face. "What kind of an anchor is it?" he innocently inquired.

Biting my lip, I tried to remain calm. "Well Charley, it'll be a big one," I replied, awkwardly gesturing with my hands as if discussing the size of a fish.

He grinned at me like a Cheshire cat. "Eddie, there's a ring this big sticking out of the coral!"

We went back to the site the following day, this time with a small underwater camera. There was no question about it; it was the long lost anchor. When news of our find got out all hell broke loose. A museum curator from New Zealand flew out to verify the anchor's authenticity and a scramble ensued, with the New Zealand and French Governments – as well as Whitby, Cook's home town – all claiming ownership. As for myself, I didn't give a monkeys, I was just happy to have found it. Not someone to miss an opportunity to film something interesting, David decided he would salvage the anchor *and* shoot a forty-minute documentary about the salvage operation, with a Robert Bolt script thrown in for good measure. David was very happy for me and announced to the world that "Eddie was right and everyone else was wrong", in reference to the hundreds of so-called experts who had been unable to find the anchor.

Ever the perfectionist, David ordered that the anchor be carefully released from its coral trap and kept below the water line until he was fully set up to show it breaking the surface. He got the anchor moved to shallower waters, where the light was better and the anchor could be seen in all its glory. We also brought in massive underwater vacuum cleaners to remove the coral without damaging it. Meticulous as ever, David also had a wooden replica built on shore so that he could work out camera angles and the divers' positions before shooting a single frame of film. To cap it all, we had a welcoming party of Tahitian girls in traditional costume waiting on shore as the anchor was hoisted out of the water. The presence of a destroyer from the French Fleet was a bit too much for both David and I to stomach, however, so he rushed to include a rendition of *Rule Britannia* as a subtle riposte. I still smile thinking about it today. But the truth is we felt like we were all buggering about a bit and that the anchor was a mere sideshow to the real reason we were here.

We soon got down to the job at hand, which was to complete the exact replica of the *Bounty*. Inevitably, we used modern materials, and although the ship was clad in wood with a copper bottom, we also installed air conditioning inside for obvious reasons. At one stage we considered making the film in New Zealand and I went down to meet government officials to make them a proposition, but the abusive double taxation system put the lid on that idea. In the hope that we could strike some sort of deal I spoke to Prime Minister Muldoon at his home, who directed me to his finance minister. "If you don't get any satisfaction there come back to see me and I'll fix it," he pledged. If there was one thing I had learned in films is that it's important to have friends in high places if you want to get things done.

Meanwhile, I did a lot of reconnaissance in New Zealand, flying all round the North and South Island coasts (some seventeen times, according to my calculations). On one occasion, I instructed the pilot to buzz the sea at the height of a ship's deck so that I could take some pictures. The manoeuvre was going fine until the plane suddenly jolted, almost causing me to lose the camera. "Sorry – nearly bumped into a whale," the pilot said nervously.

When I got back, I heard that the rumours spread by John Box had taken root. It was all very unfortunate, more so because the film hadn't cost any real money yet. We sat down and carefully worked out the cost and calculated a budget of around thirty-seven million dollars to make both films. Although it vindicated David, since it was well below John's extravagant estimates, the damage had been done: Warner Brothers announced that it was pulling out, leaving us high and dry.

Unwilling to give up now that we had got this far, we looked to get independent backing. David's agent told him Dino De Laurentiis was keen to take the project on, and after contacting him he agreed to come over and see for himself. As soon as De Laurentiis arrived he asked me to go over the locations with his brother, but I don't think we got off to the best start. As he got in the car he asked me – a lifelong anti-smoker – if he could smoke a cigarette. "Ok," I replied, slamming my foot on the accelerator so hard that he was unable to light up. We drove over to the far side of the island at breakneck speed and stopped the car (much to Laurentiis' relief) beyond Cook's Anchorage at a fabulous location. De Laurentiis must have been impressed because he turned to his brother, who had recently been doing reconnaissance (in a helicopter, if you please!) for the film *Hurricane* in Bora Bora, and gave him a huge bollocking in Italian. There's nothing more humiliating than hurt pride for some and things went rapidly downhill after that. De Laurentiis came along to speak to David about the project with his daughter Raffaella in tow, but it was patently clear that the two weren't going to hit it off. They all sat in the room, with Raffaella watching as David and his Italian counterpart knocked the proverbial stuffing out of each other.

"You are not going to be the producer," David spat, "because I've got a producer – you are the presenter."

De Laurentiis was having none of it and announced his intention of placing his daughter Raffaella – who by now was in tears – in the producer's hot seat. Words were spoken and at one stage David even accused Laurentiis of being a Mafioso. As they came out of the meeting, and once De Laurentiis was gone, David turned to me and said in a matter-of-fact way, "I think I've just sabotaged the movie." As he recounted the meeting, I was unable to suppress a wry smile, imagining David calmly telling a man of De Laurentiis' stature who was boss. Despite the unpleasant exchange De Laurentiis agreed to send out his man with me to do a recce and budget for the movie. But it was all a smokescreen. As soon as he got back to Los Angeles, Dino told him to close the project down, saying it was going to be too expensive to film.

Determined to keep the project alive, David was now spending his own money, but he knew it was an unsatisfactory arrangement that could not last. He now turned to me for ideas, just as he did whenever a problem cropped up during filming. It was a last ditch attempt to salvage David's dream but I told him I would personally speak to Lee Katz, the United Artists' chief and producer of *The Vikings*, knowing that we got on well and would probably be receptive to his proposals. I flew over to Los Angeles to meet Lee, and once I had outlined David's ideas he was sufficiently convinced about the feasibility of the project to agree to fly to Tahiti and discuss it with us. His plan was to finance the films with his partner Helen, who practically owned City Corp, one of the ten largest banks in the US at the time.

To smooth the path, I pulled out all the stops to make their stay as pleasant as possible and arranged for them to stay with us at the best hotel in Fiji – I even got them to meet the finance minister of Fiji. It was all going great when one night, in a hotel by the beach while having dinner with David and Sandy, Helen complained that the fifty million dollars needed to produce the film was too high. Alarm bells began ringing once again; she was quoting the figure John Box had been talking about in Hollywood almost three years before. It's as if she hadn't been paying any attention to us.

David was naturally incensed, certain that they had been plotting behind his back. "You stay out of it - I'll talk to Lee about the cost," he cut in, angry by this 'upstart's' interference – a female one at that! "You know nothing about making films. Nothing." David's insulting remarks had got the better of him. This was the final blow for *Bligh*, and he knew it. "I think I've stuffed the picture again," he said afterwards. Yet, he still could have salvaged the situation. The next morning Lee asked David to apologise to Helen, warning that he would otherwise have no option but to abandon the project. I knew what David's response would be. "I'm not going to apologise. I don't apologise if I'm not wrong," he said stiffly.

David's one last throw of the dice was his old pal Sam Spiegel. Once again I was asked to mediate, this time to persuade Sam to produce the film. Happy to oblige, I flew back to the UK and met Sam at his Dorchester Hotel apartment. After a short chat Sam agreed to produce the film, but only on condition that full artistic control of the project be handed over to him. This would mean that Spiegel would be able to choose the cast. In effect, he was forcing David into a humiliating climb down, knowing that David always insisted on having full artistic control over all his films. It was a sneaky stunt to pull because he knew David would never agree to such terms. And that was the end of that.

We went our separate ways, with David and Sandy flying back to LA and us jetting to London by Concorde. The fact was I could never tell how David reacted to disappointment, and this was no exception. But true to his character – and by way of a parting gift – David and Sandy bought Kathleen a Merc in Tahiti and had it shipped to the UK. It was a nice touch and once again proof of their generosity. We stayed in a plush apartment in Chelsea for a good while until David and Sandy arrived back at The Berkeley, while they got on with building their riverside home in Limehouse. We spent a lot of time together and had a pleasant time, despite what had happened in Tahiti. David's pride had got the better of him but there's no doubt in my mind that John Box had a lot to answer for as well. It was no surprise that the two became sworn enemies for years afterwards.

CHAPTER 23

Indians... Indians everywhere

A Passage to India, 1984, 163 minutes. HBO.
Producer: John Brabourne, Richard Goodwin. Director: David Lean. Writer: David Lean (based on the novel by E.M. Forster). Music: Maurice Jarre.
Cast: Judy Davis, Victor Banerjee, Peggy Ashcroft, James Fox, Alec Guinness, Nigel Havers, Richard Wilson, Art Malik.

I wasn't back in Spain for long when David phoned and asked me to meet him in London. He said he wanted to give us a surprise, and once there he revealed that he wanted all four of us to put the disappointment of *Bligh* behind us by arranging a driving trip across the southern US states. We all took a leisurely cruise on the QE2, and when we arrived in LA it soon became clear it would be no ordinary drive. David decided he and I would be driving in his Royal Red Rolls, while Kathleen and Sandy were to tag behind us in Sandy's own Rolls. It was a chance to clear our minds and take in the hurly burly of civilisation once again, although in hindsight setting off from Las Vegas wasn't perhaps the best idea.

Dining at Caesars Palace, we watched how scantily clad girls got old men excited by sitting on their laps and feeding them titbits. It was brash, noisy and sort of sad – just like Las Vegas, in fact. We'd seen enough and headed for the open road…only to get into trouble with the Highway Patrol for speeding. We were made to feel like naughty schoolchildren, and the officer – not content with his prize catch – made us drive all the way to a small western town where we were slapped with a ninety-dollar fine. He then told us, quite sternly, that we would not be allowed to leave unless we agreed to appear in court at a later date. We nodded dutifully, but I have to confess there is still an outstanding court appearance pending to this day. It was as if we had stepped into one of those cheap B-movies where strangers drive into a Godforsaken mid-western town and are never seen or heard of again – not that David would have appreciated the irony.

We exchanged some rueful looks before setting off…and promptly got into trouble once more for upsetting a group of Indians at a reservation in Monument Valley. Our crime this time had been to bring a bottle of Johnny Walker to our restaurant table, not knowing that there was a ban on alcohol at the reservation. The natives went ballistic, and for a moment I thought we would be lynched as they swarmed around our table shouting and hollering at us. The head man of the reservation suddenly grabbed the bottle and stormed out, probably to drink the entire bottle all by himself, the swine. While they were contemplating whether or not to take our scalps we hot-footed it to our cars and escaped by the skin of our teeth. What with randy old men, overzealous cops and irate Indians I was beginning to wonder whether the trip had been worth the bother. But there was no doubt in my mind the break had been good for David. It recharged his batteries and provided him with the inspiration to come up with new ideas.

Once in New York, he booked a return trip on the QE2 and shipped both cars over. We all took an extended trip to Switzerland and lived the life of Riley, staying at the top Grand Hotel Dolder until we all decided that you could have too much of a good thing. We were all getting itchy feet by now and, keen to get back to work, we parted company. Sandy and David pressed on with their new home in London and we went back to Spain. I got back into the swing of things and worked on a few, quite forgettable films. Just as boredom was beginning to creep in, David phoned, asking me to fly to London urgently as he was thinking of putting together an idea Lord Brabourne had had about making *A Passage to India*.

The trip had indeed recharged his batteries. The project was all the more appealing because one of the conditions writer E.M. Forster had insisted on regarding a possible film adaptation of his work was that David should direct it. I was sent off with Kathleen to do the reconnaissance and we flew to India to look for caves and train stations similar to those which appear in the story. We covered thousands of kilometres, travelling east to west and north to south in a small rented car without any air-con and with driver included, as self-drive hire was not allowed at the time.

Back in London I showed David and the producers my Kodachrome shots. His first impressions were good and decided to see the locations for himself. With both our partners we reprised our

American trip in India, driving around for months and visiting every location I had photographed.

While in Delhi, David dropped a subtle hint that he was willing to forgive John Box and give him a second chance. "After all, he is the best Art Director," he said thoughtfully. I was glad and very relieved David had actually reconsidered his actions – it was not something he often did once his mind was made up. John was sent for at once and I went with David to meet him at the airport. I stood back as they came together in what was a very emotional meeting. Shortly afterwards, David said he wanted to go to the Kashmir to start work and check the other locations as it was the only way we could gain a feel for the real India.

In Bombay, one of the production managers, Shama Habibullah, on hearing about our planned trip, asked if we had a gun. "Don't be silly," we naively replied. We didn't give it a second thought, but we soon rued our decision. While the four of us were waiting for a train to go through a level crossing in Kashmir, Shama's warning became all too clear. As we sat in our big white Mercedes with tons of luggage on the roof rack, a crowd of about two hundred people surrounded the car. Squeezing their faces on the car windows to get a better glimpse, they looked at us with a mixture of curiosity and disdain. We kept the windows firmly shut and looked straight ahead. I noticed David was strangely quiet – for a change. We all breathed a sigh of relief as the last wagon went past and the barrier to the level crossing was raised. Tense moment over, but it was the first time we realised the dangers of filming in the region. That night we stayed in an old fort. Yet, despite travelling for all those months looking for locations with David and Sandra, I didn't find out any more about the person behind the mask. Not that that made him any less generous a person. He showed immense interest in me and was kindness itself, to the point that, if I had wanted anything, he would have given it to me.

Travelling the length and breadth of India I took David back to the location I am most proud of in the Savandurga Hills between Bangalore and Mysore. I discreetly guided David to one of the world's largest monoliths; a solid piece of strawberry granite (it would appear in one of the film's most memorable scenes). The key with David was not to give the impression you had come up with the idea yourself, so I never told him that I 'had it' when looking for locations. This time I drove round the area knowing full well that he would 'discover' it for himself. It was a question of pride, but I had no problem with that; I knew how to play him, because no one ever told David Lean anything – you had to plant a seed. It was something I learned early on while making *The Bridge on the River Kwai*. David was beside himself with excitement. In fact, I couldn't keep up with the bugger as he raced up the hill to get a better view – and he was already a 75-year-old pensioner.

All was not well, though. It was while looking for locations that I believe David began developing his cancer symptoms. He started complaining of a pain in his neck but none of us gave it much thought at the time. Perhaps it was some sort of omen because it wasn't a happy picture to work on. John Box had brought down his camera crew, including a chap by the name of Ernie Day who used to be a camera operator and was now a camera chief. We went to see the rushes amounting to the previous week's work but David was not impressed with Ernie's contribution. "You're no good at lighting close ups," he said scathingly. If David was anything, it was being forthright. Then again, if a man like David Lean said you were no good at something the comment usually went in like a knife, so Ernie's discomfort was understandable. Alec Guinness also came under the cosh after an elaborate dance he went to the trouble of learning was discarded by David without a second thought. In fact, he took the scene out even before we shot it! Judy Davis in particular was determined to do it her way by adding bits to the character, such as wearing black lipstick, which irritated David. The clash between them was unavoidable, but what most people don't realise is that David went out of his way to help ease her into the role.

One case in point was the final, and all important, climactic court scene. To make Davis feel more comfortable, David decided to ship the entire crew to Pinewood Studios where there was a more secluded and tranquil atmosphere in which to film the scene, but his efforts and generous gestures went unnoticed for the most part. Despite it all, David did enjoy himself and was convinced he had made a good film, in spite of all the niggling and the antagonism that came from some of the cast and crew.

Interestingly, David wanted to end filming in Kashmir and insisted on putting Sandy in the film as James Fox's new wife. She wasn't that keen and because of union rules she wasn't allowed to speak, which explains why she only appears briefly for a few seconds. The bad omens continued, however. While shooting, my damaged right leg gave way and I had a bad fall, twisting my ankle badly in the process. An Indian doctor said it was only a bad sprain. Clever quack. I took his advice and made the mistake of forgetting about it. Years later, after filming two more pictures, I realised I couldn't even walk and, much against my better judgement, decided to see a surgeon at Stoke Mandeville Hospital. I was told the bones in my foot had literally crumbled, thanks largely to the injury I had sustained in Canada many years before. He fixed it but I've now got the bone fused in place and find walking agonisingly painful.

The saddest thing in retrospect, however, was that it was to be David's last film, although none of us suspected it at the time. When shooting ended David asked Kathy and I if we would like to join him and Sandy in Kenya on a Safari. I think he realised we all needed a break from what had been quite a fraught production. We all stayed at the Mount Kenya Safari Club, a lush hotel which Bill Holden and his partner Stephanie Powers had opened some years before. Stephanie had a bungalow close by where she lived with a domesticated cheetah that spent most of its time curled up on the sofa. We lived a similar life of leisure, dipping into the pool to cool off from the oppressive heat under the distant shadow of snow-capped Mount Kenya.

In the evenings we all sat together by a log fire talking and enjoying a glass of Scotland's finest. It was like Tahiti all over again. We discussed possible film projects and David made it clear he wanted to shoot another film. He told me he was thinking of making *Empire of the Sun*. I'd read the book, which was about a British kid growing up in Shanghai just before the Japanese invasion in 1941, but David wasn't very sure and he asked me what I thought about it. "I don't really like it very much. There's not much about the kid's character, certainly not enough to build a film around." He remained silent for a moment and then told me that Steven Spielberg was going to find him the money to make it.

It was no secret that Spielberg had a burning desire to do something with David, and actually went so far as to describe him as "a God" and the reason why he took up film directing in the first place. I later discussed the project with David at his house in Narrow Street, but when Spielberg got in touch with him to announce that he finally had the finance to make it, David dropped a bombshell and told him he was no longer interested. That was that and Spielberg went on to direct the film himself down in Seville. But to Steven's credit, he did not give up on David. He made it clear that he would finance any project of his and told him he could make any film he liked. "If you want to make a film about the New York telephone guide, I'll find you the money," he joked.

With that in mind I mentioned to David that Joseph Conrad's books lent themselves to film adaptations because there's a lot of melodramatic stuff about human failings which people can relate to. David agreed, and we spent days looking for books by Conrad. *Lord Jim* had been my first foray into Conrad's work on film, but it had been an unsatisfying experience. I felt with a proper treatment his other novel, *Victory*, could be made into a far more successful movie. After some lengthy discussions we sowed the seeds for *Nostromo* but agreed to put the project on hold. For his part, David felt the lead characters had far more depth and the subject of greed seemed far more enthralling than the adventures of a child in WWII.

In the end the finance came from Warner's. David went through a couple of script writers before turning once more to Robert Bolt, who was a rather sick man by this time. He was living in Sussex and David sent out a car to collect him every day and to bring him to Narrow Street, where they worked together on the script day in, day out. This went on for ages, mostly because David – being methodical, as he was – was also a slow script writer. Then, shortly after returning to Spain, I was amazed to hear that Sandy had split with David. It was totally unexpected news, but I never got to hear David's version of it – he simply never talked about the break up and pretended it had never happened. We were not going to broach the subject, anyway; it was clear he wasn't going to be outdone by anybody, not even Sandy, so he found another woman and went away with her on a trip. It was a sad way to deal with the whole affair, but it was David's way; he wasn't used to being discarded by anyone. Strangely enough, we later found out when we were introduced that the woman's name was Sandra and it wasn't long before that she moved in with him and took over his life, employing a personal assistant for him, which he'd never had before. In my estimation he started to go downhill after that. Perhaps it was because he knew how well the four of us got on that he had kept the bad news to himself.

But life went on, and despite the pain in my foot, I kept on making films. I got on with my life and while *A Passage to India* was being edited at Pinewood the Salkinds asked me to work on a totally different type of film, *Santa Claus*. It was unquestionably a terrible script but at least I had some fun working on it. I found a factory in Norwich that still made wooden toys and had everything built to my specific requirements.

Towards the end of filming I was sitting in the bar at Pinewood when a film producer approached me and asked if I wanted to work on a comedy called *Spies Like Us*, starring Dan Aykroyd and Chevy Chase. I turned the offer down straight away because I was keen to head off back to Spain, but he then offered to pay me more than I had ever earned up to then. I didn't need asking twice. As I was about to leave the bar I spotted a familiar face, sitting alone in a corner as he clasped a half-empty beer glass. It was 'Bluey' Hill, the First Assistant Director who had left such an impression at the British Embassy in Belgrade all those years ago. We soon got chatting and it turned out Bluey had since worked on all the Bond films for 'Cubby' Broccoli. With his reputation enhanced, work came thick and fast, and everyone clamoured around him for a job. It should have been a happy story with an even happier ending but his dishevelled clothes and glum face painted a very different picture. I asked what was up and he said he was destitute. I looked closely at his face and grimaced when I saw he only had one eye.

"What happened?" I innocently enquired.

"It fell out," he responded dryly. After a pregnant pause he went on. "I'm now living in a slum, you know. I've come to put the bite on Cubby to see if he can give me a job," he said, downcast.

During the whole time we were there no one came near, as though Bluey had a touch of the plague. It was in stark contrast to the way people had treated him years ago. Then, everyone wanted to be seen with this fun-loving Australian rogue. I recalled my chance encounter with Tom Morahan in a pub, both situations were eerily similar.

Filmed in Norway and at Pinewood Studios, *Spies Like Us* also took me closer to my childhood haunts, and we shot a scene at the old Bankside power station on the south bank. In its heyday it had been a wonderful building with its huge engines and dials before it was all destroyed to make way for a hideous new art gallery. It made me think about what people consider to be art nowadays. If Tracey Emin can get away with calling her unmade bed 'art' then I, and many like me, could quite rightly claim to being artists for having achieved considerably more. I was never influenced by artists, but Brunel was such a creative engineer that I also thought of him as a craftsman. His great iron structures were unquestionably beautiful; look at the wonderful Firth of Forth bridge – it doesn't take much to realise that it's far more impressive and more beautiful than a dirty bed. Unless it is way-out stuff like a Picasso painting (which has depth and can be analysed) modern art is pretty absurd.

I went back to Spain shortly afterwards and felt relieved to be leaving London behind, with all its modernist pretension, its noise, and crowded streets. My next project, *The Return of the Musketeers*, was also a return to working in Spain with Richard Lester and many of the actors who had starred in the original film more than fifteen years earlier. It should have been a happy experience but tragedy struck when Roy Kinnear was killed falling off his bloody horse while filming a scene. The awful thing about it was that he should never have been on the horse in the first place because he wasn't that good a rider. We were in Toledo at the time and in the scene he had to come across at full gallop. Poor old Roy had a great big bulk and the horse was supposed to stop suddenly, which it did. He came crashing down and was rushed off to hospital. His wife Carmel went to see him and was horrified to see that his testicles had bloated and gone all black. The staff seemed unconcerned and simply told her that it was normal. Of course, we later found out that he was haemorrhaging inside. Roy's death upset Lester so much that he never made a film after that.

CHAPTER 24

The curtain falls

The first I heard we had been given the go-ahead to film *Nostromo* was when I got a call from Warner Brothers asking me to look for locations. The wait had been long but I was overjoyed at the prospect of working with David once again, particularly after having discussed Conrad's work at length with him. I phoned to get more details and noted how energetic he sounded, as he always did when starting a new project. His instructions were clear, "Read the book but forget the first hundred pages – they're mostly boring. I'll make a film based on what follows."

Almost as though he knew he was on borrowed time, David was eager to get things moving as quickly as possible. John Box had once again been hired as the film's Production Designer and it was nice to think we'd be getting most of the gang of 'Dedicated Maniacs' together again. David arranged screen-tests with actors Tilda Swinton, Imogen Stubs and Georges Corraface, and locked himself away in an office every day, bashing away at a script with Robert Bolt, whom he used to bounce his ideas off. It's never been widely recognised to this day, but while Robert provided the dialogues it was actually David who wrote the scripts and constructed the storylines. It was just as well because Robert was in a very bad state, having suffered a heart attack some years before. Despite earning himself an undeserved reputation for being cold and ruthless, David was in fact generous to a fault and paid all of Robert's hospital bills while in Los Angeles. He now sent a car to collect him from his country home every morning while working on *Nostromo*.

Not long afterwards, David told me that they had enough of a script for me to start searching for film locations. I flew out to Mexico with Kathleen and John Box, but I knew exactly which locations we'd be using – I'd already worked that out long ago while staying at Baja California. John returned home after two weeks, but I thought I would 'spread' my time a bit. A phone call from the studios came through to my hotel room days later. The conversation went along these lines:

"Hiya Eddie, how's it going down there?"

"Very busy, very busy," I said, trying to sound solemn.

"Well, have you found anything?" the voice at the other end asked impatiently.

"I'm not too sure yet. I'll be staying out a bit longer, so you'll have to send out more money."

"Will $10,000 be enough?"

"Yes, that should see me through for now. Put it in my bank account."

"Right on, then."

Kathleen kept a strict control on the cash with her own account books in case Warner became a bit more curious as to how their money was being used and began asking questions. As it was, they didn't – and it turned out to be a wonderful five-month holiday for us.

David eventually came out to see the locations in Warner Brother's own private jet and okayed everything. But things weren't OK. I felt the emphasis in the script was wrong. Conrad's stories are always about a man who has regrets in life, but I thought the theme got confused in *Nostromo*. To kill time, I wrote my own version for fun, starting with the end; the bell tolling at Nostromo's funeral, almost like David did with *Lawrence of Arabia*. Aside from the problems with the script, David had another run in with a producer and a new one had to be found. He pulled me to one side, muttering that there were potential problems with the unions in Mexico. To my surprise, he asked me to look for locations in Spain instead. This delayed the project further and increased filming costs (not to mention the fact that we had already spent quite a lot of money) but fortunately, and thanks to my knowledge of Spain, I quickly found all the new locations on the south coast in Almería, many of which, like the white sand dunes of Cabo de Gata, had already been used in *Lawrence of Arabia*. David came over and we both visited the same sand dunes where almost thirty years before we had filmed the train derailment scene in Lawrence. There was an eerie silence as a warm wind blew across our faces. We stood still, picturing hoards of extras streaming forth once more to assault the train as the horses bolted across the dunes. David stretched out on the warm sand to daydream. I left him to it for some twenty minutes, thinking that he seemed more subdued than normal.

Later on it was decided that we would film the interiors in Nice, and while the sets were being built I showed David how some of the effects would be done. He wanted to see how I was going to present the discovery of the silver in the cavern under the mountain. "Do something magical like you did for the Ice Palace in Zhivago," he whispered. It didn't matter if that wasn't the way silver was really mined – it was the subtle but unforgettable visual details which David was keen to capture.

While walking around the sets, however, I couldn't help noticing a change in his attitude. He seemed strangely distant, disinterested even. Noticing my discomfort he turned to me, shrugging his shoulders. "I've got to go back to London…I'm having trouble with these teeth," he said, pointing to his jaw. He left, saying he was going to see his dentist in London and never came back.

The next thing I got was a message telling me that the film was folding up and that I should fly urgently to London to see David. That's when I heard he had cancer. I hurriedly got rid of all the sets and went with Kathleen to visit him at his home in Narrow Street. It was a shock seeing how fast the disease had spread. David, who was now living with Sandra Cooke, the woman he had met at Harrods, was now confined to his bed. He looked defeated but uncomplaining. His doctor said he had throat cancer – perhaps from all the cigarettes he had smoked years ago – and that his epiglottis was badly damaged, which explained why he couldn't swallow. Kathleen and I were given a bedroom but she made herself scarce while I spent weeks sitting beside David, reading *The Sunday Times* and talking to him for hours while he lay listening, mostly in silence, as he now couldn't even speak. Sandra had now taken over his life completely – even the furniture had been changed.

For the first time in David's life, he now also had a P.A., in addition to a maid, a cook and his wife, and a house boy (although he was definitely a man); all full-time employees and friends of Sandra's. I made no bones about the fact I didn't get on with her at all because I suspected she was only eager for a bit of David's fame and success to rub off on her. But nothing got on my nerves more than seeing her wander into David's room smoking. Seeing her seemingly indifferent to David's pain and suffering was more than I could bear. I was about to suggest – reasonably nicely – that she stub the cigarette out. "If you say anything to me I shall leave," she said, sensing my irritation.

"That would be a bloody good thing to do," I replied, shifting uncomfortably, aware how upsetting this must be for David to witness. When she left I turned to him, unable to contain my rage any longer. "Why don't you chuck her out?"

"Then I'd be all on my own," he groaned pitifully. I felt indignant that this great man should be reduced to begging for company.

"No you wouldn't, you can come down and live with me," I awkwardly suggested.

"Very kind, but no," he replied.

The room went quiet and I gave up trying to convince him. This went on for some time until David confessed that "she" – as he called her – was nagging him so much that it was getting unbearable. He looked at me with pleading eyes and asked Kathleen and I to stay longer, but he needn't have tried so hard. We immediately moved into the Tower Bridge Hotel – paid for by David – and every day I would walk to his Narrow Street home as before. In the meantime Sandra bought a large house near Nice in the south of France and spent quite a lot of time there having major work done on the house pool and garden. Without David's knowledge she also had his red Rolls shipped over, before shipping him over as well for a surprise wedding. It was a surprise for everyone, indeed. Kathleen and I weren't invited but what irked me most was the haste with which it had all been done, given David's weakened state.

He was soon back in London along with his two male nurses, looking worse than before. They would unceremoniously lift him to the toilet everyday as part of their 'hands-on' care, but determined not to throw the towel in, I bought him a nice wheelchair to help him move about in. When Sandra saw it she went spare. "I will not have a wheelchair in my house!" she screamed.

"It's not your fucking house yet." I snapped. It was clear we would never get on and I returned to Spain, thinking nothing more could be done.

I went to visit David once more while Sandra was away in Nice, but when I got there I found him almost choking and in a terrible state. I rushed to the phone and called one of his doctors, worried that he wasn't getting the care he needed. When the doctor arrived, he took one look at him and said he should be urgently admitted into hospital to "pump him out", whatever that meant. David was totally against the idea. "I'm not going," he said stubbornly, but no one was listening and we called an ambulance. As obstinate as ever, he refused to lie on the stretcher and motioned towards the wheelchair I'd given him, much against Sandra's wishes. As he was being taken out down the lift he turned to me. "I want my flowers," he muttered, referring to the sunflowers in his room – his favourites.

"They're wilting a bit, David, I'll bring you some fresh ones in hospital," I suggested.

"I want those. I'm not leaving until I have them." he insisted, raising his voice to a painful croak. *Still directing*, I thought.

Poor David was so ill he probably knew he wasn't coming back, but he was a determined fellow to the end. He was admitted to King Edward VIII Hospital where I sat with him almost till the very last day, only leaving his side when his lawyer turned up and asked him to sign away the vast bulk of his wealth to trusts. I dreaded going to his cremation in Putney Vale because I knew it was going to be a bloody circus. Arriving just before the service was due to begin, I stood at the back of the crowded church, just inside the doorway, straining for a view of the pulpit and David's coffin. All I could see were the tops of the heads of famous people, including Richard Attenborough and David Puttnam, half of whom had probably never even met David and who were evidently more anxious about uttering a few well-rehearsed speeches about what a great film maker he had been. *What a bunch of hypocrites*, I thought, remembering how the film industry had treated him over the years. It was all too much. I quietly uttered a few words to myself and bade farewell as the curtains closed on my friend.

Months later I heard they were organising a ceremony in his honour at St Paul's Cathedral. It had all the trappings of show-business, including an overblown orchestra backing. Needless to say, I stayed away. Fortunately, David left a lasting legacy beyond the films he made and gave most of his money to a trust and the David Lean Film Foundation film school. The funny thing is that neither David nor I ever went to a film school.

CHAPTER 25

Leaky ships

Christopher Columbus: The Discovery (1992). 120 minutes. Quinto Centenario.
Producer: Ilya Salkind, Alexander Salkind. Director: John Glen.
Writer: Mario Puzo. Music: Cliff Eidelman.
Cast: Georges Corraface, Tom Selleck, Marlon Brando, Catherine Zeta-Jones, Rachel Ward, Benicio del Toro.

David's loss was very hard to bear, and I was sad we would never get to complete *Nostromo*. But, despite the pain in my foot, which was quite unbearable at times, and the subsequent lack of mobility that made it harder for me to continue, I made a conscious decision to get back to work. My next film, *Christopher Columbus: The Discovery*, brought me together once more with period ships and my Spanish colleague Gil Parrondo, a wonderful man who's widely regarded as the best film designer in Spain. Great a technician though he is, he wasn't keen on looking for locations and would not go out to Malta, so I went instead.

The film was directed by John Glen, better known at the time for having directed a few of the James Bond films, but I didn't think he was much of a romantic director and I certainly wouldn't rate him in the top ten. He was also handicapped by having to work with such a poor script that there wasn't even enough material to shoot a film. I got the impression that it was a bit of a rushed job, timed to coincide with the 500th Anniversary of the discovery of America – all the evidence pointed to that view. Inevitably, their ships and the movie were all heading for the rocks long before we shot a single frame of film.

The only high point for us, professionally speaking, was filming a scene in what was one of the biggest tanks in the world at the back of an old fort. We rebuilt full-scale ships without a bottom and put them on wheels in a big tank, that way we could move them around and create waves in a controlled setting. The problem was that the main ships were so badly made that you couldn't shoot them too

257

close or you risked revealing their all too-obvious flaws. Maybe it was the onset of old age but I didn't have the heart to tell them that it looked like the set of a cheap TV advert. Making these things is not as easy as it looks, unfortunately they all think they can do it. Light relief was provided by Catherine Zeta-Jones, who only joined the film set when we moved to Evora in Portugal. It's a sign of how desperate the producers were to make a box office success of this film that they hired her just for the name and her looks. While they postponed shooting I went up and down Portugal looking for more locations.

Meanwhile Georges Corraface, who was playing Columbus, was told to improve his looks by working out in the gym. But it soon became clear that no amount of pumping iron would save the film. I was quite relieved when shooting ended and I went back to Carboneras for a well earned break. Then an offer came to work with John Box on *Black Beauty* at Pinewood Studios. Having overcome my abhorrence of the unions (mostly, it has to be said, because they were nothing like as militant as they used to be) I agreed to do it. For one thing, I was keen to work with John again. But my broken foot was so bad by this time that I could hardly walk. It seems time had finally caught up with me and for the first time in my life I seriously began to consider retiring. At least the producers decided to double my salary, which I didn't argue about.

Beyond physical limits

The opportunity to work with Director John Boorman on *Beyond Rangoon* stirred my old body into action once more. One of the reasons I decided to do the film is that Boorman actually bothers to listen to people. I was able to speak my mind and if I had an idea I was able to put it to him without worrying about the consequences. Now that was something new. No one ever asked for my opinion, not even David – he'd have probably shot me. The key with David was to stand back and hint at the possibilities, either by standing close to where a camera could go, or by showing reels and reels of the best locations mixed with a few of the more average sites.

As it turned out, *Beyond Rangoon*, starring Patricia Arquette, was the last film I did on location. This old body of mine, used to trekking thousands of miles across the world many times over; ready to double for actresses in small boats during storms; or to drive for days across desert sandstorms or freezing Arctic winds, had had enough. It was now excruciatingly painful to walk around the set. My feet were literally crumbling from two old fractures and despite John's benign and sensitive direction I trailed behind the other crew members like a wounded lion: unwilling to appear weak but aware that everyone else knew the painful truth and that I was running out of steam.

One pirate film too many

Back in Spain I got a very interesting call from Warner Brothers in Los Angeles, asking me if I wanted to make another pirate film. I wasn't keen at first (I made it clear to them that because of my legs I would be unable to do any location work) but they made me an offer I couldn't refuse. In fact, the figure was large enough for me to retire on. I was flown first-class and when I got there I was shown into a huge office with a splendid view of Santa Monica Boulevard. Standing in front of me were twenty-five people from the art department alone (I know, I counted them). They went off to look for the locations themselves, boasting that they were going to Santa Lucia, which also happened to be one of the most expensive and mosquito-infested islands to film in. Smiling benignly at me, they reasoned that it was a "nice American place to go to", no doubt also encouraged by the proximity of five-star hotels to the film set; a prerequisite no Hollywood star can do without these days. They then started talking about having ten boats in the movie.

"Ten boats?" I gasped. "We only had one boat when we filmed!" You didn't need ten boats, all one had to do was alter the one you had to turn it into another boat. Worried that the film had fallen into the hands of incompetent amateurs I went to see the producer to find out why the hell I'd been hired. "Can you tell me why I'm here? You're all Americans and I'm the only Brit."

"Warner Bros wanted you on, because you've done a lot of movies with boats."

"But we're already one-hundred million dollars over budget."

"Don't worry about it. Arnold Schwarzenegger is going to be *Captain Blood*," he replied, as if that would solve all our problems. *Jesus Christ*, I thought. *There's no way he's playing the lead role, is he?* Hard as I tried, I couldn't picture a cumbersome Schwarzenegger in the role of a beer-swilling English pirate, swinging from yard arm to yard arm while waving a sword. The fact that Errol Flynn, a lithe and elegant actor by anyone's reckoning, had played the role years before should have told them that Arnie was not the best man for the part, but Arnie was unquestionably a big box-office draw and was seen as a more obvious choice by the accountants. I decided to adopt a practical approach: if they wanted to fuck the whole thing up, it was their money. After all, I was getting paid double. But it was obvious that this couldn't last. Soon afterwards, we were told it was all finished, wrapped up, and that the film wasn't going to get made because Arnie didn't want to do it. Despite the huge budget, much of which had already been spent, everything had effectively gone down the plug hole because of an actor's whim. I tried to inject a dose of sanity in the proceedings, relatively speaking. "Why don't we get Andre Agassi to play Captain Blood alongside Brooke Shields (who was his girlfriend at the time)?" They weren't listening. The film industry had definitely changed and I didn't like what I saw. I put the fiasco of Los Angeles and Arnie firmly behind me and went back home.

My love affair with films ended that day. I concluded that no amount of money, and certainly no amount of computer effects and green screen backgrounds, could replace a skilled film director. I returned to Spain to reflect on my own life. I may not have made a packet in films and ended up with no pension or insurance, but I was lucky to have met Kathleen that fateful day in Ireland while filming *Ryan's Daughter*. She has helped me in every possible way and we've had a great life together. Since then, I'm also very happy to say that Sandy returned to the fold as part of the 'family' and is still very much a close friend of Kathleen's – I'm convinced David would have been over the moon about that. The three of us still often talk about him while I look back on the absent member of our family.

There were many reasons why David and I were close. David felt he could speak his mind and not worry about being betrayed or judged in any way. Perhaps my attitude to life, free of the class restraints which tied him down, also appealed to his sense of freedom. Without any doubt, he was a Director in a class of his own, right up until that last moment in the studios in Nice when he'd been forced to pack it all in. Funnily enough, I'll always remember he offered me the chance to direct on many occasions, promising that he'd find the money for me. I never took him up on the offer, but I felt no need to. Simply to have worked with him was enough.

And anyway, how could I complain? It had been an epic journey ever since I walked past the gates at Warner Brothers'. Life can be an adventure...if you're prepared to grab the moment and shake it for all it's worth.

GLOSSARY OF TERMS

Stage hands were called 'stag hounds', just as carpenters were 'chippies' and electricians were 'sparks'. Anybody in the property department – whatever he did – was a 'prop'. A 'grip' was someone who moved and looked after the camera crew, pushing a vehicle called a 'dolly' for the cameraman and his operator, which later became a contraption called a 'crab' that had the added advantage of being able to go sideways. Both were almost always on tracks.

Electricians were mostly lamp minders, many of whom spent most of their time above the sets on cradles or 'boats' that were suspended from the roof girders. They had lamps which they put shutters on and worked to the orders of the gaffer – or head spark – according to the requirements of the chief cameraman, who was the lighting cameraman or cinematographer. With the shutters on the front of the lamps – called barn doors – they could open or close to cut the light sideways.

'To make it Chinese' meant to swivel the barn door to make the slit of light go horizontal. On the stage floor there would be 'pups', 'inkey dinks' and so on which were all different types of lamps.

We also had names for various pieces of black cloth that were used to create shadows, such as a 'Charley Bar' to draw a discreet shadow across a girl's cleavage. All was black and white. Even the bed sheets had to be tinted blue. In the prop room we would dip anything white in tea. There were a multitude of words to know and tricks to learn.

If you go onto a film sound stage it may appear to be total confusion and noise with obstructions everywhere and miles of cables strewn across the floor. But it is not. Everyone knows what to do.

When a scene is about to be shot the assistant director might call out for a red light. Red lights and a bell would sound inside the stage and outside. After the scene is shot and if the director is happy enough to shout "Print it!" the assistant shouts "Kill the red!" (This, by the way, doesn't mean killing one of the shop stewards).

Eddie Fowlie died peacefully at his
home in Spain on January 22, 2011.